Biblical Patriotism:
An Evangelical Alternative to Nationalism

Biblical Patriotism:
An Evangelical Alternative to Nationalism

Adam Wyatt

An Imprint of the
Global Center for Religious Research
1312 17th Street • Suite 549
Denver, Colorado 80202

info@gcrr.org • gcrr.org

GCRR Press
An imprint of the Global Center for Religious Research
1312 17th Street Suite 549
Denver, CO 80202
www.gcrr.org

DOI: 10.33929/GCRRPress.2021.03

Typesetting/Proofreading: Kimberly Dell
Cover Design: Abdullah Al Mahmud
                fiverr.com/mahmuddidar

Library of Congress Cataloging-in-Publication Data

Biblical patriotism: an evangelical alternative to nationalism / Adam Wyatt
p.   cm.
Includes bibliographic references (p.)
ISBN (Print): 978-1-7378469-0-1
ISBN (eBook): 978-0-578-80731-7
1. Bible—Hermeneutics—Criticism, interpretation, etc.   2. Hermeneutics—Religious aspects—Christianity.   3. Christianity and politics.   4. Patriotism.   5. Nationalism.   5. Church and state.   6. Evangelicalism.   I. Title.

BV629-631   .W938   2021

ℭ

Mom and Dad, thanks for giving me a love for Jesus and His church.
Laurie, thanks for loving me like Jesus and for serving His church with me.
Abby, Lily, and Sophie, may you fiercely love Jesus and His church in the
coming years.

Contents

Preface

I'm a military kid. My dad served faithfully in the Air Force, which led me to live in various parts of the world. I was living in West Germany as a child when the Berlin Wall came down, and I used to have pieces of it but, being a child, I did not truly understand the cultural and historical significance of a few pieces of concrete, so they are now lost. I still remember as a child going on to the military base to watch a movie. Instead of the normal movie trailers that many of us love to see, we stood for the national anthem that was played. Moments like these helped shape my understanding of patriotism.

My dad was also a pastor, so standing for the anthem before movies was a big deal, but, more so, was the picture of the local church that I saw. Although the church was made up of mostly military families, it was truly diverse. Our congregation had people from all over the United States and there were so many ethnicities that gathered to worship together. Seeing a diverse church made up of mostly military families also helped shape my understanding of patriotism.

When I started my Ph.D. in 2015, I had no idea what I wanted my dissertation to focus on, but I knew that I wanted something *current* to help keep me motivated. Enter July 16, 2015: the day Donald Trump entered the race for president of the United States. I did not know it then, but this was the beginning of my study on patriotism. To be honest, Trump came out of nowhere. But, slowly and methodically, his vision to "Make America Great Again" gathered much support, especially among evangelicals. He argued that America was not what it once was but it could be again. He made the case that America needed to be better. This resonated with many. It resonated with me. I have always wanted the best for my country and my people and this has always influenced my thoughts on politics. So, I understood the draw of someone like Trump. However, I also saw something else, something that I couldn't quite put my finger on.

Making America great again was a wonderful ideal but what would that entail? That was the question. As it became more obvious that Trump was going to secure the Republican nomination, patriotic sentiment rose to the forefront of the American consciousness. This patriotic sentiment filtered into the local church and, for the first time in my ministry, politics became something that I had to consistently address in conversations. I finally had a *current topic* for my dissertation; I finally had a topic to research.

When I first started researching, I had no idea just how much the cultural, political, and theological landscape would change in regards to patriotism. I knew that it was a valid and worthy topic to study, but I was not fully prepared for the topic to dominate so much of my personal and spiritual world. Patriotism, something that I always felt was a virtue, slowly became something altogether unrecognizable to me or, at the very least, something that was distorted. When you added the firebrand, Donald Trump, to the mix, you had a blurring of nationalism with patriotism, which many could not differentiate. However, I thought that it was increasingly important to be able to distinguish nationalism from its healthier counterpart, patriotism. This book attempts to bring to the forefront some of the questions that I started to prayerfully work through at the local church level, but it is also just a small drop in the bucket of the valuable theological study that needs to be done in the area.

During the last year of writing, it became even more apparent that patriotism within the church was going to be a topic that needed more clarification. George Floyd's death, BLM and a new civil rights movement, professional athletes kneeling during the national anthems, COVID-19, and the subsequent church closings and mask mandates made it clear that people have a broad way of viewing their place in the political landscape. So, this topic continued to remain *current.* People's thoughts on marches, riots, kneelings, church closings, and masks were influenced by their flavor of patriotism. This made my project challenging.

My hope is, quite simply, that we will be willing to engage with the concepts in a way that both challenges our modern conceptions of patriotism and what a patriotic Christian should be while also embracing the good that patriotism can offer. After all, America is a great country. She is marred by her past, but she also has a noble history. Though the landscape will change, I truly believe that the Bible offers the best way to embrace the good of our own country while also offering us a proper critique of it. Hopefully, this book will stir you to a proper affection for the United States, but, more importantly, I hope that it stirs you to a deeper affection for the God of the Bible who makes us all citizens of Heaven. May Jesus' name be the one we shout for in the coming days.

The Context and the Problem

What is patriotism? A simple definition of "patriotism" is having a love of one's own country.[1] While simple, the term "patriotism," at least for many Americans, is one that is difficult to fully understand due to its connection with nationalism; and for many, patriotism cannot be divorced from nationalism, which leads to a negative view of patriotism.[2] Many claim patriotism as a virtue because it leads a person to seek out the good for one's country.[3] However, is loving one's country all that is needed for someone to be patriotic? Further, what does it take for someone to truly love his country? For some, patriotism implies the love for one's country, but for countless others, it implies something much more significant. For others, nationalism is often connected in terms of racism, ethnocentrism, and bigotry and, as a result, is not virtuous.[4] What is needed is an understanding of what patriotism is

---

[1] Mitja Sardoč, "The Anatomy of Patriotism," *Anthropological Notebooks* 23 (2017): 44; Margaret Gilbert, "*Pro Patria*: An Essay on Patriotism," *Journal of Ethics* 13 (2009): 322; Ryan LaMothe, "The Problem of Patriotism: A Psychoanalytic and Theological Analysis," *Pastoral Psychology* 58 (2009): 152.

[2] Peter Alter argues that nationalism is "one of the most ambiguous concepts of the present-day vocabulary of political and analytical thought." Peter Alter, *Nationalism* (London: Arnold, 1985), 1. This ambiguous nature of terminology of both "nationalism" and "patriotism" gives rise to a misunderstanding of what it means to be patriotic.

[3] See Alasdair MacIntyre, "Is Patriotism a Virtue?" in *Patriotism*, ed. Igor Primoratz (New York: Humanity, 2002), 43–58.

[4] While patriotism *is* closely associated with nationalism, it will be argued that it is something altogether different. Qiong Li and Marilynn Brewer argue that there is a clear differentiation between the two terms. See Qiong Li and Marilynn Brewer, "What Does It Mean to Be an American? Patriotism, Nationalism, and American Identity after 9/11," *Political Psychology* 25 (2004): 727–739. See also, David Crittendon, "Differentiating Patriotism and Nationalism: Influence of Valence of Primes," *The New School Psychology*

and what it entails to see if it has any connotations with biblical virtue.

Much overlap exists between the concept of country and nation within the concepts of patriotism and nationalism, but the interest in patriotism and nationalism is a relatively modern phenomenon.[5] A resurgence of nationalist "movements" in the global world has combined with challenges of modernization, migration, and the resulting multiculturalism to provide for an increased interest in a philosophical understanding of both patriotism and nationalism.[6] Both terms involve the love and identification of a nation or entity along with a concern for it. In patriotism, the object of love and identification is one's country, or *patria*, but for nationalism, the object of love is one's nation, or *natio*. Igor Primoratz argues that both terms are connected and understood as being the same set of beliefs and feelings but with a different object.[7]

Since people are born in a specific country, they tend to have a natural affinity toward their country.[8] However, this does not answer the question of whether patriotism is a virtue or something a

---

Bulletin 15 (2018): 1–10. The varying definitions, understandings, and misunderstandings of the two terms show the need for further study on the topic. Amélie Mummendey, et al. argue, "In a nutshell, nationalism is seen as inherently related to out-group derogation, whereas patriotism is expected to reveal a positive relation to own group *independent of* out-group derogation." Amélie Mummendey, et al., "Nationalism and Patriotism: National Identification and Out-Group Rejection," *British Journal of Social Psychology* 40 (2001): 160. On how nationalism can hide ethnonationalism, see Farida Fozdar and Mitchell Low, "'They Have to Abide by Our Laws . . . and Stuff': Ethnonationalism Masquerading as Civic Nationalism," *Nations and Nationalism* 21 (2015), 524–543.

[5] Steven Grosby, *Biblical Ideas of Nationality: Ancient and Modern* (Winona Lake: Eisenbrauns, 2002), 13.

[6] Andrew Tan, *U.S. Strategy against Global Terrorism: How It Evolved, Why It Failed, and Where It Is Headed* (New York: Palgrave, 2009), 85.

[7] Igor Primoratz, "Patriotism and Morality: Mapping the Terrain," *Journal of Moral Philosophy* 5 (2008): 205–206.

[8] Anthony Smith, *Ethno-Symbolism and Nationalism* (Routledge: London, 2009), 26–27. Anthony Smith argues that ethnic ties create associations of people that grow into self-defined ethnic communities. These self-defined communities allow a people to share a common ancestry, memories, and other elements of a common culture.

person should, at the very least, possess if he is to be a good citizen. These are questions that sociologists, philosophers, and historians have researched and argued for years. However, a further question exists: is patriotism something that a "Christian" should possess, and if so, to what end? For many, being a faithful Christian is associated with being patriotic.[9]

For a long time, patriotism was a neglected topic in the academy and major philosophic writings.[10] As already stated, there is a connection of patriotism to nationalism, which is a significant reason for the academy's lack of interest or desire in looking at nationalism.[11] Despite patriotism's significance to the pantheon of political philosophy, it remains a broadly challenged concept due to the misunderstanding of its connection to nationalism. This misunderstanding stems from a highly generalized understanding of nationalism with its connection to national pride.[12]

American patriotism seems a simple matter; however, as Wilfred McClay posits, "[I]t is simple only until one actually starts to think about it, inquire about its sources, and investigate its manifestations."[13] Patriotism, in its contemporary scope, along with its connection to nationalism, is a political philosophy that makes

---

[9] For example, Robert Jeffress, pastor of the historic First Baptist Church in Dallas, Texas, has church services throughout the year celebrating freedom in Christ *and* freedom as Americans. Michael Lienesch shows that American Christian leaders throughout history have connected civil religion to patriotism; and as a result, neither is going away. Michael Lienesch, "Contesting Civil Religion: Religious Responses to American Patriotic Nationalism, 1919–1929," *Religion and American Culture* 28 (2018). Alexis de Tocqueville noticed the connection of Christianity and patriotism in America, "In the United States religion is therefore commingled with all habits of the nation and all the feelings of patriotism; whence it derives a peculiar force." Alexis de Tocqueville, *Democracy in America*, trans. Henry Reeve, vol. 2 (New York: Colonial, 1900), 6.

[10] Igor Primoratz, ed., *Patriotism* (Amherst: Humanity, 2002), 9.

[11] Ibid., 19.

[12] Rui de Figueiredo Jr. and Zachary Elkins, "Are Patriots Bigots? An Inquiry into the Vices of In-Group Pride," *American Journal of Political Science* 47 (2003): 172; Sardoč, "The Anatomy of Patriotism," 43.

[13] Wilfred McClay, "America—Idea or Nation?" *The Public Interest* (2001): 44.

many people uncomfortable.[14] Regardless of the seemingly implied connections to nationalism, patriotism is a worthy topic of academic study. Further, the misunderstanding of the topic is not a reason to be reluctant in pursuing academic knowledge in this field. Instead, this misunderstanding of the topic makes it clear that there is a need in research. To that end, Daniel Holst argues the academy has "scholarly hostility" toward the topic of patriotism because of the academy has an "incomplete analysis" of what patriotism truly is.[15] This modern, incomplete analysis is a result of several contemporary issues.

Historical Underpinnings of American Patriotism

Puritanism

The issue of patriotism in America is much more complicated than the issue of patriotism in general.[16] The early settlers of America had a distinct understanding that God had ordained the colonization of the New World as an extension of His sovereign will in all of the world. In 1630, John Winthrop, one of the leading founders of the Massachusetts Bay Colony and eventual governor of the state, preached "A Modell of Christian Charity" showing how they fully believed that the hand of God was upon their journey to the New

---

[14] Stephen Nathanson, "In Defense of 'Moderate Patriotism,'" in *Patriotism*, ed. Igor Primoratz (Amherst: Humanity, 2002), 87. Harry Brighouse notes that some have fears that national loyalties eventually lead to disregard for universal obligations that are owed to all people; additionally, he sees that some see these patriotic loyalties having a "disruptive effect" in how nations exist in the world. Harry Brighouse, "Justifying Patriotism," *Social Theory and Practice* 32 (2006): 553. Jennifer Wolak and Ryan Dawkins posit that Americans show so much patriotism in surveys that the question can be raised whether this patriotism is simply blind allegiance or an genuinely held belief. Jennifer Wolak and Ryan Dawkins, "The Roots of Patriotism across Political Contexts," *Political Psychology* 38 (2017): 391.

[15] Daniel Holst, "From Patriotism's Christian Narrative to Ironic War Poetry" (master's thesis, Western Illinois University, 2018), 5.

[16] Mark Noll, *One Nation under God? Christian Faith and Political Action in America* (San Francisco: Harper & Row, 1988), 7.

World. "We shall be as a City upon a Hill, the eyes of all people are upon us; so that if we shall deal falsely with our god in this work we have undertaken and so cause him to withdraw his present help from us."[17] This concept of America being a "city on a hill" has been used for generations to imply that God is specifically behind the inner workings of America, but more than that, has been used to imply that America is to exist as a nation that all the world can imitate.[18]

Puritans left England to settle the New World partly because of their desire to worship freely but partly because of their Calvinist theology. While not the only religion in the colonies, Calvinism was the dominant influence in the early period of American history known as the Puritan period.[19] The Calvinist understanding of God's sovereignty meant that for the Puritans, God had given the early Americans a national mission and became a central tenet to the American sense of religion and helped form the foundation of its sense of patriotism and public life.[20] Since God had given the Americans a clear mission, any attempt at halting that mission was a direct attack on God's plans. Thus, the Puritans identified themselves with the cause of Christ, and as a result, the kingdom of

---

[17] John Winthrop, "A Modell of Christian Charity," in *Political Thought in America: An Anthology*, ed. Michael Levy (Prospect Heights: Waveland, 1992), 12. All citations from this sermon have been Anglicized from the original while maintaining original capitalization and punctuation.

[18] George Marsden, *Religion and the American Culture* (New York: Harcourt, 1990), 22. Marlana Portolano states, "America rhetoric from Winthrop's 'City on a Hill' to Reagan's 'shining city' to Barack Obama's rhetoric of hope relies on underlying utopian metaphors" that are distinctly Christian and, at the same time, "American." Marlana Portolano, "The Rhetorical Function of Utopia: An Exploration of the Concept of Utopia in Rhetorical Theory," *Utopian Studies* 23 (2012): 120.

[19] Noll, *One Nation under God?* 23. Mark Noll states, "Puritanism is the only colonial religious system that modern historians take seriously as a major religious influence on the Revolution." Mark Noll, *America's God: From Jonathan Edwards to Abraham Lincoln* (New York: Oxford, 2002), 32.

[20] Anatol Lieven, *America Right or Wrong: An Anatomy of American Nationalism* (Oxford: Oxford University Press, 2012), 30. Puritanism "was not merely a religious creed and a theology, it was also a program for society." Perry Miller, *Errand in the Wilderness* (New York: Harper, 1954), 191.

God and the nation became synonymous.[21] Further, the American republic was seen as the primary agent of redemptive history; the Puritans saw themselves, and the nation by extension, chosen by God to fulfill a special mission in the world.[22] Puritans saw themselves fulfilling this mission most clearly by seeking to influence the culture around it; and one way they attempted this was through political endeavors. Christian political involvement, primarily influenced by this Puritan theology, was "direct, forceful, and unqualified" and "played a very important part in securing independence from Great Britain."[23]

George McKenna understands that to the Puritans, God had ordained everything in early American life, and this had a broad impact on its politics. This Puritan "narrative" was the underlying "scaffolding" of an American culture that was a heroic story of a people attempting to exist and thrive as God's country.[24] This Puritan narrative had at least four characteristics that helped to steer the historical framework of America. First, Puritans saw America as paralleling ancient Israel. In this way, Americans were God's chosen people who had been sent into the wilderness to carry out His mission and to set an example before the watching world.[25] Second, the Puritans believed that their faith should be more than contemplative but activist. By carrying out God's mission in the world, they were giving evidence of God's grace upon them. Third,

---

[21] Noll, *One Nation under God?* 49; Nathan Hatch, *The Sacred Cause of Liberty: Republican Thought and the Millennium in Revolutionary New England* (New Haven: Yale University Press, 1977), 143.

[22] Hatch, *The Sacred Cause of Liberty*, 155. Seventeenth century Puritan understanding of "chosenness" was a factor that "contributed largely to America's view of themselves as a people set apart by God." John Wilsey, *One Nation under God? An Evangelical Critique of Christian America* (Eugene: Pickwick, 2011), 98. The rhetoric of early New England Puritanism was two-sided: On the one hand, they clearly saw the colonization of the New World as an example of their "chosenness," but on the other hand, they had an extreme fear that God might judge them in its colonization if they were not faithful. McKenna, *Puritan Origins of Patriotism*, 41.

[23] Noll, *One Nation under God?* 35.

[24] McKenna, *The Puritan Origins of Patriotism*, 48–51.

[25] Puritans compared themselves to Israel also because they saw themselves as seeking to leave England, whom they saw as a tyrannical empire, to settle in a promised land. Wilsey, *One Nation under God?* 80.

the Puritans believed in covenant theology that stressed that the country would prosper if they continued to hold to that mission but would be punished if they were unfaithful.[26] Fourth, the Puritans understood that America was at war with England; this was a war with the Antichrist, so the American Revolution was, in essence, a holy war.

The American Revolution was seen as a religious experience to much of early American culture, and it provided the fundamental basis for much of historical and modern American civil religion as Puritan theology shifted.[27] First, Americans stopped seeing themselves as people who were fleeing persecution but as people who were meant to evangelize the world. Second, many turned into people who were committed to defending their God-given freedoms from the British. As America won their independence from the British, they saw themselves as having won their freedom from an evil empire and having God-ordained legitimacy given to them as a result. Third, the early Puritan fathers became concerned with keeping watch over the new nation in an attempt to see it committed to practicing habits of lawfulness and hard work. As these shifts happened, the foundations for patriotism were laid.[28]

Civil Religion

Civil religion in America further allowed patriotism to be a staple in American culture.[29] "Civil religion" is the "religious way of thinking about politics and a country or nation due to broadly held

---

[26] John Carlson and Jonathan Ebel stress that the biblical covenant helped shape the American identity from colonial times. John Carlson and Jonathan Ebel, *From Jeremiad to Jihad: Religion, Violence, and America* (Berkeley: University of California Press, 2012), 64.

[27] Catherine Albanese, *Sons of the Fathers: The Civil Religion of the American Revolution* (Philadelphia: Temple University Press, 1976), 6.

[28] McKenna, *The Puritan Origins of Patriotism*, 42, 76.

[29] Robert Bellah's excellent article on the issue makes the case that American civil religion is a well-institutionalized religious system in America that should be looked at in much the same way as all other forms of religion in America. Bellah went on to stress that American civil religion is clearly "differentiated" from the religion found in its churches. Robert Bellah, "Civil Religion in America," *Dædalus* 96 (1967): 1–21.

beliefs about its history and destiny." Civil religion provides a culture with a sense of meaning, which, in turn, allows people to look at their political community in a distinctive sense. This distinctive way of looking at a country helps to bring about a sense of collective purpose, which helps it to bring about social assimilation. In short, civil religion is the "social glue" that connects a given society.[30] Civil religion in America built upon the Puritan narrative that held a belief in a personal God who gave America a special mission intervened in its history and was using it as a way to redeem the world.[31]

Civil religion was introduced by philosophers such as Machiavelli and Hobbes and was further defined by Rousseau. However, it found its contemporary definition, at least in its American context, in Robert Bellah's landmark essay, "Civil Religion in America."[32] While not explicitly defining "civil religion," Bellah described it as something that is revealed through the way American people experience the world around them. Specifically, his understanding of civil religion saw God as the central symbol in America; and as such, God had a specific national mission for America and her citizens. This mission was most clearly seen in specific periods of American trials or difficulties.[33]

---

[30] *Dictionary of Christianity in America*, s.v. "civil religion"; John Coleman, "Civil Religion," *Sociological Analysis* 31 (1970): 67, 70.

[31] McKenna, *The Puritan Origins*, 369.

[32] Bellah, "Civil Religion in America," 1–21. Bellah's importance to the topic cannot be understated. Lienesch notes that the essay has been cited in no less than two thousand five hundred academic and scholarly writings. Lienesch, "Contesting Civil Religion," 92.

[33] Bellah, "Civil Religion in America," 15. Bellah fleshes his understanding of these periods of "trials" in Bellah, *The Broken Covenant: American Civil Religion in the Time of Trial* (Chicago: Chicago University, 1970), 176–180. Here, he lists three periods of American trials that have helped shape civil religion. First, the trial of the American Revolution brought about the writing of the Constitution and the Declaration of Independence. In this period, America was seen as a nation created by God with the divine mission. The second period of trial was the time of the Civil War. This period was defined by concepts such as sacrifice and death, most notably shown by Abraham Lincoln and his Gettysburg Address. The third period of trial was during the civil rights movement and the Vietnam era. Martin Luther King was the "champion" of this era with his rhetoric that spoke to civil and religious themes that chastised the nation for not

Civil religion finds meaning and expression in meaningful cultural symbols, and this is especially true in America.[34] There are national saints like George Washington, Abraham Lincoln, and Martin Luther King; sacred spaces like Arlington National Cemetery, Gettysburg, and the sites of the 9/11 attacks. There even exists in the context of civil religion in America the sense of sacred time like July 4 and Memorial Day.[35] The Declaration of Independence and the Constitution both, according to the concepts of American civil religion, have secured a sense of sacredness; the Declaration of Independence symbolizing the sacred act of revolution and the Constitution symbolizing the sacred institution of the government following the victory of the holy war against Britain that God had ordained.[36]

The belief that God played a "constitutive" role in the founding fathers and helped to set the tone of civil religion as it is in America today cannot be understated. Archetypes like America as a "chosen people" and a "promised land" and a "new Israel" began in the Puritan period but continue to play a prominent role in American culture today. God has been a central symbol in American civil religion and continues to be.[37]

Early American Puritanism played a distinctive role in the founding of America, but when coupled with American civil religion, the groundwork was made for a distinctly patriotic nation. How could Americans not be patriotic when its citizens saw God's

---

being true to its divine mission. Jermaine McDonald argues that America is deep within a fourth trial that has arisen due to the perceived threat of Islamic terrorism. Jermaine McDonald, "A Fourth Time of Trial: Towards an Implicit and Inclusive American Civil Religion," *Implicit Religion* 16 (2013): 50.

[34] John Wilsey, *American Exceptionalism and Civil Religion: Reassessing the History of an Idea* (Downers Grove: InterVarsity, 2015), 23. The American flag may be the most prominent symbol in all of American civil religion, and this topic will be addressed later in this project.

[35] Catherine Albanese, *America: Religions and Religion* (Belmont: Wadsworth, 1981), 296–297; Conrad Cherry, "Nation, Church, and Private Religion: The Emergence of an American Pattern," *Journal of Church and State* 14 (1972): 232; Clifton Black, "American Scriptures," *Theology Today* 67 (2010): 127–168.

[36] Albanese, *Sons of the Father*, 184, 216.

[37] Bellah, "Civil Religion in America," 6–7, 17–18.

hand in its settling, founding, and revolution from its enemies? Civil religion in America has thrived because of religious freedom and the disestablishment of a state-sponsored church; this has meant that no specific religious sect can define America's religious identity.[38] The notion of civil religion in America is an essential backdrop for the discussion on patriotism because it sees America as something more than a nation; it posits that America is a nation that loyalty is owed to due to its unique relationship with God. As such, to not be patriotic can be seen almost as sin.

Civil religion is a "strange beast" in that it can appear to mean almost anything to anyone at almost any time.[39] Regardless, civil religion promises to persist and is perhaps the best starting point for considering the future of American patriotism.[40]

Contemporary Issues Regarding the Need
for a Proper Understanding of Patriotism

While American patriotism is not a new development, four contemporary events show the need for a proper understanding of patriotism: the attacks on 9/11, the subsequent war on terror, the election of Donald Trump, and a wave of professional athletes protesting the national anthem. All four, in various ways, have brought the topic of patriotism to the mainstream and deserve to be used as a rationale for discussing the topic.

The September 11 Terrorist Attacks

In the first significant attack on American soil since the surprise attack by the Japanese on Pearl Harbor, the September 11 terrorist

---

[38] Wilsey, *American Exceptionalism and Civil Religion*, 24.

[39] Raymond Haberski Jr., *God and War: American Civil Religion since 1945* (New Brunswick: Rutgers, 2012), 5. Haberski states that civil religion is a "hybrid of nationalism and traditional religion" and "has an ideological flexibility that is intoxicating because it is so evocative, elastic, and deceptively complex." Haberski, *God and War*, 5.

[40] Lienesch, "Contesting Civil Religion," 116; Philip Gorski, *American Covenant: A History of Civil Religion from the Puritans to the Present* (Princeton: Princeton University Press, 2017), 13.

attacks killed 2,986 people from over eighty different countries and reasserted patriotism into American politics. The aftermath of the attacks on September 11, 2001, led to a dramatic upsurge of patriotism in the United States. Until the 9/11 attacks, the single most lethal and deadly terrorist attack had been the attack on the Abadan theater in Iran that killed over four hundred people in 1978.[41] These attacks on the United States brought a stark realization to most Americans: they had been attacked, wounded, and hurt.

The 9/11 attacks were unique because they were seen not just as an American event but one that affected the entire world: it was a global event. Philosopher Jürgen Habermas noted this as significant when he stated that the attacks "could be called the first historic world event in the strictest sense."[42] The media pointed out repeatedly that America had come under attack and, as a result, was no longer safe. How would America respond? The attacks on America, while tragic, gave rise to a patriotic narrative that came to dominate the American political landscape that continues largely unchallenged today.[43]

After the 9/11 attacks, there was a sense of emergency that befell the American people that had not been felt in some years. As Aviel Roshwald notes, the attacks "shook up most Americans' assumptions about their nation's place in the world," which led to a brief feeling of despair but was quickly followed by a robust patriotic response.[44] The attacks did something to the core of the American public. As commentator Seth Mandel notes, the attacks "posed a discomfiting challenge to the tolerance on which liberal

---

[41] Tan, *U.S. Strategy against Global Terrorism*, 1–2.

[42] Giovanna Borradori, *Philosophy in a Time of Terror: Dialogues with Jürgen Habermas and Jacques Derrida* (Chicago: University of Chicago, 2004), 28.

[43] Richard Jackson, "The 9/11 Attacks and the Social Construction of a National Narrative," in *The Impact of 9/11 on the Media, Arts, and Entertainment: The Day That Changed Everything?* ed. Matthew Morgan (New York: Palgrave, 2009), 26–30.

[44] Aviel Roshwald, *The Endurance of Nationalism: Ancient Roots and Modern Dilemmas* (Cambridge: Cambridge University Press, 2006), 199.

democracies pride themselves."[45] The attacks gave rise to a "conservative shift" that could only be explained by the increased anxiety caused by the attacks.[46]

The time that immediately followed the 9/11 attacks created an unfamiliar set of conditions that tested the different meanings of what it meant to be an American. Patriotism in America, as well as other countries, is often visible in times of catastrophe, emergency, or war; however, before 9/11, America's national attachment had often been visible in the frequent flying of the American flag in times of peace. Now that the attacks made it clear that America was no longer in a state of peace, American flags waved in a new sense of patriotism. American stores quickly sold out due to this increased notion of patriotism.[47]

From the events of 9/11 until today, the American flag has stood as a symbol of national pride and "primes the core essence of what it means to be an American."[48] The tragic events of 9/11 served as a way to bring the national consciousness to a sense of togetherness and unity that had not been seen in recent generations. To be patriotic was to display the flag, and alternatively, not to display the flag was to be seen as unpatriotic. The public display of the American flag became a source of support and strength for the average American by promoting national unity through public displays of patriotism via flying the American flag.[49]

---

[45] Seth Mandel, "The Failed War on the 'War on Terror': Everybody Hates It and It's Not Going Anywhere," *Commentary*, November 2013, 19.

[46] George Bonanno and John Jost, "Conservative Shift among High-Exposure Survivors of the September 11th Attacks," *Basic and Applied Social Psychology* 28 (2006): 311.

[47] Markus Kemmelmeier and David Winter, "Sowing Patriotism, but Reaping Nationalism? Consequences of Exposure to the American Flag," *Political Psychology* 29 (2008): 859–860. Phillip Bratta notes that American retailer Walmart sold 116,000 American flags on September 11 and 250,000 on September 12 compared to only 6,400 and 10,000 on the same days the year before. Phillip Bratta, "Flag Display Post-9/11: A Discourse on American Nationalism," *The Journal of American Culture* 32 (2009): 232.

[48] Crittendon, "Differentiating Patriotism and Nationalism: Influence of Valence of Primes," 3.

[49] Bratta, "Flag Display Post-9/11," 238.

The War on Terror

The 9/11 attacks suggested that a massive terrorist threat posed a real and existential threat to America and the American ethos. As a result, on September 15, 2001, just days after the 9/11 attacks, President George Bush, in a radio address to the United States, launched "a broad and sustained campaign to secure our country and eradicate the evil of terrorism," and thus the global war on terror had begun.[50] A few weeks later, on October 7, the United States, with a coalition of other allies, invaded the country of Afghanistan to root out and destroy the Taliban, a terroristic group who were sought out as architects of the 9/11 attacks. As soon as the culprits were identified, President Bush stated the total defeat of Al-Qaeda and all terrorist groups with global reach to be the primary goal of the United States and her efforts at protecting America.[51] Within a month of 9/11, the United States had carried out attacks on various Taliban and Al-Qaeda bases in the country of Afghanistan and had formally invaded them.

While there were significant national debates about the invasion of Afghanistan, it had broad support from the international community; however, in February 2003, President Bush shifted his philosophy and called for a more "preemptive" approach to the global war on terror.[52] As a result of this shift, on March 19, 2003, the United States, under orders from President Bush, began phase two of the war on terror by turning his attention toward Saddam Hussein via an invasion of Iraq due to the alleged presence of weapons of mass destruction, which, the American public was told, were to be used in eventual attacks on America. This move was seen as controversial, and in response, much of the same international community that was supportive of the invasion of Afghanistan opposed the invasion of Iraq.[53] The invasion was short, ending on April 9, 2003, with the fall of the city of Baghdad.

---

[50] Tan, *U.S. Strategy against Global Terrorism*, 2.

[51] Erik Goepner, "Measuring the Effectiveness of America's War on Terror," *Parameters* 46 (2016): 108.

[52] Goepner, "Measuring the Effectiveness of America's War on Terror," 107; Tan, *U.S. Strategy against Global Terrorism*, 4.

[53] Tan, *U.S. Strategy against Global Terrorism*, 3, 107.

While public displays of the flag decreased in the months after 9/11, they increased with the invasion of Iraq.[54] The global war on terror helped build the sense of patriotism partly because it was seen in the television viewing habits of many Americans. Not only did Americans see consistent reports of the ongoing efforts on the war on terror, but they were also consistently reminded of it through the efforts of the Bush administration. In the three years following the start of the war on terror, the administration made, on average, through speeches, interviews, and official communications, ten mentions per day of something relating to the war on terror.[55] In this way, the war on terror was always before Americans, and as a result, the American public was consistently reminded to be patriotic by supporting the troops. To do so was a patriotic duty.

Patriotism contributed to the early support of the war on terror.[56] Over the past fifteen years, there have been almost ten thousand military personnel killed with almost 2.5 million servicemen and women being sent to fight. Furthermore, there have been over 675,000 disability claims as a result of the war on terror. The prolonged war has become the longest in the history of America. Additionally, trillions of dollars have been added to the American national debt.[57] The money spent, combined with over 137,000 civilian casualties, has led support for the war on terror to wane despite the patriotic leanings of many Americans.

The Presidency of Donald Trump

A third event that brought the discussion of patriotism to the forefront of American culture was the election of Donald Trump as

---

[54] Gerald Webster, "American Nationalism, the Flag, and the Invasion of Iraq," *The Geographical Review* 101 (2011): 14.

[55] Brigitte Naws, *Mass-Mediated Terrorism: The Central Role of the Media in Terrorism and Counterterrorism* (New York: Rowman and Littlefield, 2002), 148–149.

[56] Daniel McCleary, et al., "Types of Patriotism as Primary Predictors of Continuing Support for the Iraq War," *Journal of Political and Military Sociology* 37 (2009): 78.

[57] Goepner, "Measuring the Effectiveness of America's War on Terror," 107; Joseph Masco, "Auditing the War on Terror: The Watson Institute's Costs of War Project," *American Anthropologist* 115 (2013): 312.

the forty-fifth president of the United States. Running with the campaign slogan "Make America Great Again," many saw in Trump a politician who was more than patriotic: he was a candidate "for" the people. The "Make America Great Again" slogan popped up everywhere: on hats, posters, social media, and in everyday conversation.

The "Make America Great Again" slogan became one that many perceived as the start of a patriotic—and for some, a nationalist—movement. Trump, from the campaign trail to the White House, used the terms "patriot" and "nationalist" synonymously, thereby keeping the discussion of both patriotism and nationalism at the forefront of political discussion both in America and abroad. For many, Trump's campaign was widely seen as a part of a nationalist resurgence in the Western world.[58]

In an astonishing victory and upset, Trump was elected the forty-fifth president of the United States. Most analysts gave him no chance of securing the Republican nomination, let alone winning the presidency. In fact, Trump was given a one-hundred-to-one long shot of winning by a popular betting firm when he announced he was running.[59]

One of the critical reasons for Trump's surprise election was the fact that he received the collective vote of American evangelical voters.[60] Even though there was a considerable pushback against

---

[58] James Antle, "Trump's Nationalist Moment: Voters Are Speaking up for Country, Border, and Sovereignty," *The American Conservative* 18, no. 1 (2019): 14.

[59] Michael Nelson, *Trump's First Year* (Charlottesville: University of Virginia, 2018), 5.

[60] Sarah Bailey, "White Evangelicals Voted Overwhelmingly for Donald Trump," *Washington Post*, November 9, 2016, washingtonpost.com/news/acts-of-faith/wp/2016/11/09/exit-polls-show-white-evangelicals-voted-overwhelmingly-for-donald-trump/?noredirect=on&utm_term=.9b754341acf1. See also, Jessica Martinez and Gregory Smith, "How the Faithful Voted: A Preliminary 2016 Analysis," Pew Research, https://www.pewresearch.org/fact-tank/2016/11/09/how-the-faithful-voted-a-preliminary-2016-analysis/. For a more comprehensive look at how the votes of American evangelicals helped Trump win the presidency, see Angela Denker, *Red State Christians: Understanding the Voters Who Elected Donald Trump* (Minneapolis: Fortress, 2019); Andrew Whitehead, et al., "Make America Christian Again: Christian

Trump during the early period of securing the Republican presidential nomination, eventually, Trump secured the nomination. Additionally, most evangelicals supported Trump as the lesser of two evils in a head-to-head race against Hillary Clinton.[61] While it can be argued this lesser-of-two-evils approach had its merits in a head-to-head race against Hillary Clinton, what about in the primaries? According to some researchers, the reason that so many evangelicals supported Trump from his initial announcement or, at the very least, the early period of his candidacy, was that many of these voters were "Christian nationalists."[62]

  The Christian nationalist ideology that influences some notion of political discourse is unique in that it calls forth a defense of America through a mythological narrative that connects it directly to a Christian tradition. Therefore, voting for Trump, for many claiming to identify with Christian nationalism, was seen as a "symbolic defense" of the United States and her national heritage.[63] These Trump supporters were connecting their vote for him with a particular eschatological view that saw America as a once-great nation that had suffered rapidly under the presidency of a seemingly "un-Christian" and unpatriotic Barack Obama and his "un-American" policies. The only choice, for Christian nationalists, was

---

Nationalism and Voting for Donald Trump in the 2016 Presidential Election," *Sociology of Religion: A Quarterly Review* 79 (2018): 147–171.

[61] Philip Gorski, "Why Evangelicals Voted for Trump: A Critical Cultural Sociology," *American Journal of Cultural Sociology* 5 (2017): 340.

[62] Gorski, "Why Evangelicals Voted for Trump," 340; Andrew Whitehead, et al., "Make America Christian Again," 164. According to Philip Gorski, white Christian nationalists who supported Trump had four major characteristics. First, they exhibited signs of racism; second, they believed in a sense of "sacrificialism" where one should sacrifice for the nation; third, they had a sense of "apocalypticism" because they viewed Clinton's potential election as a disaster that must be avoided at all costs; fourth, they had a sense of "nostalgia" that was most readily identified with the notion of "American exceptionalism." Gorski, "Why Evangelicals Voted for Trump," 339–347.

[63] Whitehead, et al., "Make America Christian Again," 147. Also, see Evan Stewart, "Public Religion and the Vote for Donald Trump: Evidence from Panel Data," paper presented at the American Sociological Association Annual Conference, August 11–14, Philadelphia, PA. Stewart argues that Christian nationalism was among the strongest predictors of voting for Trump.

to wholeheartedly support Trump, because to do so was to secure America's place as a "Christian" nation.[64]

While Americans have almost always considered themselves patriotic, it seems the term "patriotic" has become much more prominent in the media, social commentary, and the life of the church with the election of Trump as the forty-fifth president of the United States. With his promise to make America great, there seems to have been another increase of people claiming, if not flaunting, their patriotism of a seemingly Christian nation.[65]

Professional Athletes'
Protesting of the National Anthem

Another issue surrounding patriotism has been the recent development of seeing professional athletes kneel during their respective sports' playing of the national anthem before their games or matches. On August 26, 2016, Colin Kaepernick of the San Francisco 49ers chose not to stand for the playing of the national anthem of a preseason football game and gained immediate national attention for doing so. At first, Kaepernick sat during the national anthem, but after making his reasoning for sitting clear to the media, he began to kneel during the anthem. His reasoning? He was attempting to present his kneeling as a symbolic gesture protesting

---

[64] Whitehead, et al. go on to stress that white Christian nationalism "provides a metanarrative for a religiously distinct national identity." Further, white Christian nationalists holding "this narrative and perceive threats to that identity overwhelmingly voted for Trump." Whitehead, et al., "Make America Christian Again," 152, 165. Angela Denker makes the case that Christian nationalism was one of the main reasons that Trump was elected. Denker, *Red State Christians*.

[65] Andrew Whitehead and Samuel Perry argue that the election of Trump was due to Americans who believed that America was a Christian nation and who saw Trump as a way to ensure the protection of American values. As a result, they argue that "Trumpism" will outlast the Trump presidency because of the way that Trump has transformed the Republican party. Andrew Whitehead and Samuel Perry, "Is a 'Christian America' a More Patriarchal America? Religion, Politics, and Traditionalist Gender Ideology," *Canadian Review of Sociology* 57 (2018): 173.

perceived social injustices in the United States.[66] In the months before Kaepernick's protest, there were several high profile deaths of African American men at the hands of police, and many athletes found themselves using their status as a way to spotlight the perceived injustices. While these athletes responded by doing interviews, wearing clothes with political messages, and writing editorials, it was Kaepernick who was able to exhibit more influence on these issues due to the media coverage surrounding the National Football League (NFL).[67] Some have even argued that during this time, Kaepernick has "exerted more influence on American society" than any other popular culture star.[68]

Kaepernick was standing up for his understanding of racial discrimination and police brutality; the quarterback continued to kneel throughout the season stating simply, "I am not looking for approval. I have to stand up for people that are oppressed."[69] Kaepernick's protest and message grew into something much bigger. By September 2017, more than two hundred NFL players were kneeling, and by 2018, the NFL team owners passed a rule that all players would have to stand for the national anthem or stay in the locker room.[70] Throughout the 2016 and 2017 NFL seasons, many

---

[66] Karen Smeda, "Foul on the Play: Applying Mediation Strategies to Address Social Injustice Protests in the NFL," *Dispute Resolution Journal* 73 (2018): 51.

[67] Eric Hall, "Policy Point—Counterpoint: Do African American Athletes Have an Obligation to Fight against Racial Injustice?" *International Social Science Review* 93 (2017): 1.

[68] Sean Gregory, "Colin Kaepernick," *TIME Magazine*, 2017, 100.

[69] Kofie Yeboah, "A Timeline of Events since Colin Kaepernick's National Anthem Protest," *The Undefeated*, September 6, 2016, theundefeated.com/features/a-timeline-of-events-since-colin-kaepernicks-national-anthem-protest/.

[70] Austin Knoblauch, "NFL Player Protests Sweep League after President Trump's Hostile Remarks," *USA Today*, September 24, 2017, usatoday.com/story/sports/nfl/2017/09/24/donald-trump-nfl-player-protests-national-anthem-week-3-response/697609001/; Austin Knoblauch, "NFL Expected to Enact National Anthem Policy for 18," NFL, nfl.com/news/story/0ap3000000933952/article/nfl-expected-to-enact-national-anthem-policy-for-18.

NFL players showed solidarity with Kaepernick by joining in the protests.[71]

However, this political movement split other players and many fans. In a poll during the protests, 47 percent of Americans thought that the athletes should stand during the anthem, while 51 percent thought that there should not be a specific rule requiring them to do so.[72] Public opinion polls suggested that fans began to boycott the NFL as a result of these protests, and viewership and support of the NFL began to decline.[73] Further, it was not just the fans and players that were torn on the issue—many team executives, owners, and coaches were as well. Some supported the athletes' right to protest, while others were silent.[74]

While credited with igniting the recent trend of athletes kneeling during the playing of the national anthem, this is not to say that Kaepernick was the first to bring national attention to political issues. African American runners Tommie Smith and John Carlos famously angered many Americans by raising black-gloved fists while on the podium for winning gold and silver, respectively, in the two-hundred-meter sprint during the 1968 Olympics in Mexico City. Many athletes protested during the national anthem in the sixties as a way to protest the war in Vietnam.[75] Muhammad Ali, one of the most recognized American sports figures of all time, famously protested the war in Vietnam and refused to register for the draft. Ali immediately lost his boxing license and was labeled as unpatriotic and received death threats.[76]

---

[71] Smeda, "Foul on the Play," 52.

[72] Gregory, "Colin Kaepernick," 102.

[73] Chloe Kaufman, "Speaking about Politics, a Fireable Offense? The Legality of Employee Speech Restrictions in the Entertainment Industry," *Journal of Intellectual Property and Entertainment Law* 8 (2019): 381.

[74] Smeda, "Foul on the Play," 58.

[75] Joseph Connor, "Off Key: America's National Anthem was a Lightning Rod for Controversy Long before Colin Kaepernick Stayed in His Seat," *American History* (February 2017): 50. Dave Zirin argues that the sixties and seventies were the "golden age" of political athletes. Dave Zirin, "Taking a Knee," *The Nation* 305 (2017): 3–4.

[76] Thomas Etan, "What Kaepernick Started: A Former NBA Player Reflects," *The Progressive* (November 2016): 30. Also see Travis Boyce, *Radical*

In much the same way, Kaepernick's protests were perceived as an assault on American patriotism and values. At the same time, Kaepernick brought to the forefront the understanding that American was deeply divided over the issue. While being labeled unpatriotic by many, his cultural icon status rose. While some questioned whether or not he should use his career to protest during the anthem, others called it a "timely" action due to the polarized issues of race relations within the United States.[77]

If Kaepernick lit the match to the discussion through his use of kneeling during the anthem, then Trump poured the gas.[78] On September 22, 2017, Trump stoked the polarization even further when he said in reference to Kaepernick, "Wouldn't you love to see one of these NFL owners, when somebody disrespects our flag, to say, 'Get that son of a [expletive] off the field right now'?" while speaking at a political rally in the very conservative state of Alabama.[79] The Trump administration also made suggestions that individual on-air employees should be terminated for their role in protesting during the playing of the national anthem.[80] Trump's comments thrilled not just the conservatives in the audience but his conservative base and sparked a national discussion of what it means to be patriotic.[81]

It is not surprising that the protests taking place in the NFL were the ones most responsible for bringing the issue of patriotism to the forefront. The NFL is the professional sport league most

---

Teacher: A Socialist, Feminist, and Anti-Racist Journal of the Theory and Practice of Teaching 109 (2017): 21–28.

[77] Boyce, *Radical Teacher*, 23–24.

[78] Zirin, "Taking a Knee," 3.

[79] Greggory, "Colin Kaepernick," 102.

[80] Kaufman, "Speaking about Politics," 408. Kaufman gives an excellent summary of the legal challenges presented in whether or not sports figures have a First Amendment right to protest during the anthem.

[81] Denker argues the issue with Trump and Kaepernick showed that much more was at stake: "Somehow, American pride, Jesus and pigskins got conflated, and the NFL came to represent all that is sacred about the America Trump was elected to represent . . . While the NFL has come to represent conservative patriotism and the sort of 'God and country' Christianity popular across southern and rural America . . . [it] brought to the fore a conflict that was not only about politics and sports but also about religion and about who has the final word on Christianity in America." Denker, *Red State Christians*, 124–126.

correlated with conservative politics.[82] In 1942, Congress codified rules on rising for the national anthem, and after Japan's surrender in WWII, former NFL commissioner Elmer Layden made clear the NFL's commitment to patriotism and the anthem by saying it should be "as much a part of every game as the kick-off."[83] So, for more than a generation, the NFL has been seen through a patriotic lens, at the very least, before kickoff due to the league's commitment to the national anthem.

The issue of patriotism within sports was made more obvious in the months after the 9/11 attacks because sports were seen as a type of political "discourse." Immediately after 9/11, Americans saw sports as a way to escape from the current terrorist threat, and the media helped to fuel this escape. On television, sports exhibited themes communicating the importance of unity and patriotism.[84] Sports became a way to present a narrative of cultural politics as well as communicating a particular vision of America. For example, in the third game of the World Series of professional baseball, just weeks after the 9/11 attacks, then-president Bush threw out the opening pitch in New York. Wearing a pullover that features the New York Fire Department's logo, Bush's pitch was arguably one of the most significant opening pitches in baseball history. This served as a patriotic moment, inspiring unity but also a belief that things were seemingly getting back to normal in the United States. This moment in sports was significant.

Other moments in sports over the coming months were significant as well. Super Bowl XXXVI, played on February 3, 2002, featured a highly patriotic theme: "Hope, Heroes, and Homeland." Throughout the television broadcast, the Fox Network connected American football with strands of patriotism and nationalism with its ties to the military who were now fighting

---

[82] Zirin, "Taking a Knee," 3. For a more comprehensive look at the history of how the pledge of allegiance and national anthem came to be standardized, see Richard Ellis, *To the Flag: The Unlikely History of the Pledge of Allegiance* (Lawrence: University Press of Kansas, 2005).

[83] Connor, "Off Key," 49–50.

[84] Mark Falcous and Michael Silk, "Manufacturing Consent: Mediated Sporting Spectacle and the Cultural Politics of the 'War on Terror'," *International Journal of Media and Cultural Politics* 1 (2005): 59–60.

overseas in the war on terror. With American flags seen throughout the broadcast and talks from American heroes, it was obvious to all viewers that American pride and unity were strong.[85]

Sports have an almost sacred connotation with Americans, and the ritualism around it feeds this connotation.[86] Sports have become central to the American culture; it is no surprise athletes have achieved such a prominent role.[87] When looked at together, athletes and their social influence and the patriotic lens through which much of sports is now looked at post-9/11, it is no wonder that athletes kneeling during the playing of the national anthem are looked at as taboo. Kaepernick (and Trump) have forced the American public to grapple with the difficult questions about patriotism, political protest, and the right to free speech.[88]

Rationale for Research

Due to the contemporary political culture of the United States, there is much polarization on issues of what it means to be an American; and as a result of this polarization, there is much discussion on what it means to be a "patriotic" American. What does being patriotic mean, and is it a character trait that all Americans must have? This contemporary polarization within the American political, social, and ecclesial landscape shows the need for such a discussion.

With so much contemporary discussion on the topics of patriotism due to issues like the continued war on terror, national anthem protests, and even the current president, citizens must have

---

[85] Falcous and Silk, "Manufacturing Consent," 59–61. Additionally, the opening ceremony of the Winter Olympics in Salt Lake City, Utah, in 2002 featured athletes along with various members of both NYPD and FDNY. Normally a patriotic event, the opening ceremony was made more somber by the inclusion of an American flag from New York that had survived the 9/11 attacks. This continued to serve as a reminder to the American public that the war on terror was not over.

[86] For a summary of the connection between ritualism and sporting behavior, see Oscar Fernández and Roberto Cachán-Cruz, "An Assessment of the Dynamic of Religious Ritualism in Sporting Environments," *Journal of Religious Health* 53 (2014): 1653–1661.

[87] Hall, "Policy Point," 8.

[88] Gregory, "Colin Kaepernick," 100–102.

a proper understanding of what patriotism is and what it is not. Its connection to the concept of nationalism—which has also become of contemporary importance—also brings a misunderstanding of the term, which makes any discussion of patriotism problematic. Due to the differing understandings and misunderstandings of patriotism, there are different understandings of the loyalties that people should have toward their country. Complicating this is the fact that Christians have been called to be citizens of the kingdom of God.

With this in mind, what is a Christian's responsibility to the state? Does a Christian *have* to be patriotic to be a good citizen of both the nation and the kingdom? Further, where does the church fit into the political discussion of patriotism? These are issues that can only be addressed by considering a biblical assessment of patriotism. These issues do not seem to be going away in contemporary American culture; the need for a biblical assessment of patriotism is great.

Scope of the Project

There is much work needed on the topic of patriotism. Many definitions, understandings, criticisms, and affirmations of patriotism exist. Additionally, patriotism today is often associated with nationalism, which can give it a negative connotation in the public and political square. The American concepts of patriotism run deep into its spiritual and cultural heritage; and as such, a biblical definition of patriotism must exist if the church is to be biblically faithful in an extremely divided culture rather than exist as an extension of American civil religion. This work proposes that patriotism, when properly defined, is a biblical alternative to both nationalism and cosmopolitanism. Patriotism will be shown to have three main characteristics: a sense of loyalty toward a person's particular country, a singular loyalty toward a person's country, and a personal identification with a person's country and culture. These characteristics will form the framework for a biblical understanding of patriotism. A biblically defined patriotism serves the church well as she exists in a politically divided culture; further, it assists to keep her more focused on her mission by keeping her away from merely existing as American civil religion.

The purpose of this book is to define a framework of patriotism in America and to give a proper biblical assessment of it. Because patriotism is so closely connected to nationalism, early work will be done to distinguish the terms from one another. The methodology of this project is: first, to give a brief historical sketch of the contemporary issues surrounding American patriotism and its connection to nationalism; second, a definition of patriotism will be given that will serve in later chapters as a framework for a biblical assessment; third, patriotism will be shown as a biblical alternative to both nationalism and cosmopolitanism, which will be shown to be untenable for the Christian. This framework of patriotism will then be assessed biblically while looking through an American lens.

Chapter 2 will give an assessment of the historical underpinnings of the American conception of patriotism. Because the research on these topics is so vast, special attention will be given to specific periods of American history. Special attention will be given to contemporary influences on political philosophy while looking at the following periods of American history: the Puritan era, the revolutionary period, the constitutional era, the era of the Civil War, World War II, and the Vietnam era.[89]

Chapter 3 will present a biblical definition of patriotism as a loyalty to one's particular country that involves a personal identification with his country, culture, and people. By developing a definition of patriotism that is rooted in loyalty, one can assess and evaluate what a biblical understanding of patriotism entails. Chapter 4 will seek to posit the case that patriotism is a biblical alternative to both nationalism and cosmopolitanism. Building on the work of defining terms and assessing previous literature, this project will show both nationalism and cosmopolitanism as untenable for the Christian leaving patriotism as the proper alternative. Additionally, a summary of the various types of patriotism will be given, which will help show the importance of having a biblical definition. Building on the need for a biblical definition of patriotism, Chapter 4 will give a definition that can be assessed biblically. The definition

---

[89] It is beyond the scope of this project to deal with these topics and eras comprehensively, but special care will be given to consider the major points of political writings that are germane to the topic.

will consist of three characteristics. First, patriotism is concerned with love and loyalty toward a person's home country; second, patriotism is concerned with a person's love and loyalty for his home country and not other countries; third, patriotism is concerned with a person's identification with his country and culture. These three characteristics will make up the framework of patriotism and will be looked at biblically throughout the rest of the project.

Chapter 5 will discuss the life and ministry of Paul as a test case of a biblically informed concept of patriotism. Paul, as a Roman citizen, understood what it meant to have loyalty to a country. In this way, Paul will be shown to be a person who understood his role as a citizen of a state while also being a citizen of the kingdom of God. Chapter 6 will consider contemporary issues regarding patriotism for the American church and give practical conclusions and further areas of study. Finally, Chapter 7 will give a summary of the main thesis and takeaways from each chapter.

2

Historical Underpinnings
of American Patriotism

To properly understand how America became such a patriotic country, it is essential to understand some of the historical developments that guided the country to embrace such an importance on being patriotic. There are several periods of American history that help set the stage for the contemporary setting that sees patriotism as a vital bedrock of American culture; in the early periods, Americans connected their country directly with God and His mission on earth. In this way, Americans developed a sense that their country was being particularly blessed and used by God, which necessitated patriotic belief in the country.

The first period that serves as a historical underpinning of contemporary patriotism is the Puritan era of America's founding. During this period, the settling of America was understood as a heroic journey into the wilderness where Christians were being sent out to do God's work in the world. As such, America was a metaphorical "city on a hill." The next period that is important to understand is the time surrounding the Revolutionary War. As Americans sought their independence, they saw themselves as doing the Lord's work in establishing a "new Israel" in the world. For the revolutionaries, defending America from the evil British Empire was the only way to ensure that God's new kingdom would survive. The only option then for patriots who feared God was to fight. The third historical period is the Civil War era. During this era, both the North and the South wrestled with concepts of national identity that saw both sides as being under the lordship of God and, via extension, His providence. This continued after the Civil War was over, and as a result, the national consciousness shifted from seeing the United States as a collection of individual states to a truly "united" country. The fourth era is the WWII era. During this period, the United States became a world power. As a result of her eventual involvement in WWII, America's economy and military became the strongest in the world and became a symbol for good in the world. The last period that is important for an understanding of patriotism is the Vietnam War era. While not a particularly positive era in American history, Vietnam led Americans to be critical patriots who supported the military despite her military efforts.

The Puritans

The American concept of faith and country was initially shaped and developed by the Puritans.[1] Of all of the religious systems that existed in the early days of the founding of America, Puritanism is the only one that modern historians take seriously.[2] It would be a mistake to understate how important the religious culture of New England was to the evolving American ethos and, more particularly, the influence of Puritan rhetoric on the American identity. Puritan theology remained the dominant theology in New England from the time of the first settlement in 1620 to the time of American independence in 1776.[3]

For a variety of reasons, the Puritans saw themselves as a people set apart by God attempting to fulfill a specific mission in the world. As a result, the Puritans helped contribute to a particular worldview that saw themselves as chosen explicitly by God. This "chosenness" rhetoric, specifically in New England, was two-sided. On the one hand, the Puritans understood that this chosenness was important enough to influence all particulars of daily life; on the other hand, there was a real fear that God might judge them for being unfaithful to their mission.[4] More than that, out of this sense of

---

[1] Cathleen Kaveny, "The Remnants of Theocracy: The Puritans, the Jeremiad and the Contemporary Culture Wars," *Law, Culture and the Humanities* 9 (2013): 60.

[2] Mark Noll, *America's God: From Jonathan Edwards to Abraham Lincoln* (New York: Oxford University Press, 2002), 32.

[3] Harry Stout, *The New England Soul: Preaching and Religious Culture in Colonial New England* (Oxford: Oxford University Press, 2012), 9.

[4] George McKenna, *The Puritan Origins of American Patriotism* (New Haven: Yale, 2007), 41; John Wilsey, *One Nation under God? An Evangelical Critique of Christian America* (Eugene: Pickwick, 2011), 98. Noted Puritan

chosenness grew a sense that Americans saw themselves as the primary agent of redemptive history.[5] The concept of God's choosing of America is evident in one of the most important early American sermons by John Winthrop.

America as the "City on a Hill"

In 1630, aboard the ship Arbella, probably before landfall, John Winthrop delivered a sermon entitled "A Modell of Christian Charity."[6] While not published in his lifetime, this sermon stands as a testament to the belief that the journey to America was vital because it was a way to fulfill God's mission.[7] Winthrop drew parallels between the settlers and the ancient Israelites who were crossing the ocean to settle the Promised Land. This journey was a sacred story tied intimately to their unique chosenness much like the

---

scholar Perry Miller remarked that Puritanism "was not merely a religious creed and a theology, it was also a program for society." Perry Miller, *Errand in the Wilderness* (New York: Harper, 1954), 191. Thus, Puritanism was a worldview with wide applications on the American people.

[5] Nathan Hatch, *The Sacred Cause of Liberty* (New Haven: Yale University Press, 1977), 155.

[6] Recent research suggests that this sermon was actually written "before" Winthrop's departure and was subsequently circulated within the Puritan community in written form. Philip Gorski, *American Covenant: A History of Civil Religion from the Puritans to the Present* (Princeton: Princeton University Press, 2017), 40. For more on modern research on this sermon, see Hugh Dawson, "John Winthrop's Rite of Passage: The Origins of the 'Cristian Charitie' Discourse," *Early American Literature* 26 (1991): 219–231.

[7] Alan Heimert and Andrew Delbanco, eds., *The Puritans in America: A Narrative Anthology* (Cambridge: Harvard University Press, 1985), 81. Richard Gamble argues that this sermon was not as important to the early American people. He states that from 1630–1838, there was little, if any, importance to the sermon because there is no evidence of any preacher, politician, or significant member of the American public who quoted it before 1858. However, Gamble does see the significance of the Puritan concept of America being a city on a hill. While this sermon was not as significant to the early American people, it cannot be argued that the themes included in the sermon are not. Further, there is lasting importance on this sermon as it still used as a prophecy of America's future greatness and exceptionalism. See Richard Gamble, *In Search of the City on a Hill: The Making and Unmaking of an American Myth* (New York: Continuum, 2012), 68–70.

nation of Israel. Winthrop saw the people overseeing the establishment of Massachusetts Bay as entering into a special covenant with God. Winthrop's understanding was that if the people were obedient to this covenant, God would "please to hear us, and bring us in peace to the place we desire"; however, if they were disobedient, "the Lord will surely break out in wrath against us."[8] For Winthrop and the Puritans, the people were establishing a Christian colony that would seek to be a city on a hill, a beacon that would be a source of inspiration of Christian community to the world based upon God's righteousness and justice.[9]

This concept of America as a city on a hill still proves rhetorically useful for describing America as a nation.[10] From this concept arose the development of a distinctly spiritual and intellectual understanding of the American spirit; America was chosen but also existed as a light to the world. In this way, Puritans stressed that the colonists must support the new nation because it was an extension of God's mission; as such, to be a faithful colonist, one must, in essence, be patriotic, because to be so was to support God and, by extension, his new instrument in the world.

The Puritan "Errand into
the Wilderness"

In order for the Puritans to achieve the notion that America was a city on a hill, the wilderness needed to be tamed. In the colonial

---

[8] John Winthrop, "A Model of Christian Charity," in *The Puritans in America: A Narrative Anthology*, ed. Alan Heimert and Andrew Delbanco (Cambridge: Harvard University Press, 1985), 90–91.

[9] Conrad Cherry stated that the Puritans sought "to build a holy commonwealth in which the people were covenanted together by their profession of religious faith and were covenanted with god by their pledge to erect a Christian society." Conrad Cherry, *God's New Israel: Religious Interpretations of American Destiny* (Chapel Hill: University of North Carolina Press, 1998), 26; Gorski, *American Covenant*, 41; John Wilsey, "America as the City upon a Hill: An Historical, Philosophical and Theological Critique of the Historiographical Construal of America as a Christian Nation" (PhD diss., Southeastern Baptist Theological Seminary, 2009), 72.

[10] Gorski suggests that this sermon is now a part of the "national canon" because it still very much used today. Gorski, *American Covenant*, 59.

period, the New England Puritans had an eschatologically oriented conception of the wilderness they found themselves. Puritans saw America as the woman mentioned in Revelation 12:6 and saw the wilderness as the unexplored land of the New World. The woman flees from the dragon after the deliverance of her son so the dragon will not destroy her. The woman represents the church who is now on earth and not in heaven because she now represents the true people of God on earth.[11] The Puritans thought of the church in America as taking shape as a garden in the wilderness of the New World.[12] In essence, the Puritan's journey into the wilderness was seen as an attempt to reclaim the faithful nature of the church as a retreat from the world. The Puritan's "errand into the wilderness" was seen as a literal extension of the Israelite's exodus from Egypt, where they were heading out in the wilderness to inherit the land that was promised to them. In this way, the Puritans saw the New World as both land to be conquered but also land full of promise.

The Puritans not only believed the New World was their blessing; they also believed the New World was to be a beacon of hope for the mission of God. As Perry Miller notes, the Puritans "came to America, where they could establish a society in which the one and only truth should reign forever."[13] The Puritans sought to establish their colonies in the new wilderness and worked extensively to "carve out a civilization on a new and barely explored continent."[14] Rooting their allegorical reading in the Old Testament, Puritans saw themselves as a special people in much the same way as ancient Israel; they embraced being sent as a consecrated people on their own version of an exodus, or an errand, facing particular challenges as ways to demonstrate their faithfulness.[15]

---

[11] G. K. Beale, *The Book of Revelation: A Commentary on the Greek Text*, New International Greek Testament Commentary (Grand Rapids: Eerdmans, 1999), 642.

[12] George Williams, *Wilderness and Paradise in Christian Thought: The Biblical Experience of the Desert in the History of Christianity and the Paradise Theme in the Theological Idea of the University* (New York: Harper & Brothers, 1962), 99.

[13] Perry Miller, *Errand into the Wilderness* (Cambridge: Belknap, 1956), 144.

[14] Wilsey, "America as the City upon a Hill," 98.

[15] Kaveny, "The Remnants of Theocracy," 63–64.

As troubles came, the Puritans held to their belief in the sovereignty of God. They understood that the settling of the New World would be difficult, but they also understood that God would be with them and provide everything that they needed. This errand into the wilderness would be the foundation for making America the city on a hill that Winthrop foresaw. In this way, Puritan ideology helped form a national consciousness that was deeply indebted by the Bible that saw God as being the one who was ordaining everything that happened to fulfill His mission in the world. As such, America was the new Israel sent into the new Promised Land.

The Puritan Concept
of the National Covenant

No matter how much the Puritans wanted success for the new American community, they understood this new Israel needed to be faithful to God because He was the one who had chosen them. Because they understood God had chosen them, they saw in the settling of America a covenant between them and God. God would be faithful to them in their errand and journey into the wilderness as long as they continued to be faithful to Him. In this way, the Puritans saw this covenant as a conditional one: God would continue to bless them because of their chosenness only as long as they continued to be faithful.[16] As the colonists were members of a covenanted society, all of life was to be submitted to God and His sovereign will under the authority of Scripture. Ultimately, for the Puritans in New England, all of society was made up of this cohesive system where all of life would be thoroughly and biblically interwoven together.[17]

Like the covenant made between God and ancient Israel, this national covenant promised temporal blessings and prosperity on a strict quid pro quo basis. As long as man obeyed God's commandments, he would live in relative tranquility and peace.[18]

---

[16] Kaveny, "The Remnants of Theocracy," 68.

[17] Wilsey, "America as the City upon a Hill," 11.

[18] Mary Morrissey, "Elect Nations and Prophetic Preaching: *Types and Examples* in the Paul's Cross Jeremiad," in *The English Sermon Revised: Religion, Literature and History, 1600–1750*, ed. Lori Ferrell and Peter McCullough (Manchester: Manchester University Press, 2000), 46–47.

This national covenant obliged the community only to outward acts of holiness and required that God would punish all violations with punishment, but it also promised that all outward repentance and reformation would secure an immediate deliverance from impending doom.[19]

Major Developments of Patriotism
during the Puritan Era

One of the most important developments of the American conception of patriotism that occurred during the Puritan era was the concept of the chosenness of America. Puritans, and subsequent Americans, have often considered America to be specifically chosen by God to be a light in the world. Heavily influenced by Puritan thought, this concept is one that continues today. America is often seen in terms of God's providence; America exists, from its very founding, to be a blessing to the world. The notion that America is a city on a hill is crucial to the development of patriotism because when looked at through a lens of divine providence, as a result, failing to be patriotic would be failing to recognize God's providential plan in the world.

Revolutionary War Era

The revolutionary crisis helped transform the theological errand into the wilderness into a political venture. The American Revolution adapted apocalyptic language to refer to political ideas, and as a result, Americans saw the American Revolution as a means to bring about God's coming kingdom in the world. They viewed eschatology not merely as a formal theological framework that explained God's remote plans for the world but also as a description of the world that the faithful Christian soldier was to do battle in.[20] At the beginning of the American Revolution, religious colonists

---

[19] Perry Miller, "Preparation for Salvation," in *Essays in American Colonial History*, ed. Paul Goodman (New York: Holt, 1967), 156.

[20] J. F. Maclear, "New England and the Fifth Monarchy: The Quest for the Millennium in Early American Puritanism," *William and Mary Quarterly* 32 (1975): 226.

held common beliefs about the providence of God, seeing God as having uniquely blessed the New World and given her a special mission in the world.[21] In this way, New England Puritans held a millennial view that saw the American Revolution as a part of their errand into the wilderness and merged it with the seeking of American development.[22] As these views merged, patriotism became a Christian duty.

Millennialism in the
Revolutionary War Era

The belief in the coming millennial reign of Christ is one of the oldest and most lasting patterns of Western thought. While scholars of millennialism have disagreed over its historical role, American historians have understood millennialism as an essential theme in early American politics, especially in regards to the American Revolution.[23] The American Revolution was seen through a millennial lens because it saw America as the principal seat of the coming kingdom of God. American revolutionary millennialism was not just about destroying the British; it was seen as bringing about the "creation of a heavenly paradise," and as a result, American patriots conceived history as having a gradual movement towards this paradise.[24] Millennial interpretations of prophecy were thus filled with patriotic and nationalistic overtones because of their religious themes that existed from their very origin in American political culture.[25]

As soon as the American Revolution began, there was immediately an argument about what its goal was. Was the goal to

---

[21] John Berens, "'Good News from a Far Country': A Note on Divine Providence and the Stamp Act Crisis," *Church History* 45 (1976): 310.

[22] Sacvan Bercovitch, "How the Puritans Won the American Revolution," *The Massachusetts Review* 17 (1976): 606. Sacvan Bercovitch would go on to call this the "eschatology of errand . . . American millennialism." Sacvan Bercovitch, "The Typology of America's Mission," *American Quarterly* 30 (1978): 137.

[23] Ruth Bloch, *Visionary Republic: Millennial Themes in American Thought, 1756–1800* (Cambridge: Cambridge University Press, 1985), xi–xii.

[24] Bloch, *Visionary Republic*, 3–5.

[25] Bloch, *Visionary Republic*, 12.

recover the past, or was it meant to initiate a new age in the world?[26] Millennialism was a compelling component of the revolutionary political culture in America through the 1770s that added the critical element of eschatological resolve to the patriot cause because it turned a war for independence into a just and holy war against the British. In this way, millennial interpretations moved from resistance to revolution, and these "millennial aspiration became a prominent feature of American revolutionary consciousness."[27]

New England's clerical and political leaders taught on eschatology regularly and believed it was vital for them and the people of New England to place themselves into the "unfolding and accelerating course of historical eschatology" as seen through biblical symbolism.[28] In late eighteenth-century America, most religious and millennialist understandings invoked the prophetic symbolism of the Bible. Hopes for the future became symbolized in biblical millennial language and were a crucial characteristic of American culture in the revolutionary era.[29] Millennialism and its connection with America being the new Israel have become essential topics in the historiography of the American Revolution.[30]

---

[26] Catherine Albanese notes that "Puritans both held to their view of the past and looked from past and present to the future. In this double identity, they would make a lasting mark on the American religious future." Additionally, she notes, "[I]n the New World wilderness, Europeans felt that they could re-experience the time when the church was new and strong. In America, they thought, they could restore the ancient order, uneroded by time or change." Catherine Albanese, *America: Religion and Religions* (Belmont: Wadsworth, 1992), 117, 152.

[27] Susan Juster, *Doomsayers: Anglo-American Prophecy in the Age of Revolution* (Philadelphia: University of Pennsylvania Press, 2003), 135; Bloch, *Visionary Republic*, 75.

[28] Thomas Kidd, *The Protestant Interest: New England after Puritanism* (New Haven: Yale University Press, 2004), 137.

[29] Ruth Bloch, "The Social and Political Base of Millennial Literature in Late Eighteenth-Century America," *American Quarterly* 40 (1988): 378–381, 389. According to one historian, more publications featured apocalyptic elements during the 1750s than at any other time in the history of colonial America. Kerry Trask, *In the Pursuit of Shadows: A Study of Collective Hope and Despair in Provincial Massachusetts during the Era of the Seven Years War, 1748–1764* (Minneapolis: University of Minnesota Press, 1971), 199.

[30] Melvin Endy Jr., "Just War, Holy War, and Millennialism in Revolutionary America," *William and Mary Quarterly* 42 (1985): 3. The Puritans

The concepts of America being a city on a hill while at the same time existing in the wilderness was fed by what Nathan Hatch termed "civil millennialism."[31] This civil millennialism combined millennial theology with republican virtues and became central themes in the relationship between religion and politics in much of revolutionary New England.[32] Ruth Bloch stresses the importance of the relationship between religion and politics in noting that revolutionary millennialism "infused the highest political ideas of the patriotic movement with transcendent religious significance and gave contemporary actions a pivotal place in the cosmic scheme of history."[33]

The significance of millennialism that flourished at the start of the Revolutionary War did not lessen after the war. The nation had taken a beating during the war, but there was also a serious belief that the kingdom of God was going to advance because of it. This millennial expectancy rose to greater heights after the war. New England clergy were emphatic in celebrating the American Revolution as the central event in millennial eschatology because they connected it to the kingdom of God, but they also saw that with this new kingdom came both civil and religious liberty.[34] Additionally, the new American republic was now seen as the primary agent of redemptive history in the world because it was seen as the principal seat of the kingdom.[35] Through the war's connection to millennialism, Christianity was infused with nationalism. In the developing concept of American civil religion, the defense of the nation was seen as a sacred obligation, and Christians who did not

---

made numerous parallels between themselves and the ancient Israelites: liberation from slavery, the delivery across the water, the sealing of the covenant, the errand into the wilderness, and many others. Philip Gorski, *American Covenant: A History of Civil Religion from the Puritans to the Present* (Princeton: Princeton University Press, 2017), 38–39.

[31] Hatch, *The Sacred Cause of Liberty.*

[32] Hatch, *The Sacred Cause of Libert,* 3. Ruth Bloch argues that without millennialism, it would be impossible for American revolutionary ideology to come into existence. Bloch, *Visionary Republic,* 93.

[33] Bloch, *Visionary Republic,* 86.

[34] Hatch, *The Sacred Cause of Liberty,* 146–148.

[35] Hatch, *The Sacred Cause of Liberty,* 155; Bloch, *Visionary Republic,* 11.

fully support this new concept of civil religion were out of the conventional way of American thinking.[36]

The Role of the Clergy
during the Revolutionary Era

The vital role of the clergy during the revolutionary era has not received the attention of many political theorists, but to their contemporaries, it was clear.[37] A member of the clergy in early America was, in most cases, the leading man in the community, and in all of America, not just in New England, they helped mold political opinion.[38] While the clergy were divided into various aspects of theology, they were united in the familiar perspective of government: they understood that liberty was essential to a healthy society.[39] The clergy were public spokesmen for Christianity but also in promoting the seeking of liberty in America. As such, from at least the 1770s, they rendered excellent service to the patriot cause during the American revolution.[40]

Ministers of the revolutionary era opposed tyranny and did so in God's name; they hailed liberty as the virtue of the "New

---

[36] Jon Alexander, "Christian Attitudes toward War in Colonial America," *Church and Society* 64 (1974): 22–23.

[37] Ellis Sandoz, ed., *Political Sermons of the American Founding Era, 1730–1805*, vol. 1 (Indianapolis: Liberty Fund, 1998), xii. Harry Stout, in his work on preaching in colonial New England, states, "Historians who minimize the clergy's determinative role in shaping New England's revolutionary mentality, pointing out that they drafted no official resolutions in their associations miss the points at which ministers made their vital contributions." Stout, *The New England Soul: Preaching and Religious Culture in Colonial New England* (Oxford: Oxford University Press, 2012), 291.

[38] Samuel Child, *The Colonial Parson of New England: A Picture* (New York: The Baker and Taylor Co, 1896), 81; Patricia Bonomi, *Under the Cope of Heaven: Religion, Society, and Politics in Colonial America* (New York: Oxford University Press, 1986), 209.

[39] Hatch, *The Sacred Cause of Liberty*, 8. Patricia Bonomi states, "The sermon literature of the 1770s—North and south, evangelical and rationalist—shows a striking uniformity of language and belief. Nearly every sermon addressed the political crisis." Bonomi, *Under the Cope of Heaven*, 212.

[40] Mark Noll, *One Nation under God? Christian Faith and Political Action in America* (Cambridge: Harper, 1988), 35.

American Israel" and declared that in sharing these values with all humanity, America would become the principal seat of Christ's coming earthly rule.[41] For America to become the principal seat of Christ's earthly rule, the British would have to be defeated; and since the clergy wanted their congregation to be obedient to God's plan, they encouraged the politics of the revolution. Samuel Child understands the apparent connection, "It was the natural course for the minister to pursue—this taking active part in the politics of the new country."[42] So while the Puritans popularized the concept of the sacred history of New England, the eighteenth-century clergy established the concept of America's mission of setting up a new millennial kingdom that saw the founders as champions of freedom, both civil and religious.[43] The clergy became "social guardians" and "watchmen" who were "responsible for being on the lookout for divine warnings" and who told the people and the nation "who they were and what they must do to retain God's special covenant interest."[44] As Melvin Endy Jr. summarizes the importance of the clergy in leading the people during the American Revolution:

> While it is true that holy war themes are marked in the writings of about one-fifth of the ministers, including a number of prominent men, the Revolutionary clergy for the most part presented themselves not as priests of a holy people but as the religious and moral leaders of a body politic fighting what they perceived to be a just war.[45]

---

[41] Hatch, *The Sacred Cause of Liberty*, 409.

[42] Child, *The Colonial Parson of New England*, 75.

[43] Bercovitch, "The Typology of America's Mission," 135; Michael Hughey, "The Political Covenant: Protestant Foundations of the American State," *State, Culture, and Society* 1 (1984): 125. Melvin Endy Jr. states that possibly one-sixth of all documents dealing with public events during the American Revolution by pastors placed the nation squarely in the context of millennial history. Endy, "Just War, Holy War, and Millennialism in Revolutionary America," 17.

[44] Stout, *The New England Soul*, 27, 28.

[45] Endy, "Just War, Holy War, and Millennialism," 10.

Sermons of the Revolutionary Era

Crucial to understanding early American culture is understanding the "enduring spirituality in the pulpit and pew."[46] Due to the vast territory that America encompassed, it is crucial to understand that sermons served as the only regular form of mass communication in the new republic.[47] As such, their importance cannot be understated. Clergy and their accompanying sermons played a determinative role in helping form the American notion of patriotism. Patricia Bonomi makes this point clear, "Patriots never doubted the influence of the clergy in forming public opinion."[48]

Sermons existed as a model of how religion came to permeate America's national identity because they allowed the pastor—widely considered the most important person in the community—a way to connect contemporary issues to the people showing them where they fit into God's mission. Clergy interpreted contemporary events through a lens of political theology, and as a result, the sermons became a distinctive type of political speech.[49] Revolutionary sermons played a distinctive role in arousing public sentiment and "firing the souls of men with patriotism."[50] Additionally, these sermons connected patriotism with furthering the achievement of God's mission for America.[51]

While there is no overall synthesis of sermons during the American Revolution, many were published. A vast majority of sermons were of the occasional variety (85 percent), meaning that they were not specifically the main Sunday sermon. As such, these occasional sermons cannot necessarily be the best indicator of the overall political leanings of the clergy. By the time the American Revolution was in full swing, the occasional sermons had rivaled regular Sunday sermons in terms of importance.[52]

---

[46] Stout, *The New England Soul*, 6.

[47] Stout, *The New England Soul*, 3.

[48] Bonomi, *Under the Cope of Heaven*, 209.

[49] Sandoz, *Political Sermons*, xii.

[50] Child, *The Colonial Parson of New England*, 86.

[51] Bercovitch, "The Typology of America's Mission," 135.

[52] Stout, *The New England Soul*, 30.

There were various other types of sermons that were influential during the American Revolution. Fast sermons were preached to get the congregation and, by extension, the nation to seek the Lord's face as they encountered specific hardships during the American Revolution. In fast-day sermons, clergy would interpret current catastrophes as God's judgment for sins and encourage repentance.[53] Fast sermons also expressed the idea that God would ordain an American victory through their faithfulness, inaugurate the millennial kingdom of Christ, and use America to spread the kingdom to the ends of the earth.[54] Election sermons were significant as well because they coincided with the election of local leaders widely viewed as the most important day of the year; it was when free men gathered throughout the colonies to elect representatives.[55] These were annual events, and after the election was over, prominent ministers would deliver a "state of the covenant" sermon to all of the politicians gathered. Contained in these sermons were responsibilities of the covenant and reminders and warnings of what would happen if the covenant was not kept.[56]

Artillery sermons were also crucial in stirring up patriotism. The artillery sermons were given directly to soldiers and dealt with various moral issues relating to their duties but usually "climaxed" by urging them to fight under the banner of Christ, who was "the great captain of their salvation."[57] As Stout explains, the artillery sermons were "some of the most radical and violent sentiments in all Puritan preaching, and some of the most self-assured statements about New England as a superior people who need fear no mortal enemy."[58] The militarism of these sermons fostered a strong sense of the patriotic duty of the Christian soldier who was fighting to achieve God's mission. By destroying the enemies of America, the soldier was helping to bring about God's kingdom in the new world.

---

[53] Sandoz, *Political Sermons*, xxi. Often, fast sermons coincided with the Continental Congress's request for prayer and fasting. This was done at least sixteen times during the American Revolution. Sandoz, *Political Sermons*, xxi; Kaveny, "The Remnants of Theocracy," 64.

[54] Bloch, *Visionary Republic*, 79, 85.

[55] Stout, *The New England Soul*, 29.

[56] Kaveny, "The Remnants of Theocracy," 64.

[57] Endy, "Just War, Holy War, and Millennialism," 20.

[58] Stout, *New England Soul*, 83.

The Jeremiad

Of all the sermon styles that helped lead the early American nation toward patriotism, none was as influential as the jeremiad. Taking allegories from Scripture, especially of the Old Testament, jeremiads supplied common interpretations of contemporary events through the lens of apocalyptic and millennial literature.[59] A jeremiad was a sermon of woe and promise. Its name originated from the Old Testament prophet Jeremiah and became prominent with the Puritans who based it on a belief in a past golden age from which subsequent generations had departed. The jeremiads brought attention to contemporary moral failures and natural disasters and endeavored to create a sense of anxiety that would lead to moral and social reform and renewal of the national covenant.[60]

Through these sermons, the clergy reminded Americans of the mission of liberty their ancestors had begun through the settling of America and of their responsibility in defeating the British.[61] Jeremiads played a decisive role in the community, especially in terms of fostering patriotism; as such, jeremiads became the primary form of political rhetoric of the day.[62]

Jeremiads sought to use an apocalyptic lens to interpret contemporary events. Disasters were seen as God's punishment for sins and as manifestations of God's wrath toward the country and her people.[63] Jeremiads became a form of religious-political rhetoric

---

[59] Bonomi, *Under the Cope of Heaven*, 214.

[60] Daniel G. Reid, et al., *Dictionary of Christianity in America* (Downers Grove: InterVarsity Press, 1990). Christopher Grasso also argues that jeremiads helped preach the concept of the national covenant. Christopher Grasso, "Images and Shadows of Jonathan Edwards," *American Literary History* 8 (1996): 690; Edmund Morgan, "The Puritan Ethic and the American Revolution," *William and Mary Quarterly* 24 (1967): 6.

[61] Hughey, "The Political Covenant," 125.

[62] Cathleen Kaveny, "The Remnants of Theocracy: The Puritans, the Jeremiad and the Contemporary Culture Wars," *Law, Culture and the Humanities* 9 (2013): 65–66. Ellis Sandoz states they were central to the American consciousness. Sandoz, *Political Sermons of the American Founding Era, 1730–1805*, xxi.

[63] Perry Miller, "Preparation for Salvation," in *Essays in American Colonial History*, ed. Paul Goodman (New York: Holt, 1967), 154.

in which prominent pastors chastised the American people for violations of the national covenant and urged repentance to avoid the continuation of God's wrath displayed in national setbacks such as defeats in battle, bad crops, earthquakes, or sicknesses.[64] By highlighting the sins not of individuals but the entire nation, the jeremiad allowed all Americans to indicate repentance of their sinful ways by participating in what at the outset seemed the cause of God.[65] By stressing repentance, the people were to see success; in this way, jeremiads became a way to make sense of adversity and encourage people to seek the Lord as they sought to fulfill their patriotic duty.

While jeremiads saw national setbacks as a judgment from God, they also saw victories as divine blessings for obedience. The clergy interpreted military victories as rewards, and as a result, the jeremiad could be extremely optimistic. Michael Lienesch stresses the potential for optimism in the jeremiad by stating early patriots were "proud of the successful revolution, boastful about the recent founding, and captivated by the seemingly limitless potential of the new nation."[66]

The clergy's widespread use of jeremiads helped transition the nation toward a sense of patriotism and civil millennialism. At first, the jeremiads were regional, but they spread steadily to the entire country uniting the people in solidarity as they sought to be faithful to God's mission. Second, as the jeremiads spread, they crossed denominational lines. At first, they were more prominent in the Calvinist circles, but they soon were opened to pulpits of various types because the revolution had grown from a regional setting to a

---

[64] Kaveny, "The Remnants of Theocracy," 62, 64; Bercovitch, "How the Puritans Won the American Revolution," 601.

[65] Alan Heimert, *Religion and the American Mind: From the Great Awakening to the Revolution* (Cambridge: Harvard University Press, 1966), 424. Alan Heimert argues that jeremiads "reflected belief that all difficulties came as punishments for a society's sins, that these afflictions could be removed only by repentance, and that their removal was occasion for demonstration that such repentance had been sincere." Heimert, *Religion and the American Mind*, 284.

[66] Michael Lienesch, "The Role of Political Millennialism in Early American Nationalism," *The Western Political Quarterly* 36 (1983): 449.

national one.[67] Third, the language of the jeremiad—"the language of American critique and progress"—began to encompass previously marginalized groups such as slaves.[68] This allowed for the revolution and the patriotism that followed it to be engaging to all classes of people. Fourth, as the jeremiads spread, the responsibilities of the covenant became less clear. In other words, the jeremiads became less about being faithful to God but more about being faithful to the country.[69] They became an essential strategy for motivating people to renew their faith to the church with the hope that by doing so, the destiny of American freedom would be theirs.[70]

Sermons gave people hope in their present circumstances, but more than that, they were meant to show the importance of the providence of God in the chosenness of America. Americans saw themselves as God's new Israel and were reminded about this almost every time they heard the clergy preach. This constant reminder fostered a strong sense of patriotism that, when combined with civil

---

[67] "The clergy extended membership in the covenant beyond the genuinely pious and reborn to include all God-fearing, liberty-loving, white Protestant colonists—in short, to the entire political community." Michael Hughey, "The Political Covenant: Protestant Foundations of the American State," *Culture and Society* 1 (1984): 125–126. He goes on to state, "[W]hile Americans dispensed with divine laws as the basis of their national covenant, they retained the conception, though its strictly religious content was diminished." Hughey, "The Political Covenant," 142.

[68] For how slaves used the jeremiad, see Willie Harrell Jr., *Origins of the African American Jeremiad: The Rhetorical Strategies of Social Protest and Activism, 1760–1861* (Jefferson: McFarland, 2011); David Howard-Pitney, *Afro-American Jeremiad: Appeals for Justice in America* (Philadelphia: Temple University Press, 2005).

[69] Kaveny, "The Remnants of Theocracy," 66–67. The rapid development and spread of the concept of the national covenant combined with preaching led to the American concern of a "conquest of power" rather than the "pursuit of holiness." Miller, "Preparation for Salvation," 162.

[70] Deborah Madsen, *American Exceptionalism* (Jackson: University Press, 1998), 12; Nathan Hatch, "The Origins of Civil Millennialism in America: New England Clergymen, War with France, and the Revolution," *William and Mary Quarterly* 31 (1974): 408. George McKenna also agrees with this assessment stating that jeremiads were a "reminder of the community's holy mission and an exhortation to remain faithful to it." George McKenna, *The Puritan Origins of American Patriotism* (New Haven: Yale, 2007), 73.

millennialism, set the stage for civil religion in America for generations to come.

Significant Developments of Patriotism
during the Revolutionary War Era

The Revolutionary War furthered the notion that God had chosen America by connecting current events to God's millennial plan in the world. Looking through an apocalyptic lens, the founders and citizens saw America as God's new Israel that existed to bring God's plan to the world. Looking at early success in America's achievement of freedom from England, Americans saw the hand of God not just in her founding but in her advancement. American destiny was tied to God directly, and as a result, patriotism flourished.

The American Civil War

The Civil War is essential to understanding American national identity and purpose. Indeed, it can be said that America was born during the American Revolution; it can also be said that it was reborn during the Civil War.[71] This rebirth was due to the Civil War's place as a watershed of forming American identity in the United States.[72] America was a young nation when the Civil War began, and as such, the nation had not been tested nor had a genuine sense of nationhood been established. Before the war broke out, Americans were loyal to their local communities, cities, and towns and had little interaction with the national government outside of

---

[71] Agnieszka Monnet, "War and National Renewal: Civil Religion and Blood Sacrifice in American Culture," *European Journal of American Studies* 7 (2012): 2.

[72] The Civil War has been the subject of more books on the history of the United States than any other individual topic. Kimlyn Bender, "The American Experience of a Darkening and Receding Providence: The Civil War and the Unmaking of an American Religious Synthesis," *Cultural Encounters* 9 (2013): 109. Kimlyn Bender states that it is approaching, if not surpassing, one hundred thousand books on the subject.

national elections.[73] The people felt national loyalty was based on a social contract guaranteeing the people a particular body of rights, and if the state violated those rights, the contract could be broken. Thus, the people's loyalty was less directed toward the nation as it was to the people who embodied the virtues of the country.[74]

Slavery

It is beyond the scope of this project to discuss in full the issues and concepts of the Civil War. Instead, careful attention must be taken to look at various parts of the Civil War to see how it affected the sense of patriotism in the United States as a whole. When looked at individually, these parts helped form a sense of patriotism and nationalism that still exists in modern American culture today. Historian Mark Noll notes that slavery debates drove the political history of the United States since its founding, and these debates continued to intensify as war threatened.[75] This is not to say that all soldiers who fought in the Civil War did so because of their own views on slavery, but it eventually became the central issue of the war's continuance.

Few Union soldiers mentioned slavery as the central issue of their enlistment. Ironically, one significant way that Southerners used the issue of slavery as a reason for enlistment was not to defend chattel slavery but rather to fight against those who would seek enslavement over them.[76] Additionally, it was not only Southerners who did not see the issue of slavery as the main reason to enlist. Most Northern soldiers also did not think the abolition of slavery to be the primary reason for enlistment. For many in the North, the fight was not about the sin of slavery but the sin of secession. Many Northern soldiers fought to preserve the republic of their founding

---

[73] Melinda Lawson, "'A Profound National Devotion': The Civil War Union Leagues and the Construction of a New National Patriotism," *Civil War History* 48 (2002): 340.

[74] Lawson, "'A Profound National Devotion,'" 340.

[75] Mark Noll, *God and Race in American Politics: A Short History* (Princeton: Princeton University Press, 2008), 14, 43.

[76] James McPherson, *For Cause and Comrades: Why Men Fought in the Civil War* (New York: Oxford University Press, 1997), 19–21.

fathers.[77] Southerners saw themselves as fighting to preserve their way of life and to reject Northern influence. In essence, the fight was about varying understandings of patriotism.[78] As Andre Fleche notes, the Civil War "called into question American greatness and threatened the nation's place among the powers of the world. . . . The frustrated patriot feared the inability of the nation to maintain its integrity disgraced the United States."[79] Both the North and the South fought to maintain their understanding of what it meant to be a nation with a specific national culture.[80]

---

[77] Judkin Browning, "'I Am Not So Patriotic as I Was Once': The Effects of Military Occupation on the Occupying Union Soldiers during the Civil War," *Civil War History* 55 (2009): 220–223.

[78] For a broad treatment of why men fought in the "brothers war," see McPherson, *For Cause and Comrades*; Gerald Linderman, *Embattled Courage: The Experience of Combat in the American Civil War* (New York: Free Press, 1989); Earl Hess, *The Union Soldier in Battle: Enduring the Ordeal of Combat* (Lawrence: University of Kansas, 1997). McPherson, using a broad and comprehensive survey of personal correspondence during the Civil War, notes that 66 percent of Confederates affirmed patriotism at one time during their enlistment, and 68 percent of Union soldiers did as well. McPherson, *For Cause and Comrades*, 100–101.

[79] Andre Fleche, *The Revolution of 1861: The American Civil War in the Age of Nationalistic Conflict* (Chapel Hill: University of North Carolina, 2012), 70–71.

[80] This statement is not meant to endorse or negate the horrific injustices inflicted by the sinful institution of slavery in the United States. The institution of slavery ultimately *became* the reason the Civil War endured to its completion because Abraham Lincoln understood that the only way to bring the end to the war was to destroy the institution of slavery, while the South began to see slavery as a Southern way of life and to stop it would be a direct attack on their culture. Ultimately, slavery was an evil in the history of the United States, but there is not enough space here to deal with it in this manner. The main issue as it relates to this project is how the Civil War is a historical underpinning to American patriotism. For a historical summary of how the early church thought of slavery, see John McGuckin, "Church and Slavery in an Age of Oppression," in *The Path of Christianity: The First Thousand Years* (Downers Grove: InterVarsity, 2017), 1056–1089. For a look at the Southern biblical basis for slavery and a Northern case for abolition, see Mitchell Snay, "Slavery Defended: The Morality of Slavery and the Infidelity of Abolitionism," in *Gospel of Disunion: Religion and Separatism in the Antebellum South* (Cambridge: Cambridge Press, 1993), 53–77. For a look at how both Northern and Southern Civil War theologians used the Bible in the debate over slavery, see Willard Swartley, *Slavery, Sabbath, War and Women: Core Issues in Biblical Interpretation* (Scottdale: Herald, 1983), 31–64.

Civil Religion during the Civil War

From the American Revolution to the Civil War, religious adherence grew twice as fast the population did. As a result, the period preceding the Civil War was marked by strong religious characteristics.[81] During the Civil War, religion held a dominant position in American culture, and it heavily influenced politics.

Not only was the overall culture influenced by religion, but the militaries of both the North and South were influenced as well. James McPherson notes, "Civil war armies were, arguably, the most religious in American history."[82] Military leaders mirrored religious sentiments of the people they fought for. Additionally, soldiers' faith unquestionably helped sustain morale on both sides. Civil War soldiers saw themselves as fighting for their hometowns, and as a result, were serving to help spread their national cause.[83] However, religion and faith were also used by both sides to justify the killing of their American enemies and to deal with death.[84]

Christian faith was central to the culture and society of the antebellum South and, in particular, was the most fundamental source of legitimation for the young Confederacy. By embracing Christianity as the central inspiration of the Confederacy, and by claiming it as their legitimating authority, Southerners attempted to strengthen their cause before the watching world and within the eyes of their people.[85] In this way, religion played an essential role in the formation of a distinctly Southern national identity.

---

[81] Noll, *God and Race in American Politics*, 29; George Rable, *God's Almost Chosen Peoples: A Religious History of the American Civil War* (Chapel Hill: University of North Carolina, 2010), 7.

[82] McPherson, *For Cause and Comrades*, 63.

[83] James Silver, *Confederate Morale and Church Propaganda, Confederate Centennial Studies*, no. 3 (1957): 32; Rable, *God's Almost Chosen Peoples*, 8; McPherson, *For Cause and Comrades*, 63; Samuel Watson, "Religion and Combat Motivation in the Confederate Armies," *The Journal of Military History* 58 (1994): 34.

[84] Phillip Paluden, "Religion in the American Civil War," in *Religion and the Civil War*, ed. Randall Miller, et al. (New York: Oxford University Press, 1998), 30.

[85] Drew Faust, *The Creation of Confederate Nationalism: Ideology and Identity in the Civil War South* (Baton Rouge: Louisiana State University Press,

Religion was also important to the people and armies of the North. While the North was far more religiously diverse, the war helped bring unity. Where before different denominations were divided on both political and theological issues, now they were united.[86] Northern churchgoers declared their loyalty to the Union both in the pulpit and the pews, and as a result, their churches became highly patriotic.[87]

The Role of the Clergy
in the Civil War

Just as the clergy were influential during the Revolutionary War, they held a significant role in the North and the South before and during the Civil War.[88] The enormous impact the clergy had during the Civil War cannot be understated.[89] During colonial times, clergy tended to spend the majority of their ministry at one church. However, during the immediate era before the Civil War, a shift took place. Many clergy began to change pulpits and churches.[90] Additionally, churches began to remove pastors with far more ease than had been used during colonial times. Clergy left to pursue

---

1988), 22–23; Mitchell Snay, *Gospel of Disunion: Religion and Separatism in the Antebellum South* (Cambridge: Cambridge Press, 1993), 3.

[86] Paluden, "Religion in the American Civil War," 23, 30.

[87] Rable, *God's Almost Chosen Peoples*, 191–192.

[88] The critical place the clergy had in culture can be seen even in their financial compensation. The average for a white non-slave in the United States at the time was $2,580.00. However, the clergy in the North, on average, earned $4,376.00. This is dwarfed in comparison to the clergy of the South who had amassed, on average, wealth of $10,177.00. The clergy during the war were paid exceedingly well during this time. E. Brooks Holifield, "The Penurious Preacher? Nineteenth-Century Clerical Wealth: North and South," *Journal of the American Academy of Religion* 58 (1990): 17.

[89] Most of what follows traces the importance of clergy during the Civil War. However, chaplains also played an essential role in the shaping of civil religion during the Civil War. For more on chaplains during this period, see George Rable, "The Shepherds and Their Sheep" in *God's Almost Chosen Peoples: A Religious History of the American Civil War* (Chapel Hill: University of North Carolina, 2010), 107–126.

[90] James Silver notes that many churches exchanged clergy to have someone fill the pulpit who more closely aligned with their political views on the war and slavery. Silver, *Confederate Morale and Church Propaganda*, 22.

opportunities with more prominent churches and more money, and along with this came more pressure to conform to the existing church culture.[91] In this way, members of the clergy stoked the fire of whatever flavor of patriotism existed in the local church that they served.

Clergy probably played the most significant role in keeping the faith in the Confederate cause.[92] Religion held sway in much of the Southern culture, and clergy were seen as "arbiters and upholders of a virtuous social order."[93] They were so effective in merging Christianity with Southern culture that one "could not exist without the other."[94] With the merging of Christianity with Southern culture, the clergy helped make the church the most powerful and influential organization in the South before and during the Civil War. Historian Harry Stout stresses the importance of the Southern church: "Without the clergy's active endorsement of secession and war alongside that of the statesmen and generals, there could not have been a Confederate nation. By the 1840s and 1850s, Christianity represented the most powerful cultural system in the Old South."[95]

While not all Southern clergy were supportive of secession or war, the clergy who were had a heavy heart.[96] It was clergy and their belief that the cause of the Confederacy was just that helped pave the way for secession. Clergy identified the Confederacy as a Christian nation, and this helped to sanctify the war itself.[97] At the outbreak of the Civil War, the clergy of the South proclaimed that the honor of being God's chosen nation belonged to the Confederacy

---

[91] George Frederickson, "The Coming of the Lord: The Northern Protestant Clergy and the Civil War Crisis," in *Religion and the American Civil War*, ed. Randall Miller, et al. (New York: Oxford University Press, 1998), 111–112.

[92] Paluden, "Religion in the American Civil War," 31.

[93] Harry Stout, *Upon the Altar of the Nation: A Moral History of the Civil War* (New York: Viking, 2006), 10.

[94] Stout, *Upon the Altar of the Nation*, 37.

[95] Stout, *Upon the Altar of the Nation*, 43. Silver states, Southern clergymen were "responsible for a state of mind which made secession possible." Silver, *Confederate Morale and Church Propaganda*, 10.

[96] Silver, *Confederate Morale and Church Propaganda*, 19, 23.

[97] Rable, *God's Almost Chosen Peoples*, 314.

alone. In this way, clergy became "vanguards in the movement of countless Southerners away from Unionism and toward Confederate identity, nationalism, and loyalty." In essence, clergy became "chief promoters of Confederate nationalism."[98]

Influence of Sermons
in the Civil War

In the same way that sermons served to communicate public sentiment about the Revolutionary War, sermons continued to be influential cultural commentaries during the Civil War. Many sermons from the Civil War era were highly political; were deeply passionate about numerous social issues, not just slavery; and were examples of powerful and beautiful rhetoric. The most vigorous defense of slavery was seen in Southern pulpits, while Northern pulpits were never unanimous in their condemnation of slavery. Regardless of personal thoughts of slavery, clergy on both sides of the Mason Dixon Line were influential in fanning the fires of regionalism, which divided the nation.[99]

Despite potential reasons for staying quiet on the issue of the war, most clergy felt it was their duty to engage with the topic of war to help sustain and strengthen their congregations during these difficult times. In so doing, the clergy used a patriotic call for resolve and dedication to the war efforts. In this way, sermons became the most effective means of maintaining the morale of the people, used to "rekindle the sacred fires of patriotism."[100] Clergy who joined patriotism with religion helped transform the Civil War into more than a political conflict but into a holy war.[101]

---

[98] Timothy Wesley, "The Politics of Faith: Religious Authority and Politics during the American Civil War" (PhD diss., Pennsylvania State University, 2010), 191, 195.

[99] David Chesebrough, "The Civil War and the Use of Sermons as Historical Documents," *OAH Magazine of History* 8, no. 1 (1993), 26–27.

[100] James Silver, *Confederate Morale and Church Propaganda*, 15, 37.

[101] Stout notes, "By 1863, political preaching in the North and South had virtually completed the apotheosis of "patriotism" into a full-blown civil religion." Stout, *Upon the Altar of the Nation*, 248. For a comprehensive look at Civil War preaching, see Wesley, "The Politics of Faith"; Jeremy Crawford,

The Concept of Divine Providence
in the Civil War

Just as during the Revolutionary War, people—both Northern and Southern—saw themselves as being on a divine mission. For the Northerners, they were sent to maintain the precious Union that their forefathers had fought the evil British for. In so doing, the North was attempting to continue the mission of God that had been so readily clear less than a hundred years earlier. The Southerners also saw themselves as fighting to continue the Lord's mission that began during the American Revolution, and as a result, they were seeking to claim American identity for themselves.[102] Since both sides believed they were fighting for the Lord, they both anticipated a divinely given victory.

The North and the South held firm assertions of their own moral "rightness," which led to a deep sense of divine providence during the war.[103] Northern clergy continually reminded their churches that their purpose in the war was just. The fight initially was to preserve the Union, and only later did it become to free the slaves. The Civil War revived the sense of millennial anticipation for the Northern clergy because they saw that out of national difficulty and trial, the nation would rise to greater heights than ever before. In this way, the North had a sense that divine providence was going to help them achieve their God-ordained mission. In the South, clergy supported the war with at least equal force encouraging their congregation to fight the good and noble fight, whatever happened, because they also were fighting the Lord's battle.[104] Both sides of the Civil War looked for signs of the Lord's favor during the war. Every battle, no matter how minor, tested the providence of God.[105] Celebrations of victory became celebrations

---

"God's Will in Warfare: An Investigation of American Civil War-Era Preaching" (PhD diss., Mid-America Baptist Theological Seminary, 2016).

[102] Faust, *The Creation of Confederate Nationalism*, 14.

[103] Bender, "The American Experience of a Darkening and Receding Providence," 115.

[104] Chesebrough, "The Civil War and the Use of Sermons as Historical Documents," 28.

[105] Rable, *God's Almost Chosen Peoples*, 74–75.

of patriotic virtue that combined with a sense of belief in God's providential guidance.

The Civil War stands as an important indicator and event in the history of America and of its concept of patriotism. Due to both the North and the South's belief in providence, there was a secularization of American culture that came about because Christianity was replaced with civil religion. "[E]vangelical Christianity was thus wedded to America's power and destiny."[106] Further, the Civil War belief in divine providence led to a belief that God now ordered American exceptionalism, which ultimately led to Manifest Destiny.[107]

The Civil War's Influence
on American Patriotism

Political understanding changed drastically during the Civil War. Before the war, the United States did not honestly share a sense of national identity. When the war started, the Union grew to see the importance of the nation and was willing to fight to reclaim it while the South saw the importance of culture and fought to keep it. The North saw the importance of the nation, while the South saw themselves as "a nation among nations."[108] One way to see the shift in nationalistic thinking is to see how people spoke of the republic. Due to the war's influence and the following Reconstruction, they went from saying that the United States "are" a Republic to the United States "is" a Republic.[109]

Civil War Americans saw that only through a shared collective national identity could people properly have a relationship with their country. The North built a sense of national identity that saw the nation as an organism whose growth was natural and good while the South built a culture of sacrifice, celebrating the deaths of "noble soldiers" who fought for their culture, thus connecting

---

[106] Bender, "The American Experience," 118.

[107] Bender, "The American Experience,"121.

[108] Faust, *The Creation of Confederate Nationalism*, 11.

[109] Monnet, "War and National Renewal," 3.

soldiers to fellow citizens.[110] This shared identity of people in the North and the South stressed the importance of patriotism. During the Civil War, no matter where a person lived, patriotism was incredibly valuable, and "lukewarm patriotism was no patriotism at all."[111] Patriotic convictions were critical to both civilians and soldiers and played an essential role in sustaining both of their motivations during the Civil War.

Another issue that arose during the Civil War was the importance of national symbols. Before the Civil War, there were few valid symbols of national patriotism. Both Union and Confederates saw themselves fighting for "abstract symbols" such as the flag, the country, or the Constitution.[112] Fighting for an abstract symbol became vital because it helped make sense of the chaos surrounding soldiers in the trenches. While the flag was an abstract symbol, it became a significant symbol as a result of the war. Flags, even the national one, were rare and mainly reserved for naval and merchant ships. This changed at the start of the war. National flags of both the North and the South became "transcendent" symbols of patriotism.[113]

Flags symbolized the pride and honor during the Civil War and "acquired a special mystique for Civil War soldiers."[114] The American flag in the North added a new depth as a symbol of nationalism in the early days of the war because it reminded people of the importance of the United States being a unified republic.[115] Since the Confederacy was a new nation, they felt a need to create a symbol of national unity and did so with the creation of their

---

[110] Lawson, "'A Profound National Devotion',"358; Aaron Sheehan-Dean, *Why Confederates Fought: Family and Nation in Civil War Virginia* (Chapel Hill: University of North Carolina, 2007), 66, 70.

[111] Wesley, "The Politics of Faith," 79. This is illustrated by a sermon by Henry Ward Beecher, "God hates lukewarm patriotism as much as lukewarm religion and we hate it too. We do not believe in hermaphrodite patriots." Henry Ward Beecher, *Freedom and War* (Boston: Ticknor & Fields, 1863), 121.

[112] McPherson, *For Cause and Comrades*, 21.

[113] Stout, *Upon the Altar of the Nation*, 28–29.

[114] McPherson, *For Cause and Comrades*, 84.

[115] Alice Fahs, *The Imagined Civil War: Popular Literature of the North and South, 1861–1865* (Chapel Hill: University of North Carolina, 2001), 68.

national flag, the Stainless Banner.[116] Using the religious symbol of the cross on the flag, Southerners attempted to convey a message that their fight was a holy one, and in so doing, they attempted to reassure people in the South that their cause was just.[117] In this way, the South, more than the North, modeled a sense of patriotism that was also a striking sense of religious nationalism.[118] With the connection of the flag to religious nationalism, the South was far more committed to the use of flags than the North, which set the stage for the importance of the contemporary use of the American flag today.[119]

World War II

One of the most important historical developments that affected the rise of American patriotism was its role in World War II. While initially isolated from the war, Americans eventually became embroiled in a war that came to define its nature as a real world power, and in addition, the American military became a mythological "savior" to the rest of the world. Thus, WWII was a good and moral war that helped solidify America's rise to national prominence.

President Roosevelt's Shift from
Isolation to Intervention

Initially, at the outbreak of WWII, President Roosevelt (FDR) pursued isolationist political policies.[120] WWI had ended without

---

[116] While there were several versions of the flag, the Stainless Banner is the one most used by the Confederacy. For a history of the Confederate flags, see John Coski, *The Confederate Battle Flag: America's Most Embattled Emblem* (New York: Harvard University Press, 2005).

[117] Rable, *God's Almost Chosen Peoples*, 39.

[118] Robert Bonner, "Flag Culture and the Consolidation of Confederate Nationalism," *The Journal of Southern History* 68 (2002): 296.

[119] Stout, *Upon the Altar of the Nation*, 29.

[120] The term "isolation" came about in the 1920s, along with "exceptionalism" and generally referred to the thought that the United States needed to look after national interests alone. John Lukacs, *The Legacy of the Second World War* (New Haven: Yale University Press, 2010), 140.

much benefit to the American people; it had cost much and led to the increase of isolationism's popularity and led Americans to argue in the name of nationalism to stay out of the war.[121] Americans were still recovering from the Great War and were in the midst of the Great Depression, so FDR refused to commit the United States to defend the international order.[122] World War I caused an understandable sense of disillusion of the American people that found manifestation in an overwhelming national sense of complete isolation world conflicts, and FDR constantly reiterated his similar belief.[123] Robert Divine notes how FDR's initial belief of isolation helped form public opinion on the issue of isolation:

> His belief that the United States could avoid war by denying arms to belligerents, his denunciation of war on moral grounds, his often expressed hope that the United States could best serve humanity as a passive example of democracy—all these ideas had contributed to the prevailing public mood.[124]

FDR thought the United States had to work with other nations to help establish peace in the world, but he did not want to commit to being a world-peace-keeping organization.[125] FDR personally inclined toward intervention, but he moved very cautiously, sensing the impending danger on the horizon:

---

[121] Ted Grimsrud, *The Good War That Wasn't—and Why It Matters: World War II's Moral Legacy* (Eugene: Cascade, 2014), 28, 33. Additionally, many Americans viewed the Great War as a mistake and was something that should not be repeated. Susan Brewer, *Why America Fights: Patriotism and War Propaganda from the Philippines to Iraq* (Oxford: Oxford University Press, 2009), 91.

[122] FDR had acquiesced Italy's invasion of Ethiopia, Japan's invasion of China, and Germany's invasion of the Sudetenland, showing that he had a penchant for isolation before Pearl Harbor. By the end of 1938, through these conquests, FDR had moved closer to intervention, sensing the ultimate threat to the United States that fascism—Hitler in particular—posed. Robert Divine, *Roosevelt and World War II* (Baltimore: Johns Hopkins Press, 1969), 5–6, 23.

[123] Divine, *Roosevelt and World War II*, 7.

[124] Divine, *Roosevelt and World War II*, 19.

[125] Warren Kimball, "The Incredible Shrinking War: The Second World War, Not (Just) the Origins of the Cold War," *Diplomatic History* 25 (2001): 360.

His hesitancy was not just a catering to isolationist strength but a reflection of his own inner uncertainty. Recognizing that Hitler threatened the security of the United States, he took a series of steps which brought the nation to the brink of war, but his own revulsion at the thought of plunging his country into the most devastating conflict in history held him back.[126]

FDR's political war strategy was nationally orientated but also worldwide in scope. Shifting toward intervention, he faced a challenge at home where he had to convince his fellow countrymen of what was truly at stake in this world conflict.[127] In essence, FDR's policies showed that he believed that the United States could not survive a world led by the Axis powers, so he did all that he could to "edge the country closer and closer leaving the ultimate decision to Germany and Japan."[128] The ultimate decision ultimately fell to Japan when they attacked Pearl Harbor, which removed any sense of isolation among the American people.[129]

The Role of WWII on the
American Sense of Patriotism

From early 1939, the United States military went from 140,000 soldiers to 1.25 million just sixteen months later.[130] A full sixteen million Americans would join the war, with many more millions

---

[126] Divine, *Roosevelt and World War II*, 48. FDR's Lend-Lease policy was one way that the United States helped her eventual allies, bringing her closer to war. FDR compared this to a neighborly act of "loaning a hose to the man next door when his house is on fire." Brewer, *Why America Fights*, 94. The Lend-Lease policy was named H.R. 1776, which was a patriotic callback to the year that America declared her independence and now was offering to help the world. Kenneth Davis, *FDR, The War President, 1940–1943: A History* (New York: Random House, 2000), 98.

[127] Raymond O'Connor, *Diplomacy for Victory: FDR and Unconditional Surrender* (New York: W. W. Norton, 1971), 18.

[128] Brewer, *Why America Fights*, 92; Divine, *Roosevelt and World War II*, 47.

[129] Kenneth Davis, *FDR, The War President, 1940–1943*, 348.

[130] John Lukacs, *The Legacy of the Second World War* (New Haven: Yale University Press, 2010), 145.

serving the national interest at home.[131] World War II had caused the American military complex to grow by lengths and bounds and had also affected the American economy and made her a global power. By 1945, the United States navy was more massive than all other navies combined, even though much of the United States Navy was destroyed at Pearl Harbor. Americans had developed the atomic bomb—and used it twice. Additionally, even though the United States was suffering from the effects of the Great Depression before the war, now the dollar was the single most dominant monetary unit in the world.[132] In a sense, WWII *was* a "good" war because it led to the establishment of the United States as a dominant world power. The shift from the Pax Britannica to Pax Americana had a profound impact on the American consciousness and led the American people to see their involvement in WWII as bringing peace and harmony to the world. In this way, Americans grew to see themselves as saviors on the world stage.[133]

America's entry into WWII and subsequent victory left a patriotic flavor in the mouths of most Americans because they came to see how the American spirit could be united to defeat a perceived evil in the world. Further, WWII established American military dominance in the world and forced the world to come to terms with American strength. As a result of WWII, American militarism became a way of life, and people grew to see American troops as "citizen soldiers" who were an extension of the American way of life and as a symbol of national unity and pride.[134]

Additionally, FDR's shift from isolation to intervention marked a significant shift in American foreign policy, especially when combined with America's military growth. FDR's intervention declared that the United States was not just determined to win WWII but also to obtain peace for the entire world.[135] FDR's intervention constructed and posited patriotism as a prerequisite for proper civic duty; a dutiful citizen had to be patriotic, and an

---

[131] Jacques Pauwels, *The Myth of the Good War: America in the Second World War* (Toronto: Jame Lorimer, 2015), 86.

[132] Lukacs, *The Legacy of the Second World War*, 48.

[133] Grimsrud, *The Good War That Wasn't*, 15, 95.

[134] Brewer, *Why America Fights*, 89.

[135] Brewer, *Why America Fights*, 87.

appropriately patriotic American wanted to keep democracy alive in the world.[136] This is important, for it helps explain the American concept of using the military to ensure liberty and freedom around the world. If American intervention in WWII was just, and if it was indeed a "good war," then additional military conflict in the world could continue to be justified.

The Vietnam War

While American involvement in World War II has been frequently referred to as a "good war" due to the perceived level of justification, the Vietnam War has received a different level of attention. The perceived morality of the Vietnam War haunts the American public and consciousness and has caused raging debates and has "triggered the most profound societal divisions since the Civil War."[137] More than forty years after the Vietnam War ended, it still occupies a central place in the collective American consciousness and remains an "unsettled part of the collective memory and experience" of the United States.[138]

The collective memory of America's role in Vietnam is complex.[139] In a study of American support of all American wars,

---

[136] Michelle Casey, "Working as Civic and Patriotic Duty for Consumption: A Critical Discourse Analysis of American Presidential Inaugural Speeches since World War II" (PhD diss., University of Nevada, Las Vegas, 2016), 80.

[137] Robert McMahon, "Contested Memory: The Vietnam War and American Society, 1975–2001," *Diplomatic History* 26 (2002): 160, 183.

[138] David Parsons, *Dangerous Grounds: Antiwar Coffeehouses and Military Dissent in the Vietnam Era* (Chapel Hill: University of North Carolina Press, 2017), 1; Penny Lewis, *Hardhats, Hippies, and Hawks: The Vietnam Antiwar Movement as Myth and Memory* (Ithaca: ILR Press, 2013), 3.

[139] Collective memory offers a useful tool for examining the nature of war, and nations must come to terms with collective memory to make sense of the trauma of war. This is especially true regarding the collective memory of Vietnam on American memory. While there is no consensus about the shared memory of the Vietnam War, it is crucial to recognize that these memories are constructed rather than simply remembered to meet people's needs. See McMahon, "Contested Memory," 162–163.

Vietnam had the least public support of all wars.[140] Support of the Vietnam War consistently dwindled the longer the war continued, and it became a subject of political debate and was widely opposed to people on both sides of the political spectrum.[141] While it is beyond the scope of this project to lay out the root causes of American initiation, involvement, and escalation of the Vietnam War, it has played a significant role in the development of the American notion of patriotism.

American Textbooks' Influence on
Collective Memory of the Vietnam War

One way to see the changing collective memory of the Vietnam War is to see the change in how American high school history textbooks have traced the historical development of the war. Since the issue of the Vietnam War is one that has remained unsettled, the major textbooks have been, on the whole, vague in how they treat American involvement. These textbooks have not been specifically clear on how Americans are to view its history in Vietnam; rather, they have given not a "particular series of facts but an atmosphere, an impression, a tone" that is distinctly patriotic.[142]

High school history textbooks help to inform collective memory and help shape "historical interpretations," which, in turn, significantly influence how people remember war.[143] In this way, history textbooks have helped serve as nationalistic histories because they have helped shape a patriotic understanding of American military involvement in an instructive rather than explorative way, showing how American involvement in Vietnam

---

[140] A. Dorn, et al., "How Just Were America's Wars? A Survey of Experts Using a Just War Index," *International Studies Perspectives* 16 (2015): 276.

[141] Michael Walzer, *Arguing about War* (New Haven: Yale University Press, 2004), 6.

[142] Walzer, *Arguing about War*, 18; Kevin Wilson, "From Memory to History: American Cultural Memory of the Vietnam War" (master's thesis, Miami University, 2006), 30–31.

[143] Wilson, "From Memory to History," 3, 21.

should exist in terms of patriotic virtue instead of criticism of whether involvement was justified.[144]

Textbooks that were written and published during the Vietnam War era struggled to make sense of the war. Textbook editors had no easier of a job in 1980: it was just as difficult then to write about the war as it was in earlier years to make sense of the current war and to make predictions about it.[145] As a result of the difficulties in making sense of the contested meanings of the Vietnam War, many editors choose to simply stay away from it. By staying away from many of the details of the Vietnam War, textbooks have helped to reshape public memory by taking the war and embedding a specific patriotic narrative.

American News Media's Influence on Collective Memory of the Vietnam War

In the sixties, more than 90 percent of Americans had a television, and they watched an estimated six hours of television a day.[146] In the late sixties, the news was limited to three major networks and only at limited times of the day. Without twenty-four-hour cable news options, competing views of the war between networks were limited.[147] While technology was limited, the Vietnam War allowed for the media to be involved in military action on the frontlines for the first time in American history.[148]

The results of news reports showing the nature of the conflict gave a much less optimistic view of the war, which influenced the minds of the American public in significant wars. This stood in sharp contrast to the way the national leaders had presented the war. Because Americans were able to see what was happening, public

---

[144] FitzGerald, *America Revised*, 47.

[145] FitzGerald, *America Revised*, 124–127.

[146] Brewer, *Why America Fights*, 181.

[147] Jennifer Anderson, "Prime Time Politics: Television News and the Visual Framing of War" (PhD diss., Vanderbilt University, 2011), 18.

[148] The size and portability and cost of video equipment limited what was actually caught on film. Camera crews had to carry upwards of one hundred pounds of equipment to properly film the war. So while they were able to show firsthand accounts of the war, what was shown was limited. Ibid., 19.

opinion began to change, and the American people began to mistrust both the leaders and the war.[149]

The Vietnam War and
Its Effects on Soldiers

The polarization of the Vietnam War on the American public can be best seen through its effects on American soldiers.[150] Approximately 20 percent of Vietnam era soldiers and veterans actively resisted American involvement in the war in which they fought.[151] Additionally, as the war continued, reenlistment dropped, and serious incidents of military insubordination increased in ways that had not been seen in the American military since the Civil War.[152]

Soldiers have always searched for meaning in military conflict, but it seems as if they struggled to find it during the Vietnam War.[153] Due to many Americans dodging the draft, many Vietnam veterans were "vilified" and "accorded less respect" on returning home from their service because a small minority of Americans saw the war as immoral. As a result, some saw soldiers

---

[149] Kirk Slaughter, "Gaining Momentum: How Media Influences Public Opinion to Push Civil-Military Decision Makers into Formulating Foreign Policy" (paper presented to the Air University, February 2016), 9–10.

[150] Much work has been done on the experience of Vietnam War soldiers. See Josephina Card, *Lives after Vietnam: The Personal Impact of Military Service* (Lexington: Lexington, 1983); J. A. King, et al., "Psychological Effects of Military Service in Vietnam: A Meta-Analysis," *Psy Bulletin* 102 (1987): 257–271; Ellen Frey-Wouters and Robert Laufer, *Legacy of a War: American Soldier in Vietnam* (New York: Routledge, 1986).

[151] Richard Moser, *The New Winter Soldiers: GI and Veteran Dissent during the Vietnam Era* (New Brunswick: Rutgers, 1996), 3. For a look at the underground GI protest movement, see Derek Seidman, "Paper Soldiers: The *Ally* and the GI Underground Press during the Vietnam War," in *Protest on the Page: Essays on Print and the Culture of Dissent since 1865*, ed. James Danky, et al. (Madison: University of Wisconsin, 2015), 183–202.

[152] Parsons, *Dangerous Grounds*, 89.

[153] On memory and the meaning of war, see Jay Winter, *Sites of Memory, Sites of Mourning: The Great War in European Cultural History* (Cambridge: Cambridge University Press, 2014).

as immoral for participating in the war.[154] This anti-war movement played a critical element in a "revisionist narrative" of the Vietnam War.[155]

It is important to understand that most Americans, despite their level of support of the war, generally supported the American troops. Vietnam veterans mirrored Civil War veterans who came home and were admired and honored despite the outcome of the War. This lost-cause attitude made little difference in the collective memory of the war; instead, it helped solidify the American public's view of patriotism as one that supported the military despite the rationale for war; the sharp criticism and protest at home showed that Americans owed these soldiers a great debt for serving despite the criticisms.[156] In the want of having a moral justification for American intervention in Vietnam, people focused on supporting the American troops who suffered greatly in the war as a way to be patriotic citizens regardless of the military outcome.

The Vietnam War's Influence on the
Concept of American Patriotism

Due to the overall lack of support of the war, it contradicted previous collective memory of war (WWI, WWII), in which the American military played a decisive role in the world. This only helped to splinter the overall consensus of American involvement in Vietnam.[157] Vietnam showed that while all American military operations are not necessarily morally justified, Americans, by and large, support the soldiers in the conflicts. Additionally, as a result of the moral ambiguity of the Vietnam War, Americans began to be constructive patriots who were at least open to the idea of being critical of the government. This criticalness has allowed Americans

---

[154] Wilson, "From Memory to History," 42.

[155] Parsons, *Dangerous Grounds*, 2. Popular Vietnam War movies have also played an essential role in this revisionist history. Movies such as the *Rambo* films, *Hamburger Hill, Forrest Gump, Full Metal Jacket, Good Morning Vietnam*, and others show patriotic soldiers serving in spite of ungrateful anti-war activists.

[156] McMahon, "Contested Memory," 167, 171.

[157] Wilson, "From Memory to History," 17.

to do their patriotic duty of supporting the military and the troops, even if they did not wholeheartedly endorse or support the military action in the first place. This new nature of patriotism condemned blind patriotism that required absolute obedience from its citizens.[158]

Historical Underpinnings of American Patriotism

Tracing the historical underpinnings of modern American patriotism is a challenging task. Doing so shows that America sees herself largely through a patriotic lens clouded through civil religion. In this way, America is a country that was seemingly founded by God with a purpose: to be a shining light to the world. Through the Civil War, America was able to develop a national identity that saw her as being full of noble soldiers who were always willing to fight for her noble ideals. Further, this national identity called for American involvement in later wars. Through WWII, America became the most dominant military power in the world, but more than that, she grew into a moral force for good in the world. Being a moral force for good was challenged by the difficulties of the Vietnam War, which made the American public rethink her role in the world, while also reaffirming her overall support of American troops out of a sense of collective patriotic duty. All of these underpinnings are crucial to understanding the vast influence that patriotism has on the American public consciousness.

---

[158] Moser, *The New Winter Soldiers*, 155.

3

Toward a Biblical Definition of "Patriotism"

There is much discussion centered around patriotism, and some of that is due to the varying definitions of the term. As a result, a proper definition must be given in order to be able to assess it. For this project, patriotism's definition is "loyalty to a person's particular country that involves a personal identification with his country, culture, and people." By developing a definition of patriotism rooted in loyalty, one can biblically assess and evaluate what patriotism entails. This project will show that this definition of patriotism can be biblically evaluated and maintained by a Christian under specific qualifications. Additionally, patriotism, under a proper definition, is a biblical alternative to nationalism and cosmopolitanism. Nationalism's insistence upon the superiority of one culture or nation over all others cannot be maintained biblically. Additionally, cosmopolitan's claim that a country's borders do not matter because people are citizens of the world means that their native country does not truly matter.[1] Neither of these is tenable to a Christian; therefore, a proper definition of patriotism is a better and biblical alternative. Since patriotism is loyalty to one's country, this chapter will show how loyalty develops through the Bible in three major areas: family relationships, friendships, and land. These three significant areas of loyalty develop through the Old Testament, help provide a biblical framework, and are the most important in understanding patriotism.

---

[1] Simon Keller, "The Case against Patriotism," in *The Ethics of Patriotism: A Debate*, ed. John Kleinig, et al. (Malden: Wiley, 2016), 49.

Patriotism's Core:
Loyalty

Patriotism is intricately connected to the concepts surrounding loyalty; patriots are motivated by loyalty to promote and defend their country's interests.[2] In some sense, patriotism requires putting one's own country's interests before others, which requires a certain level of loyalty from the citizen toward the country. Therefore, to truly understand patriotism, one must have a robust understanding of loyalty.[3] However, "loyalty," much like "patriotism," is a problematic term to define. A recent literature review of the term found no fewer than thirty-two different terminologies used as characteristics of loyalty showing how the term has a wide use of meanings, concepts, and values.[4]

To understand loyalty to one's country, one must understand that loyalty is a personal choice and can be taken away from one object and given to another. In some sense, patriotic loyalty is rooted in seeing a country as having certain valuable characteristics that make it worthy of that loyalty.[5] Patriotism is rooted in loyalty, and loyalty is rooted in personal choice, so patriotism must be seen as particular: it is one's *own* patriotism rooted in one's *own* loyalty for one's *own* country.[6]

Filial Loyalties

In coming to terms with a proper understanding of loyalty, one must look at various social institutions that help shape one's understanding of loyalty. The social institution most responsible for shaping loyalty is the family, where loyalty holds a central place in

---

[2] Stephen Nathanson, "Patriotism, War, and the Limits of Permissible Partiality," *Journal of Ethics* 13 (2009): 401–402.

[3] Ryan LaMothe states that loyalty is "paramount" in understanding patriotism. Ryan LaMothe, "The Problem of Patriotism: A Psychoanalytic and Theological Analysis," *Pastoral Psychology* 58 (2009): 162.

[4] Mark Rutgers and Lijing Yang, "Virtue or Vice: The Nature of Loyalty," *Public Integrity* 21 (2019): 396.

[5] Simon Keller, "Patriotism as Bad Faith," *Ethics* 115 (2005): 567, 574.

[6] Marcia Baron, "Patriotism and 'Liberal' Morality," in *Patriotism*, ed. Igor Primoratz (Amherst: Humanity, 2002), 62.

the ethical dimensions of relationships.[7] In families, there is a certain level of loyalty that develops that connects members within the family. Families are connected by a shared life that affects their worldview by a shared connection to one another. This connection is not chosen by family members but inherited from a family unit already in place. This family unit helps form views of loyalty in two ways. First, there is a sense of duty in parents' obligatory care for their children. Second, children have a sense of duty for their parents due to the care given to them by their parents. The child's feelings to the parent help construct concepts of family loyalty that, in turn, shape his understanding of loyalty in a broader way that shapes patriotism.[8]

In family structures, expectations and values help to influence loyalty within it and are transmitted to children from parents, and this results in a complex schema for developing family loyalty, which affects the way a person views loyalty.[9] How a family shapes loyalty is crucial to understanding how loyalty shapes a person's view toward patriotism.

There are four significant conceptions of how the family influences loyalty. First, there is the debt theory. The debt theory of family loyalty arises because parents have done so much for their children, bringing about a debt that needs to be repaid by children's actions, especially as parents age and need more help from their children.[10] This theory stresses that parents' sacrifices toward their children lead to a sense of inequality in the parent/child relationship that leads to the children's duty to pay back what is owed by long-

---

[7] Suus van Hekken, "Parent and Child Perceptions of Boszormenyi-Nagy's Ethical Dimensions of the Parent-Child Relationship," *Contemporary Family Therapy* 12 (1990): 530.

[8] To be sure, the concept of loyalty is intimately connected to duty. For this project, loyalty will be looked at as a choice, while duty will not. A duty is obligated, while a loyalty toward something is voluntarily chosen based upon other factors. In this way, families and their duties help shape loyalty even though they are not the same.

[9] Ann Leibig and Katherine Green, "The Development of Family Loyalty and Relational Ethics in Children," *Contemporary Family Therapy* 21 (1999): 90, 108.

[10] Simon Keller, "Four Theories of Filial Duty," *The Philosophical Quarterly* 56 (2006): 256.

term care and support of the parents. Second, the gratitude theory stresses that a child must show loyalty toward his parents to fulfill appropriate acts of gratitude toward them in response to all of the good things that his parents have done for him.[11] The gratitude theory is different from the debt theory because it does more than stress an obligation of care for parents. It focuses on a child's current loyalty more positively because it focuses on the good that parents have done on the behalf of children. Third, the friendship theory of filial loyalty lies not in what parents have done for their children in the past but in the parents' and children's relationship in the present. According to this theory, the duties between adult children and their parents are a result of friendship.[12] This theory of loyalty stresses that the concern of a child to a parent lies in the quality of the two parties' existing relationship; if an adult child and their parents do not share a strong or healthy relationship of close friendship, the adult child may not have a strong feeling of loyalty toward his parents.[13] Fourth, the special goods theory is concerned with the child's long-term care of his parents by working hard to provide special needs or goods that his parents need. If the child is in a position to provide for his parents, then the concept of reciprocity demands that he does what he can for his parents.[14]

These theories help make sense of the various components of patriotism because they help make sense of how a person understands loyalty. In much the same way as a person cannot choose the parents he has, a person cannot choose the country in which he was born. Some people see patriotism as stemming from a personal debt because of all that the country has done for them. This debt leads them to feel as if they need to sacrifice for their country. Others see gratitude as the basis of patriotism. These people are patriotic because of the sacrifice that others have paid for a country's current state, and because of these great sacrifices, a person should

---

[11] Keller, "Four Theories of Filial Duty," 257.

[12] Keller, "Four Theories of Filial Duty," 262. Also, see Simon Keller, *The Limits of Loyalty* (Cambridge: Cambridge, 2007), 115–119.

[13] William Sin, "Adult Children's Obligations towards Their Parents: A Contractualist Explanation," *Journal of Value Inquiry* 53 (2019): 29.

[14] Brynn Welch, "A Theory of Filial Obligations," *Social Theory and Practice* 38 (2012): 724.

be patriotic out of his gratitude. The friendship model of filial loyalty can help to explain patriotism due to the importance of a person looking at the current relationship that exists between a citizen and a country. Just as the friendship model emphasizes whether a parent and child have a proper and healthy relationship, some feel that patriotism should depend upon the current nature of the relationship between a country and the citizen. As such, loyalty depends entirely upon the nature of the relationship.

The Fifth Commandment
and Filial Loyalty

Walter Brueggemann rightly notes, "[I]n the world of Biblical faith, the family is the primary meaning which shapes and defines reality."[15] The proper place to start for understanding the biblical conception of filial loyalties is the fifth commandment. Society in the ancient Near East was foremost a society centered on family. It was the family who was the fundamental economic and sociological unit. This centrality is also seen in the biblical laws on filial duties, which are restricted to the family and spelled out most specifically in relation to children's duties performed toward parents. The most well-known statement concerning children's duties toward parents is found in the fifth commandment of the Ten Commandments, where children are commanded to show honor to their parents.[16] In requiring that adult children care for their parents, there is little doubt that the early Christian communities were also greatly influenced by the fifth commandment, as the New Testament authors quoted or referred to this commandment in some form multiple times.[17]

---

[15] Walter Brueggemann, "The Covenanted Family: A Zone for Humanness," *Journal of Current Social Issues* 14 (1977): 18.

[16] Jan Verbruggen, "Filial Duties in the Ancient Near East" (PhD diss., The Johns Hopkins University, 1997), 11.

[17] Warren Carter, "Adult Children and Elderly Parents: The Worlds of the New Testament," *Journal of Religious Gerontology* 12 (2001): 45; Eph 6:2–3; Mt 15:4–6; 19:19; Mk 7:10; 10:19.

Historically, three different interpretations have been given to the fifth commandment.[18] The first interpretation is patterned on Israel's patriarchal structure and stresses the parents' authority and the subsequent need for obedience from the children. In this interpretation, the child's obedience to the parents requires support for the overall family structure.[19] The second interpretation of the fifth commandment requires more than obedience and submission from the child but also respect for them as it is connected to the parents' authority.[20] The third interpretation of the fifth commandment focuses on the physical care of the elderly in the community, most notably seen through children's care of their own parents.[21] This aspect of the commandment is recognized in the Talmud: "What is honoring? Providing them food and drink, clothing and covers, and taking them in and out." Care of one's aged parents is one of the fundamental duties spelled out in adoption contracts and other documents of the ancient Near East.[22]

The fifth commandment's primary concept as a basis for the understanding of patriotism is its focus on honor. The fifth commandment commands children to honor their parents while never specifying how that is to be shown. The fact that honoring parents appears among the first five commandments, all of which deal with honoring, suggests the importance of this commandment.[23] Additionally, the honoring of parents is first

---

[18] Ranier Albertz, "Hintergrund und Bedeutung des Elterngebots im Dekalog," *ZAW* 90 (1978): 348–374.

[19] Werner Keszler, "Die Literarische, Historische und Theologische Problematik des Dekalogs," *VT* 7 (1957): 1–16.

[20] Verbruggen, "Filial Duties in the Ancient Near East," 11. Also see Karl Barth, *Church Dogmatics*, vol. 3, part 4 (Edinburgh: T&T Clark, 1969), 269–281.

[21] Verbruggen, "Filial Duties in the Ancient Near East," 11. This interpretation is fleshed out more fully in 1 Timothy 5:4–8, where Paul stressed that children are to give a recompense (ἀμοιβάς) to parents based on what they have been given.

[22] Care of one's aged parents is one of the fundamental duties spelled out in adoption contracts and other documents of the ancient Near East. Jeffrey Tigay, *Deuteronomy*, The JPS Torah Commentary (Philadelphia: Jewish Publication Society, 1996), 70.

[23] Tigay, *Deuteronomy*, 70.

among the duties toward other human beings listed in the Ten Commandments, furthering its significance.

Honor, however, cannot be commanded if it remains only an attitude or temperament. Therefore, to honor demands personal action that comes from the inner spirit. Essentially, כָּבֵד (*kābēd*) carries the nuance of weighing something down with honor or respect. It is used in Deuteronomy 5:16 with the notion of declaring to someone the quality of honor. The command to honor parents is, therefore, a command to demonstrate in concrete, empirical ways the respect people must have for their parents.[24]

The honor that must exist within the parental-child relationship is crucial to understanding patriotism for a few reasons. First, just as a person does not choose to be born within a family, he does not choose his birth country, which is the object of patriotism.[25] The command to show honor to one's parents has no qualification and does not state that a child must honor his parents only *if* they reach some sort of deserved status; no, the command to honor parents is inherent in who they are, not in what type of people they are. In much the same way, patriotism is linked to a person's country via his connection to it through birth, and there is no qualification that a country must meet in order to be one's object of patriotism.

Second, just as a person is to honor *his* parents, not someone else's, people are patriotic to their *own* country and not another. There is a certain level of ownership in both honoring one's parents and one's level of patriotism of his "own" country. A person cannot truly be patriotic toward a country that is not his own. This personal identification with one's own country is crucial to developing a sense of patriotism that is both personal and identifiable: a country is one's "own"; therefore, patriotism's object must be toward one's own country.

---

[24] Eugene Merrill, *Deuteronomy*, The New American Commentary (Nashville: Broadman & Holman Publishers, 1994), 153.

[25] While immigrants who choose to reside in a country can be extremely patriotic, most of the discussion of patriotism revolves around someone's birth country.

Friendship Loyalties

The second biblical topic that influences a proper framework of loyalty revolves around the biblical concept of friendship. As a topic, friendship has been largely ignored by Old Testament scholars, possibly on account of its complexity.[26] While the Jewish tradition is far more focused on kinship and family ties, the Old Testament does offer extensive material on friendship while not necessarily developing a serious reflection on the theme of friendship, which is in sharp contrast to the Greek and Roman traditions.[27]

A friend is a person with whom one shares affection and personal commitment. It is a voluntary association between people who enjoy one another's company and are concerned, at some level, with one another's welfare.[28] In the Bible, the term ranges from a casual acquaintance (e.g., Mt 5:25; 20:13; cf. Jb 2:11) to one who shared an intimate, personal bond (e.g., 2 Sm 15:37; cf. 1 Sm 18:1). In technical usage, a friend was one who held a position of trust, often involving an intimate association. For example, the "friend of the bridegroom" (Jgs 14:20; 15:2) arranged and presided over the wedding (Jn 3:29; cf. 2 Cor 11:2). The "friend of the king" was an essential royal court official, apparently a trusted adviser and intimate companion (1 Kgs 4:5; 1 Chr 27:33; 2 Sm 15:37).[29] Abraham was described as being a "friend" of God (2 Chr 20:7; Is 41:8; Jas 2:23), while God even spoke to Moses as a "friend" (Ex 33:11–12).

Most of the Old Testament words translated "friend," are from the Hebrew root, רֵעַ. The most common term for "friend" is רֵעַ,

---

[26] Saul Olyan, *Friendship in the Hebrew Bible* (New Haven: Yale, 2017), 2.

[27] Gary Stansell, "David and His Friends: Social-Scientific Perspectives on the David-Jonathan Friendship," *Biblical Theology Bulletin* 41 (2011): 116; Sean Kealy, "Friendship in the Bible," *Scripture in Church* 31 (2001): 508. The book of Ecclesiasticus also gives a detailed treatment of friendship in nine passages: 6:5–7; 9:10–15; 11:29–34; 12:8–9; 19:5–16; 22:19–26; 25:1–11; 27:16–21; 36:23–37:15.

[28] Olyan, *Friendship in the Hebrew Bible*, 1.

[29] Allen Myers, "Friend," *The Eerdmans Bible Dictionary* (Grand Rapids: Eerdmans, 1987), 392–393.

"friend." In the New Testament, several words appear, including φίλος, "friend"; εταιρος, "companion, comrade"; and πλησιον, "neighbor," along with a variety of kinship terms used for those outside of one's family for whom one feels a special affection. In both Testaments, "friends" and "friendship" involve three critical components: a close association, special loyalty, and affection.[30]

The Friendship of
David and Jonathan

The most notable example of friendship in the Old Testament is the story of David and Jonathan.[31] This friendship is challenging to understand because it is often viewed through Western eyes and, sometimes, with homosexual overtones. The emotional nature of the texts describing the friendship does not clarify to what extent the relationship is motivated by either politics or friendship, which gives an openness to liberal interpretations.[32] Regardless of liberal interpretations, the relationship between these two intimate friends is best understood through a lens of loyalty.[33]

---

[30] Carl Bridges Jr., "Friend, Friendship," *Evangelical Dictionary of Biblical Theology*, Baker Reference Library (Grand Rapids: Baker, 1996), 272.

[31] While it can be argued that Ruth and Naomi presented a deep friendship based on loyalty, their story lacks the breadth of the friendship of David and Jonathan. Additionally, Ruth and Naomi's relationship was based more upon marriage ties than friendship.

[32] Stansell, "David and His Friends," 117; David Abernethy, "The Heir of Saul: Jonathan's Life and Death in Theological Perspective," in *Characters and Characterization in the Book of Samuel*, ed. Keith Bodner and Benjamin Johnson (London: T & T Clark, 2020), 149. André Gide's *Saul*, originally published in 1922, is one of the most notable works stressing the homosexual nature of not just David and Jonathan; Gide suggests a homosexual triangle of David, Saul, and Jonathan. For more on a "queer" reading of David and Jonathan's relationship, see Ken Stone, *Queer Commentary and the Hebrew Bible* (London: Sheffield, 2001). James Harding looks at the vagueness of David and Jonathan's relationship as a way to interpret it in a sexual way in James Harding, *The Love of David and Jonathan: Ideology, Text, and Reception* (Sheffield: Equinox, 2013), 122–273. Regardless of these poor interpretations, there is nothing in the text that indicates any sort of homosexual relationship between the two, and to attempt to make the text say something that it clearly does not, is a foolish attempt to force a wrong hermeneutical application on a clear text about friendship.

[33] Stansell, "David and His Friends," 128.

Proverbs 18:24 says, "A man of many companions may come to ruin, but there is a friend who sticks closer than a brother." This verse implies the possibility of graduations of friendship and compares the exceptional friend to that of a brother, connecting friendship to familial loyalty.[34] David and Jonathan were not only brothers-in-law, but they also had an intimate friendship that existed under tremendous tension, since Saul, Jonathan's father, had sworn to kill David despite his service.[35] David and Jonathan's friendship was reasonable because both had much in common. Both were courageous, young warriors who possessed profound faith in the Lord and had trusted the Lord in their initiated attacks against the militarily superior Philistines that had resulted in significant victories for Israel.[36]

Jonathan, like his father Saul (1 Sm 16:21), "loved" David. This deep love inspired Jonathan to make a covenant with David (1 Sm 18:3–4). This covenantal pact was the only time in the Bible that two same-sex friends promised loyalty to each other.[37] The fact that Jonathan gave David the clothing and arms initially reserved for the heir to Saul's throne holds symbolic and thematic significance and explains how David came to possess these coveted tokens of power and becomes part of the background of his eventual kingship.[38]

1 Samuel 18:1 stresses that Jonathan's soul was "knit" (קשר) to David's. This Hebrew idiom is also found in Genesis 44:30, where it speaks of Benjamin's relationship to his father; this expression carries the idea of great affection toward someone. While readers are never explicitly told that David loved Jonathan, there is an indication that David cared for him; the narrative does, however,

---

[34] Olyan, *Friendship in the Hebrew Bible*, 24.

[35] Tony Cartledge, *1 and 2 Samuel*, Smyth and Helwys Bible Commentary (Macon: Smyth & Helwys, 2001), 240.

[36] Robert Bergen, *1, 2 Samuel*, The New American Commentary (Nashville: Broadman & Holman Publishers, 1996), 199. Jonathan and his armor-bearer famously launch a successful surprise attack on the Philistines in 1 Samuel 14. Additionally, David had just killed Goliath in 1 Samuel 17; Jonathan and David's relationship could have developed out of Jonathan's admiration for David's heroics.

[37] Philip Culbertson, *The Future of Male Spirituality* (Minneapolis: Fortress Press, 1992), 83.

[38] Bergen, *1, 2 Samuel*, 199–200.

show the emphasis surrounding their relationship is on Jonathan's love for David.[39] Jonathan pledged loyalty to David in the covenant made between these two in 1 Samuel 18. While Jonathan initiated the covenant, it became more mutual as Jonathan repeatedly demonstrated his loyalty to David.[40]

Jonathan was swearing loyalty to David at a high personal cost: to enter into a covenant with David in this way, voluntarily and symbolically giving him his weapons, was to be seen as surrendering his future kingdom.[41] Jonathan made a costly choice to stay loyal to David; he ultimately rejected his father and did not show him the culturally accepted form of honor.[42] Brueggemann is correct when he states, "In retrospect this is an act of stunning loyalty on Jonathan's part." What is more, Jonathan chose to be loyal to David much earlier when Saul's true nature was not known. "The text invites us to reflect on the cost of loyalty and the terrible ambiguities within which loyalty must be practiced."[43]

Jonathan loved his father, Saul, and was loyal to him, almost to a fault. Jonathan's frequent use of the phrase "my father" brings this familial loyalty to the forefront. However, in making his covenant with David, he shunned his rightful claim on the future kingdom and chose to be loyal to David. This level of friendship is "one of the most heart-warming stories in all of the world's literature."[44] While heartwarming, their relationship was not necessarily a celebration of friendship's virtues; it was, according to Brueggemann, "an exposé of the wrenching, risk, pain, hurt, and hope required as God brings God's new reign."[45] More than that,

---

[39] Roger Omanson and John Ellington, *A Handbook on the First Book of Samuel*, UBS Handbook Series (New York: United Bible Societies, 2001), 387.

[40] Abernethy, "The Heir of Saul," 150.

[41] Joyce Baldwin, *1 and 2 Samuel: An Introduction and Commentary*, The Tyndale Old Testament Commentaries (Leicester: Inter-Varsity, 1998), 135.

[42] While it may seem strange that Jonathan would show more loyalty to David than to Saul, it is important to remember that Saul had once tried to kill him just as he tried to kill David (1 Samuel 14). Cartledge, *1 and 2 Samuel*, 235.

[43] Walter Brueggemann, *First and Second Samuel*, Interpretation: A Bible Commentary for Teaching and Preaching (Louisville: John Knox, 1990), 153.

[44] Cartledge, *1 and 2 Samuel*, 240, 244.

[45] Brueggemann, *First and Second Samuel*, 153.

however, it was a depiction of loyalty. Jonathan asked nothing of David in the present; he simply asked David to remember him in the future, which David did.

Friendship loyalties show that a person can make a judgment call on who to be loyal to. This is different from filial loyalties derived from the family in which someone is born. Friendships, no matter how deep, are based on an individual's decision that calls for a certain level of loyalty to the recipient based upon friendship. In the same way, people chose to be loyal to their country. This choice of loyalty is a decision that must be made by an individual to remain patriotic toward his country.

Loyalty to the Land

The third biblical topic that influences the proper conception of loyalty is the land. Brueggemann is correct when he states that land "is a central if not *the central theme* of the biblical faith."[46] In the Old Testament, the concept and theme of land and its relationship with Israel is vital as a dominant theme and is an essential element in the biblical framework of promise and fulfillment and holds a central place in the overall structure of the Old Testament's narrative.[47] In the Old Testament, the word or words designating "land" appear more than one thousand six hundred times, while only fifty times in the New Testament.[48]

How one views the land affects one's theology, especially in terms of how it relates to the nation and the people of Israel. A

---

[46] Walter Brueggemann, *The Land: Place as Gift, Promise, and Challenge in Biblical Faith*, 2nd ed. (Minneapolis: Fortress, 2002), 3.

[47] Patrick Miller, "The Gift of God: The Deuteronomic Theology of the Land," *Interpretation* 23 (1969): 461; Oren Martin, *Bound for the Promised Land: The Land Promise in God's Redemptive Plan*, New Studies in Biblical Theology (Downers Grove: Apollos, 2015), 18; Jerry Frankel, *The Land of Canaan and the Destiny of Israel: Theologies of Territory in the Hebrew Bible* (Winona Lake: Eisenbrauns, 2011), 1–2.

[48] Naim Ateek, "Zionism and the Land: A Palestinian Christian Perspective," in *The Land of Promise: Biblical, Theological and Contemporary Perspectives*, ed. Philip Johnston and Peter Walker (Downers Grove: InterVarsity, 2000), 209.

proper theology of land starts in Eden.[49] Adam was created out of the dust, which implies his connection to the land, and was placed in the garden of Eden to tend it. By man's very creation, he was related to the ground, making him perfectly matched for the task of working it, which is required for proper cultivation.[50] Although Eden's location remains mysterious, the point of its description is clear for the reader: the home God has prepared is bountiful.[51] However, more than Eden being bountiful, it was the place where God resided and entered into a relationship with Adam. In essence, Eden was the first sanctuary on earth and served as the prototype "place" of the kingdom.[52] Adam, being placed in Eden, shows Eden's importance on being the dwelling place of humanity and serves as the model for humankind's need for a home in the land.

Place or Space?

Brueggemann argues that the Bible is "primarily concerned with the issue of being displaced and yearning for a place."[53] It is out of this longing for a place that the theology of the land finds its meaning. While there is a contemporary emphasis on geography regarding land, the Old Testament was concerned with something more. When God made a promise to Abram that He would bless him by giving him the Promised Land, God promised him more than just geographical land; God promised Abram that he would have a "place." Eventual possession of the land would be necessary, but only insofar as the land would be a place of memories and hope. The Promised Land was more than a space; it was a "place"; it was a storied place.[54]

---

[49] O. Palmer Robertson, *The Israel of God: Yesterday, Today, and Tomorrow* (Philipsburg: P & R, 2000), 4.

[50] Kenneth Mathews, *Genesis 1–11:26*, vol. 1A, *The New American Commentary* (Nashville: Broadman & Holman Publishers, 1996), 195.

[51] Mathews, *Genesis 1–11:26*, 208.

[52] Gregory Beale, "Eden, the Temple, and the Church's Mission in the New Creation," *JETS* 48 (2005): 7; Martin, *Bound for the Promised Land*, 38, 75.

[53] Brueggemann, *The Land*, 2.

[54] John Inge, "A Christian Theology of Place" (PhD diss., University of Durham, 2001), 68.

Israel had to go in to conquer the Promised Land, which shows that it existed as land before it existed as a home for Israel. Space exists prior to inhabitation or conquest, but space is how people come to experience land after it has given people a home. A place is thus the result of the civilization of space.[55] Land is important today because it represents something more than dirt or soil; it represents a home or a place that represents the very nature of who people are. In this way, people feel strongly about their homeland as a place rather than merely their land. In a sense, as Edward Casey argues, place is the "geographical self," which makes the self and place interdependent: one cannot exist without the other.[56] People are rooted in their country because it represents more to them than land; it represents to them their home, which leads them to feelings of deep affection and patriotism for their country because it represents to them the place where they belong.[57]

The Land was Promised

The land that Israel would eventually possess was indeed a land that was "promised." God promised Abram a special land in Genesis 12:7. This reference refers back to 12:1: "the land that I will show you." The land's identity was now firmly established. Now, the original promises of nationhood and blessings for Israel were enhanced by granting an actual national territory through which those promises may be accomplished. From this promise onward, the Jewish people's history and destiny are inseparably bound up

---

[55] Oliver O'Donovan, "The Loss of a Sense of Place," *The Irish Theological Quarterly* 55 (1989): 46.

[56] Edward Casey, "Between Geography and Philosophy: What Does It Mean to Be in the Place-World?" *Annals of the Association of American Geographers* 91 (2001): 683–684.

[57] Gary Burge sees the importance of the theme of place as "potent not simply because it represents geography we may own, but because it represents a place where we are rooted and can understand who we are. . . . Each of us wants a place that we can call home, a place we may think of as our own, where familiar things are available, where old stories may be retold, where we experience some connection with a legacy that stretches out behind us." Gary Burge, *Jesus and the Land: The New Testament Challenge to "Holy Land" Theology* (Grand Rapids: Baker, 2010), ix.

with the Promised Land.[58] However, this promise was deeper than land; this Promised Land would become the medium through which God would give Himself to the people; the land would be theirs, but only because God was theirs.[59]

The Promised Land concept is central to the Old Testament and perhaps finds its fullest expression in the book of Deuteronomy. God promised a land to Abraham (Gn 12:7; 13:15; 17:8), which was given to Israel after a long sojourn in Egypt, but it came within covenantal obligations (Dt 29:1–30:20).[60] When the nation of Israel broke the covenant, God allowed them to go into exile even though He promised they would be brought back. Thus, Israel's sojourning in a foreign land and subsequent return to Canaan became a central theme in the Old Testament. As a result, the Promised Land would always be seen as a place of rest to the Israelites (Dt 12:9–10; Jo 1:13–15).

In the same way that Israel needed a place, they needed to see a place on the horizon. This Promised Land became something that the people could and would look forward to no matter their current situation. The Promised Land motif would serve as a pattern of a greater, future reality for the people before the conquest of Canaan but would also be something that they would look forward to in exile. The Promised Land would be something that Israel would always see as vital because it would serve as their new Eden: the eventual place where they would once again live under God's lordship.[61]

---

[58] Nahum Sarna, *Genesis*, The JPS Torah Commentary (Philadelphia: Jewish Publication Society, 1989), 92.

[59] O'Donovan, "The Loss of a Sense of Place," 50.

[60] Josef Plöger argues that God setting the land before Israel was not truly a contractual obligation. Instead, it was spoken of in military usage, referring to a formula of surrender. The land was given to Israel as enemies were given over to surrender in a military operation. Josef Plöger, *Literarkritische, Forgeschichtliche und Stilkritische Untersuchungen zum Deuteronomium* (Bonn: Bonner, 1967), 61–63.

[61] Martin, *Bound for the Promised Land*, 17, 115.

The Land was a Gift

The Promised Land is continually referenced in Deuteronomy as a gracious gift from God to Israel.[62] God's people were not about to take the Promised Land from other people, but they would receive the land as a gift from its divine owner.[63] Israel was not just promised a land; they were gifted a land. The land belonged to the Lord (Lv 25:23). That God owned the land is emphasized by the prohibition that opens the section: "The land must not be sold permanently." This indicates the Israelites were nothing more than tenants of the land that belonged to the Lord since He was the one who gave the land to Israel.

Traditional land models stressed that tribal and social groups did not have any direct access to the land but had to enter into some sort of relationship with the king or ruler. God was the one who allocated the land to Israel and is pictured as a universal monarch who controls all domains, of which Canaan happens to be one.[64] As the proper landowner, God alone had the title to the property; the Israelites were simply aliens and tenants with stewardship responsibilities (1 Chr 29:15; Heb 11:13).[65] As the landowner, God had the right to grant residence to his tenants and to evict them if they did not keep their side of the covenant (2 Chr 7:20).

---

[62] Dt 1:8, 35; 6:10, 18, 23; 7:13; 8:1; 10:11; 11:9, 21; 15:4; 19:8; 25:19; 26:1, 3, 15; 28:11; 30:20; 31:7; 34:4. Patrick Miller stresses the importance of the land being a gift: Patrick Miller, "The Gift of God: The Deuteronomic Theology of the Land," *Interpretation* 23 (1969): 451–465. God also gave Israel cities (20:16), towns (16:5, 18; 17:2); and nations (19:1).

[63] Merrill, *Deuteronomy*, 68.

[64] Norman Habel, *The Land Is Mine: Six Biblical Land Ideologies* (Minneapolis: Fortress, 1995), 29, 37.

[65] Mark Rooker, *Leviticus*, vol. 3A, *The New American Commentary* (Nashville: Broadman & Holman Publishers, 2000), 306; Baruch Levine, *Leviticus*, The JPS Torah Commentary (Philadelphia: Jewish Publication Society, 1989), 174.

Boundaries of Land

All nations enjoy territorial boundaries and identity, partly because God has ordained them so.[66] Boundaries are important because they define an order of being of a nation. The land of Israel was no different. God established Israel's boundaries and, according to Ezekiel 38:12, made her the center of the earth; and according to Ezekiel 5:5, Jerusalem was the center of Israel and thus the center of the center of the world.[67]

The New Testament's View of Land

The trajectory of the land theme in the New Testament is one of the most difficult biblical themes to track.[68] In the Old Testament, the land was a special sacred space set apart from other lands in creation; the New Testament shifts the emphasis on land from literal to symbolic.[69] In the Old Testament, Israel understood the Promised Land to be a means for salvation. This is not to say that God was not with them while they were in the wilderness or exile. Still, the Promised Land, and its eventual establishment into the nation of Israel, served as a means of salvation for the people—Israel's very existence was dependent upon the land.[70] However, this is not the case in the New Testament. The land in the New Testament was seen in a mostly symbolic manner through the lens of Jesus. For the New Testament writers, the land took a definite change through the

---

[66] Esther Reed, "Refugee Rights and State Sovereignty: Theological Perspectives on the Ethics of Territorial Borders," *Journal of the Society of Christian Ethics* 30 (2010): 63, 65; Ps 74:17; Ez 47:13; Acts 17:24–26; Dt 32:8–9.

[67] Burge, *Jesus and the Land*, 1.

[68] Bruce Waltke and Charles Yu, *An Old Testament Theology: An Exegetical, Canonical, and Thematic Approach* (Grand Rapids: Zondervan, 2007), 559.

[69] Munther Isaac, "From Land to Lands, from Eden to the Renewed Earth: A Christ-Centred Biblical Theology of the Promised Land" (PhD diss., Middlesex University, 2014), 49; Walter Elwell and Barry Beitzel, "Land," *Baker Encyclopedia of the Bible* (Grand Rapids: Baker, 1988), 1307.

[70] Miller, "The Gift of God," 453.

person and work of Jesus. Colin Chapman makes this case well by stating:

> [T]he New Testament writers showed no interest in a literal interpretation. Since they were silent about the future of the land and at the same time interpreted the concept of the land in the light of Jesus and his kingdom, they must have believed that this was the only possible interpretation of the significance of the land for the Christian. Once the New Testament writers had seen the significance of the land and the nation in the context of the kingdom of God which had come into being in Jesus of Nazareth, they ceased to look forward to a literal fulfillment of Old Testament prophecies of a return to the land and a restored Jewish state. The only fulfillment of all the promises and prophecies was already there before their eyes in the person of Jesus. The way they interpreted the Old Testament must be the norm for the Christian interpretation of the Old Testament today.[71]

Israel, in the Old Testament, fled to the Promised Land for redemption. Yet in the New Testament, a redeemed people do not go to a geographical place to be redeemed; instead, they flee to Christ for their salvation.[72]

In the New Testament, it appears that the Promised Land is understood as typifying something of the future heavenly rest awaiting God's people. The New Testament indicates that it is God's purpose to prepare an eternal home for His people where the King's rule is eternally just, where all things are subject to His will, and where the needs of His people are completely satisfied (Heb 11:13–16; Revelation 21). In light of Jesus's incarnation, any statement of Scripture concerning a future for the land is interpreted as fulfilled through the church, which is seen as the new Israel and subsequent heir of the Old Testament promises. God's kingdom is now a spiritual reality and not a physical reality. To abide in Christ

---

[71] Colin Chapman, *Whose Promised Land?* (Tring: Lion, 1983), 153.

[72] Gregory Beale, *A New Testament Biblical Theology: The Unfolding of the Old Testament in the New* (Grand Rapids: Baker, 2011), 750.

is considered now a fulfillment of the physical and geographical promises of the Old Testament.[73]

W. D. Davies's study on the land in the New Testament is one of very few in-depth studies of the land in the New Testament.[74] However, Davies surveys the Old Testament background, then looks at the New Testament writings and notes that there are few explicit land references in the Pauline epistles. He notes that Paul did not include the land in the list of advantages of the chosen people in the book of Romans, nor did he make much of the promise of the land. For Paul, God's promise for the land is for all people in all places, not just for the nation of Israel.[75] The land was an essential part of God's plan for man, specifically the Promised Land. However, God always wanted to extend these blessings to all lands. For the present, the earth remains under sin's curse, which brings much pain and suffering, and although creation groans (Rm 8:22), one day, God will recreate it, and it will achieve its longed for glorious destiny.[76]

Loyalty to the Nation Itself

A fourth social institution that helps to shape a biblically informed patriotism is loyalty towards the nation itself. The OT shapes a biblical understanding of nation and nationhood but does so by describing God's relationship to Israel and Israel's subsequent relationship with the other nations of the world. The nation of Israel traced its ancestry back to the 12 sons of Jacob and was referred to variously as "Israel" (Gn. 34:7), "the people of Israel" (Ex. 1:8), "the (twelve) tribes of Israel" (Gn. 49:16, 28), and also as "the Israelites" (Gn. 32:32). "Israel" is used over 2500 times in the Bible, so it is

---

[73] Elwell and Beitzel, "Land," 1307.

[74] W. D. Davies, *The Gospel and the Land: Early Christianity and Jewish Territorial Doctrine* (Berkeley: University of California Press, 1974). Others include OP Robertson, *The Israel of God: Yesterday, Today, and Tomorrow* (Philipsburg: P & R, 2000); Habel, *The Land Is Mine*; Moshe Weinfeld, *The Promise of the Land: The Inheritance of the Land of Canaan by the Israelites* (Berkeley: University of California Press, 1993); Arie Leder, *Waiting for the Land: The Story Line of the Pentateuch* (Phillipsburg, 2010).

[75] Davies, *The Gospel and the Land*, 196–200.

[76] Joseph Fitzmyer, *Romans: A New Translation with Introduction and Commentary*, Anchor Yale Bible (New Haven: Yale University Press, 2008), 509.

clear that the Bible is written with an eye toward the importance of the nation itself and shows that Israel is a profoundly theological concept that refers to the importance of the people of God.[77]

That Israel was known as a "people" is significant. Etymologically, the word suggests that members of a people are in some way related to one another. However, there is more here than Israel merely being a people. Israel is also a nation. As Goldingay notes, Israel is "an entity that sees itself as ethnically one, a huge family, and also a political entity whose members are aware of belonging together."[78] At some point, ancient Israel saw themselves as both a people and a nation so the terminology surrounding "Israel" was fluid.[79] Israel was both a people of God and the nation of God. It is through the lens of Israel that a proper understanding of nationhood is developed.

Deuteronomy 32:8 shows that God "fixed the borders" of the people of the world.[80] This act of universal sovereignty gives clear evidence of the Lord's concern for all of the people of the world. Adding to the concepts of nationhood seen through the Table of Nations in Genesis 10, this fixing of borders is essential. Israel was central to the purposes of the Lord, which were tied to the land. So, the intent of the statement that God fixed boundaries for all peoples according to his predetermined plan for Israel means there would be a land for them carved out from the rest of the world. This geographical inheritance for Israel came through allotments of all other nations, especially those of Canaan, to accommodate that purpose.[81]

---

[77] Keith Grüneberg, *Abraham, Blessing and the Nations: A Philological and Exegetical Study of Genesis 12:3 in its Narrative Context* (Berlin: Walter de Gruyter, 2003), 168; James LaGrand, *The Earliest Christian Mission to 'All Nations' in the Light of Matthew's Gospel.* (Tampa: Scholars Press, 1995), 48.

[78] John Goldingay, *Old Testament Theology: Israel's Life* (Downers Grove: InterVarsity, 2009), 542. Also see John Goldingay, *Old Testament Ethics: A Guided Tour* (Downers Grove: InterVarsity, 2019), 153.

[79] Steven Grosby, "Religion and Nationality in Antiquity," *European Journal of Sociology* 32 (1991): 231.

[80] Paul stresses the importance of this fact in his sermon at the Areopagus in Acts 17:26; Also see Psalm 74:17.

[81] Eugene Merrill, *Deuteronomy*, The New American Commentary (Nashville: Broadman & Holman, 1994), 412–413.

The Calling of Abraham and the
Beginning of Israel as a Nation

The precise beginnings of Israel's origins as a people are problematic to determine and subject to interpretation of the biblical accounts and supplementary historical data. However, Genesis points to God's call of Abram to journey with his family to Canaan, with the promise that they would one day become a great nation.[82] Before the calling of Abraham, it is vital to understand the cultural situation that surrounded his calling. The "Table of Nations" in Genesis 10 is posited as a graphic representation, in genealogical form, of the relationship between ancient people groups with whom Israel had interactions, thus offering a historical setting for the call and life of Abraham. In this way, the Table of Nations is the bridge between the earlier part of Genesis, which expresses God's dealing with mankind as a whole, and the story of Israel's establishment as a nation.[83] From the time of the flood onward, "nations spread abroad on the earth" (Gen 10:32). The Table of Nations shows that the entire world in Abraham's day was understood politically.[84]

Genesis 11:1 shows that the world has "one language" and is thus united in a basic way despite different nations listed in Genesis 10. While people were spreading out and filling the earth, they also stopped to build a monument to themselves by creating the Tower of Babel. Mirroring the attempt of humanity in the garden of Eden to achieve power independently of God, the people attempt to reach heaven and are promptly judged for it. The "mirrored" image of the narrative heightens the focal event of God's descent to earth (v. 5), which is the point at which the fortunes of the people change. Despite the efforts of the people of Babel to reach "to the heavens" (v. 4), the Lord "came down" from heaven to witness their feeble efforts (v. 5). The overarching message is that human pride resulted in the Lord's punishment of dispersal.[85] The Tower of Babel explains how people spread out and filled the earth with different

---

[82] *The Eerdmans Bible Dictionary* (1987), s.v. "Israel."

[83] Ibid., 981.

[84] Walter Brueggemann, *Genesis*. (Atlanta: John Knox, 1982), 93.

[85] K. A. Mathews, *Genesis 1–11:26*, The New American Commentary (Nashville: Broadman & Holman, 1996), 467–68.

languages. It also explains why the nations are scattered as they are in Genesis 10. Even though God gave the people a command to increase and fill the earth (Gen 9:1), Babel shows the division into different people groups with different languages was a consequence of sin.[86] In Genesis 10, the people are scattering across the earth in order to fill it, but in Genesis 11, they are scattering in a state of confusion and division.[87]

It is against this background of the emergence of people groups, nations, and sin that Abram is called by God to become a special people and nation. God's call of Abram in Genesis 12 is in response to the sinful human situation seen in Genesis 3–11. The Table of Nations and the Tower of Babel, in the context of the sinful human situation, stand as the prologue for Genesis 12:1–3 and the calling of Abram.[88] As Christopher Wright notes, "God's promise to Abraham in Genesis 12 is God's answer to the problem of the nations in Genesis 10 and 11."[89] The call of Abram is seen as God's dealing with the nations of the world that have been scattered but will ultimately be blessed through the promise of Abram. In the same text in which God promises that Abram will become a great nation, God also promised the rest of the nations they would also be blessed.[90]

The call to Abram takes place in the context of God's dealings with all of the nations of the world who have been the focus of Genesis 10 and 11.[91] By making Abram's descendants a "great nation" who will be a "blessing," God will bring salvation to the scattered nations; so while the call is to the individual Abram, it is ultimately intended for the salvation of the people of the world. The following three phrases identify the spheres of influence in his life that Abram must leave behind, from the broad to the specific: from

---

[86] Daniel Hays, *From Every People and Nation: A Biblical Theology of Race,* New Studies in Biblical Theology 14 (Downers Grove: InterVarsity, 2003), 60.

[87] Christopher Wright, *The Mission of God's People: A Biblical Theology of the Church's Mission* (Grand Rapids: Zondervan, 2010), 70.

[88] Daniel Hays, *From Every People and Nation,* 61.

[89] Christopher Wright, *The Mission of God's People,* 70.

[90] Charles Scobie, 'Israel and the Nations: An Essay in Biblical Theology' *Tyndale Bulletin* 43 (1992): 285.

[91] Christopher Wright, Ibid., 71.

"your country," from "your people," and from "your father's household." The alliterative "from" heads each phrase reinforcing the command of separation God requires of Abram.[92] In other words, Abram has to leave everything that gave him a sense of security. However, by doing this, Abram is promised a land and is promised that his descendants will form a great nation.[93] God does not promise to make a great people of Abram but a great nation. Abram already is a people due to his family; however, Israel will become a nation among the nations.

Gaining a specific land is an important theme in Abram's call narrative as seen in verse 7. Abram is promised that the land he is in, although currently filled with Canaanites, will one day be his family's land. It seems that the point of this land promise is meant to establish the nationhood of Abraham through the covenantal promise of land. In this section, the land becomes an essential focal point of the promises to Abraham.[94] It is not just that Abraham will become a blessing to the nations; it is the nation of Abraham that will become the blessing to the nations. The land of promise would thus become a nation of promise. All that was needed was Israel to come to possess the land.

Israel's Relationship to War

The fifth social institution that helps to shape a biblically informed patriotism is a proper understanding of war. Given that the Canaanites already inhabited the land promised to Abram, war with them was inevitable. Throughout Old Testament history, warfare was an inevitable fact of life and a practical necessity for survival.[95] The first reason war was inevitable for Israel is the geography of the area. Although Palestine was not rich in natural resources, it was an

---

[92] K. A. Mathews, *Genesis 11:27–50:26*, 105, 109.

[93] Andreas Köstenberger and Peter O'Brien, *Salvation to the Ends of the Earth: A Biblical Theology of Mission*, New Studies in Biblical Theology (Downers Grove: InterVarsity, 2001), 29.

[94] Grüneberg, *Abraham, Blessing and the Nations: A Philological and Exegetical Study of Genesis 12:3 in its Narrative Context*, 164.

[95] Peter Craigie, *The Problem of War in the Old Testament* (Grand Rapids: Eerdmans, 1978), 66.

important commercial and military route. Additionally, its location between the Mediterranean to the west and the desert to the east tended to make it a prize of war in conflicts between the Egyptian or Mesopotamian empires. As a result, in the struggles involving Egypt, Assyria, and Babylonia (not to mention lesser powers such as Moab, Amalek, and the Philistines), Palestine's small land played an important strategic role and was often in military turmoil.[96] As Craigie notes, "without the use of force the state of Israel would not have come into existence."[97]

All nations had laws and customs governing aspects of war. War is a function of the state and is how nations assert themselves against other nations.[98] States exist to maintain, defend, and even extend their territories. The use of force and violence externally as well as internally is inherent to their nature and purpose.[99] War in the Old Testament was always viewed as a necessary evil in the defense of God's people from those who would seek their destruction or who would seek their property or resources. God, as the Creator and Sovereign over all things, had the right to bring these nations under his dominion by force if necessary. God chose to do so through the use of his elect people. All war by Israel was thus under divine protection and existed as "holy war" (or "Yahweh war") and, as such, was not only allowed by the Lord but instructed and carried out by him.[100]

The second reason war was a way of life for Israel was theological. The fact that God had promised judgment upon sinful human beings is frequently expressed in armed conflict through human agents in this particular area of the world. Indeed, most warfare throughout the ancient Near East had a spiritual and theological dimension, with each side in a conflict acting in the

---

[96] Allen Myers, *The Eerdmans Bible Dictionary*, 1043–44.

[97] *International Standard Bible Encylopedia* (1988), s.v. "War, Idea of."

[98] Peter Craigie, *The Problem of War in the Old Testament*, 66; John Goldingay, *Old Testament Theology*, 549.

[99] Goldingay, *Old Testament Theology: Israel's Life*, 549.

[100] Eugene H. Merrill, *Deuteronomy*, 282. General rules for warfare inside of the Promised Land do not apply. In the Promised Land, the *herem* applies where God ordered a complete and total destruction of the enemy as a type of sacrifice to God, J.G. McConville, *Deuteronomy*, Apollos Old Testament Commentary (Downers Grove: InterVarsity, 2002), 321.

name of its patron god, who would be credited with the victory. In the OT, warfare illustrates God's sovereign control over human history, guaranteeing victory to those to whom he granted it. Therefore, war was seen as a fate prescribed to Israel's enemies as a punishment for their sins (Dt 9:4–5) and a preventative and protective measure to keep Israel from going astray (Dt 7:4).[101]

In this way, war plays a significant part of the biblical story of Israel. Warfare is described in the Book of Deuteronomy, especially in chapter 20. War is not merely a human enterprise fought by kings with trained soldiers and military equipment; war, in the biblical narrative, is God's war in which he is involved together with the covenant people of Israel who are selected to fight in his name.[102] In this way, Israel's warfare was a "holy war" that was always initiated by God and never Israel. Israel experienced God as a warrior and Yahweh is referred to as "a man of war" (Ex 15:3; Ps 24:8; Isa 42:13) and Numbers 21:14 refers to a *Book of the Wars of Yahweh*, an ancient unknown that seems to be dedicated to the great victories ascribed to Yahweh the God of Israel.[103] Trusting in God was a central aspect of war in Israel because without him, Israel could not hope to win any significant skirmish or take the Promised Land. Gerhard von Rad even argues that it is "certain that the concept of faith" in God "had its actual origin in the holy war."[104]

The third reason that war was inevitable for Israel was practical in that the land would need to be defended. War was a practical necessity for survival for all states in the ancient world because resources were scarce, so while Israel would have to conquer the promised land they would also have to protect it from eventual invasion. Once the nation of Israel was established and embedded in the promised land, the allure of resources would become an enticement for invading armies. Therefore, the nation

---

[101] Alain Marchadour and David Neuhaus, *The Land, the Bible, and History: Toward the Land that I Will Show You,* The Abrahamic Diologues Series (New York: Fordham, 2007), 26.

[102] *Baker Encyclopedia of the Bible* (1988), s.v. "War, Holy."

[103] R. Dennis Cole, *Numbers*, The New American Commentary (Nashville: Broadman & Holman Publishers, 2000), 353.

[104] Gerhard von Rad, *Holy War in Ancient Israel.* Translated by Marva Dawn. Grand Rapids: Eerdmans, 1991., 71.

would have to maintain a proper sense of self-defense. As Craigie notes, "Once a state has been established, it must have the right of self-defense in order to survive, for to deny that right would be to deny the possibility of the continued existence of that state."[105]

When war is inevitable, according to the Torah, it must be carried out humanely. The Torah contained rules to ensure wars would be conducted as humanely as possible. For example, Female captives could not be violated. If a man saw a prisoner he wished to marry, her rights and feelings must be respected and she must be given time to mourn the loss of her family. If the Israelite man later grew tired of her, he could not abuse her or sell her for money (Dt 21:10–14). Additionally, before a city was attacked the law required that terms of peace be offered. If peace was accepted the city was not to be destroyed (Dt 20:11). The nature of humane war was so extensive, there were even conservation laws governing destruction of trees in a siege (Dt 20:19–20).

Life is sacred in the Old Testament and murder is a capital offense in the covenant of Genesis 9:1–7. Yet no physical life can be more important than God's redemptive purpose for the whole world through the nation of Israel. Thus, if the Canaanites had been allowed to survive unchecked, they would have slowly and painfully killed their own selves and worse, they would have been a constant distraction for the people of Israel.[106] Thus, God's command to destroy the Canaanites was his way of protecting Israel by keeping them separate. In this way, Israel was supposed to maintain their special nature before God and stay separated from the rest of the nations. This "us versus them" mentality is important in nationhood because just as land needs to be protected, so does a culture. War, at least in the political theology perspective, was meant to help keep the nation of Israel pure and protected.

The land of Israel was given to them by God and thus it was holy. Therefore, any defense of the promised land against foreign invasion was, in essence, a holy war because any invading nation was trespassing upon sacred territory that actually belonged to God's people by his decree. The punishment of doing so would be

---

[105] Peter Craigie, *The Problem of War in the Old Testament,* 71–72.

[106] *Evangelical Dictionary of Biblical Theology,* electronic ed., s.v. "War, Holy War."

the wrath of God. From this perspective the complete destruction of Israel's enemies was necessary, particularly when the enemy was sinful and morally corrupt.[107]

It does not seem to have ever been God's purpose to slaughter all the Canaanites at once. The Book of Joshua describes a few dramatic victories for a theological purpose. Exodus 23:29–30, however, indicates it was God's original purpose to drive the Canaanites out "little by little" so the land would not become desolate and wild animals multiply against them. Judges 3:1–4 informs us that Canaanites were left to test the Israelites and to keep them militarily alert. What is seen in Joshua is the rapid crushing of Canaanite capability of being an offensive threat. They were militarily crippled so there would be little chance for them to gain control of Israelite society.

Kingship and the
Professionalization of War

If wars were to be won and if the Promised Land was to be maintained, especially in light of the nations surrounding Israel, they would seemingly need a king. After all, in the ancient world, going to war was a seasonal activity of kings to expand their kingdom.[108] In light of failed Judges and the work that was seemingly ahead of the people in maintaining the kingdom in future wars, the people of Israel request a king in 1 Sam 8. Kingship, at least in the eyes of Israel, would bring about the understanding of the essence of wars, and Saul's initial kingship would be seen as a military kingship.[109]

Deuteronomy 17:14–15 points to the issue of royal power coming up only *when* the nation of Israel comes into the promised land.[110] It is only *after* the Promised Land has been entered and possessed that the people will ask for a king. After the people have

---

[107] *Baker Encyclopedia of the Bible,* s.v. "War, Holy."

[108] J.G. McConville, *Deuteronomy,* 317.

[109] Gerhard von Rad, *Holy War in Ancient Israel,* 74–75.

[110] "When you come to the land that the LORD your God is giving you, and you possess it and dwell in it and then say, 'I will set a king over me, like all the nations that are around me,' you may indeed set a king over you whom the LORD your God will choose."

been faithfully led into their promised inheritance, they will seek for themselves a king like the rest of the nations. Israel's request for a king like the other nations may have been misguided and an act of rebellion, but it does not automatically suggest that monarchy itself was wrong or that 1 Samuel 8 is meant to be read as anti-kingship. In Samuel 8, the people claim that they need a king in order to be able to defend themselves against other nations rather than rely solely on God's leadership.[111] It is apparent from the text that the monarchy is not established by the people, but it is allowed by Yahweh. O'Donovan states that 1 Samuel 8 is an *apologia* for the monarchy that "intends to leave no doubt that the monarchy came to existence by Yahweh's decision."[112] If the request for a king were inherently wrong or incompatible with following Yahweh, it would doubtless have been rejected. God permitted the people of Israel to anoint a king even though their motivations were wrong. In Deuteronomy 17, God told the people they would one day have a king, but in 1 Samuel 8, God has allowed the king to be vastly different, and seemingly the nation will suffer because of it. God does not draw up the conclusions that we anticipate. Instead of rejecting their plea for a king, God grants permission.

Saul is God's answer to the wrong motives of the Israelites. However, Saul has the opportunity to prove himself and to succeed as God's anointed king.[113] Samuel warns the people what will happen with Saul as king, but they persist in their request. In this way, to adopt kingship ran the political danger of seeing Israel's theocracy destroyed, or at the very least, undermined. Saul's kingship will run afoul of the limits placed upon kingship in Deuteronomy 17. The limits of Deuteronomy 17 existed to keep the future king from being a tyrant and make sure that the people were protected in spite of their wrong-hearted request. Having a king like the rest of the world took the chance that the ancient world's view of kingship would undermine the very faith of Israel in Yahweh,

---

[111] John Goldingay, *Old Testament Theology: Israel's Life,* 548.

[112] Oliver O'Donovan, *The Desire of the Nations: Rediscovering the Roots of Political Theology* (Cambridge: Cambridge, 1996), 61.

[113] All biblical kings were anointed by God rather than elected or chosen by the people, Michael Cafferky, "Honor the King. Yes, But Emulate the King?" The Journal of Applied Christian Leadership 4 (2012), 36–38.

which received its most faithful expression in the time when Israel had no king.[114] Saul will not be a good king and Samuel warns them: he will be a tyrant, but the people accept him and the repercussions.

A fundamental tension exists in regards to kingship in Israel. On the one hand, the request for a king in 1 Samuel is seen as a disregard to the covenant and a refusal to remain "separate" from the other nations of the world because they desire a king *like* the *other* nations; on the other hand, if it was an evil thing to ask for a king, then why did God grant it? In requesting a king, Israel seeks to be *like* other nations even though their covenant with Yahweh has made them fundamentally *unlike* all other nations.[115] The texts of Deuteronomy 17 and 1 Samuel 8 suggest a real struggle in the establishment of the monarchy that continued to exist throughout the biblical literature.

There are portions of the Old Testament that are seemingly pro-monarchic, while other sections seem to be firmly against the nation having a king. Israel had existed as a theocracy and now exists as a monarchy: there is a tension in going from having a sovereign God as their ruler to being led by a king. Goldingay argues that the OT maintains and emphasizes both a positive view of the monarchy and a negative view, and because of this, OT scholars have identified more with the tension that exists rather than claiming that it is ambiguous.[116] On the other hand, David Howard posits that God's attitude toward kingship is one in which the biblical texts appear to be ambiguous. Howard argues that *all* texts that seem to speak to the issue of kingship are pro-kingship, and any texts that appear to be anti-kingship are merely dealing with the motivations behind the issue of kingship rather than questioning the legitimacy of it.[117]

One tension that exists is that Yahweh in the OT never advocates for kingship or condones it. The book of Deuteronomy is not against or hostile to the nature of kingship and presents it in

---

[114] Bernhard Anderson, *Out of the Depths: The Psalms Speak for Us Today* (Philadelphia: Westminster, 2000), 26.

[115] Brueggemann, *Deuteronomy,* 184.

[116] Goldingay, *Old Testament Theology,* 732, 734.

[117] David Howard, "The Case for Kingship in the Old Testament Narrative Books and the Psalms," *TrinJ* 9 (1988), 19–20.

chapter 17 in a positive light. This is despite the fundamental message of the book being, as Grant claims, the sovereignty of God.[118] At best, it seems the office of kingship is presented as being optional for the people of Israel rather than mandatory.[119] This would make the king's office the only social institution whose entire existence is deemed to be optional.

Kingship, as seen through OT eyes, promised an interesting shift in looking at politics in the life of Israel because it takes the focus off of God as King to a person as king. This shift will become crucial to political theology in the future because, now, kings will lead Israel, and Israel will look to them as their official leaders. Thus, kingship will change how the kingdom is looked at and be something that changes how politics will be assessed because people will look to a singular person as the figurehead of the political institution rather than God. For coming discussions of patriotism, the Bible will now, especially in the NT, assess politics not through the lens of a theocracy but through the lens of civic government and a Christian's obligations to it.

How the Bible Shapes
Loyalty to the Land

The Bible shapes the understanding of one's home country in several ways. First, loyalty to the land is shaped by an understanding that God has given and established boundaries of all countries (Dt 32:8; Acts 17:26). God has established that people live in nations; from a biblical perspective, humanity is to rule over, care for, and enjoy God's creation. The Greek may be more literally translated as "having determined their appointed times and the boundaries of their dwelling places." The boundaries of their lands seem to

---

[118] Jamie Grant, *The King as Exemplar: The Function of Deuteronomy's Kingship Law in the Shaping of the Book of Psalms* (Atlanta: SBL, 2004), 202. Gregory Goswell also states this is the main thrust of Deuteronomy 17 in context with the overall theme of sovereignty in the book of Deuteronomy, "'David Their King': Kingship in the Prophecy of Hosea," *Journal for the Study of the Old Testament* 42 (2017), 175.

[119] Von Rad calls it an "optional arrangement," *Deuteronomy* (Philadelphia: Westminster, 1966), 121.

reference the various areas in which people live (cf. Dt 32:8). Because God has established all national boundaries, there is a collective responsibility shared by humanity in God's creation. Additionally, God has also ordained these nations to be used in achieving his special overarching purpose.[120]

Second, since Adam was kicked out of Eden, man has been wandering and searching for a somewhere to belong. When Israel was subsequently promised a land, they began to look expectantly toward the fulfillment of that promise. In essence, one's homeland is a type of promised land—or Eden—in that it is a place for him to belong. One's homeland is now seen through the lens of "place" where the relations between God and Adam's children have been partially restored. This intimate connection to one's homeland leads to an incredible sense of loyalty.

Defining "Patriotism"

Once a biblical framework of loyalty has been established, one can begin to craft a definition of "patriotism." The first major tenet of a biblically informed patriotism is loyalty toward one's own home country. Just as God has established all nations' boundaries, a person must be patriotic to the nation he is in. As John Kleinig states:

> [O]ne does not start off as patriotic and then look for a country to which to be patriotic. One's patriotism is always developed—if it develops at all—in the context of some particular country…. The person who wishes that there was country about which he could feel patriotic is not patriotic, even though he would like to be.[121]

This is true. People cannot truly be patriotic of any country that is not their own. One can only be a patriot of one's own country; to qualify as a patriot, one must do more than simply identify with a

---

[120] David Peterson, *The Acts of the Apostles*, The Pillar New Testament Commentary (Grand Rapids: Eerdmans, 2009), 497–498.

[121] John Kleinig, "The Virtue in Patriotism," in *The Ethics of Patriotism: A Debate*, ed. John Kleinig, et al. (Malden: Wiley, 2015), 21.

country but must identify a country as one's own.[122] Patriots are bound by a sentiment of connectedness that exists by nationality. Sharing in this nationality is to share a specific understanding or vision of where one fits historically and culturally in a people's story.[123] Sharing in nationality means sharing in the citizenship of one's country, and it is because citizenship assumes membership that nationality has become so imperative in the modern world.[124]

The second major tenet of a biblically informed patriotism is loyalty toward one's own country only. In other words, one's loyalty toward one's own country should always dwarf loyalty toward any other country. Patriotism requires a specific loyalty and regard toward a nation to whom a person belongs against all others. Patriotism is affection for and loyalty to one's particular place and always reflects a personal identity in one's own country.[125] A person's membership of a country, and loyalty toward it, is never truly in doubt. Even when Israel was in captivity, they remained the people of Israel, even when they were no longer residing in Israel. The third major tenet of a biblically informed patriotism is an identification with one's home country, culture, and people. Patriotism is not merely restricted to the land but also its citizens and necessitates an identification with a people and a specific way of life.[126] Patriotism is simply loyalty to the nation and social order of which one is a member, generally as a citizen.[127]

Summary

To understand patriotism, one must understand loyalty. A case can be made that loyalty is a biblical concept by looking at families, friendships, and land. These help develop a framework of loyalty that is essential to develop a sense of patriotism. "Patriotism" is

---

[122] Keller, "The Case against Patriotism," 53, 56.

[123] Kok-Chor Tan, "Patriotic Obligations," *The Monist* 86 (2003): 444.

[124] Roger Scruton, *The Need for Nations* (London: Civitas, 2004), 10.

[125] Liah Greenfeld, *Advanced Introduction to Nationalism* (Cheltenham: Edward Elgar, 2016), 43.

[126] Igor Primoratz, "Patriotism and Morality: Mapping the Terrain," *Journal of Moral Philosophy* 5 (2008): 206; Igor Primoratz, "Introduction," *The Journal of Ethics* 13 (2009): 295.

[127] Kleinig, "The Virtue in Patriotism," 29.

"loyalty toward one's own home country—and one's home country alone—and personal identification with one's home country, culture, and people." This definition of patriotism is specific enough to be separated from the notions of nationalism and cosmopolitanism and can be biblically assessed. The next chapter will show how patriotism is a biblical alternative to both nationalism and cosmopolitanism.

4

Toward an Understanding
of Patriotism

For a long time, patriotism has been a neglected subject in the area of political philosophy. However, in the last few decades, there has been a renewed interest in the term.[1] There is much overlap between the concept of country and nation within the concepts of patriotism and nationalism, but the interest in patriotism and nationalism is a relatively modern phenomenon.[2] Certain nationalist movements in the world, along with challenges of modernization, migration, and the resulting multiculturalism has offered an increased interest in a philosophical understanding of both patriotism and nationalism.[3] Igor Primoratz argues that both terms are connected and understood as being the same set of beliefs and feelings but with a different object.[4] The object in question is the loyalty toward either the state or the nation. The problem for an accurate understanding of the terms is that both may seem identical.[5]

This chapter argues that nationalism and cosmopolitanism are the bookends for the framing of a proper discussion of patriotism. Both of these terms are untenable for the Christian, while a proper understanding of patriotism is tenable. Additionally, patriotism will be discussed within the context of two major strands: extreme and moderate, noting the significant characteristics of both.

---

[1] Igor Primoratz, *Patriotism* (Amherst: Humanity, 2002), 9.

[2] Steven Grosby, *Biblical Ideas of Nationality: Ancient and Modern* (Winona Lake: Eisenbrauns, 2002), 13.

[3] Andrew Tan, *U.S. Strategy against Global Terrorism: How It Evolved, Why It Failed, and Where It Is Headed* (New York: Palgrave, 2009), 85.

[4] Igor Primoratz, "Patriotism and Morality: Mapping the Terrain," *Journal of Moral Philosophy* 5 (2008): 205–206.

[5] Anthony Smith, *Ethno-Symbolism and Nationalism: A Cultural Approach* (London: Routledge, 2009), 62.

Following the two major strands, care will be given to discuss the three major components of definitions of patriotism: loyalty, land, and culture.

The Bookends of the American Conception of Patriotism: Nationalism and Cosmopolitanism

If patriotism were to be looked at on a scale, it would be bookended by both nationalism and cosmopolitanism. Nationalism, at its core, is the belief in the superiority of a nation and can lead—not always—to a desire to dominate others, particularly in minority groups.[6] Cosmopolitanism is a liberal philosophy that seeks to ignore national ties by stressing the importance of seeing all people as fellow citizens regardless of national citizenship. In this way, all people are citizens of the world. Nationalism and its belief in superiority are on one side of extreme patriotism, and cosmopolitanism and its underplaying of particular citizenship bracket the other side of patriotism that is more moderate. Ultimately, nationalism and cosmopolitanism, while relevant to the discussion of patriotism, fail to be political frameworks that the Christian should hold to. Patriotism, on the other hand, when properly understood and defined, offers a much better alternative for the Christian.

The General Understanding of Nationalism

Due to nationalism's close ties to the understanding of patriotism, care must be taken to come to an understanding of nationalism. The nation, to quote Benedict Anderson's famous phrase, is an "imagined community" in that even though citizens of a country are not necessarily that close to one another, "in the minds of each other lives the image of their community."[7] Nationalism is the thesis that

---

[6] David Crittendon, "Differentiating Patriotism and Nationalism: Influence of Valence in Primes," *The New School Psychology Bulletin* 15 (2018): 1.

[7] Benedict Anderson, *Imagined Communities: Reflections on the Origin and Spread of Nationalism* (London: Verso, 2016), 6.

a person's first and supreme loyalty should be to the nation-state.[8] Ernest Gellner defines "nationalism" as the striving to make culture and polity "congruent, to endow a culture with its own political roof, and not more than one roof at that."[9] In this way, Gellner argues that nationalism is more of a political principle that affects the people of a nation as it binds people together. Accordingly, nationalism is dependent upon each national culture. It is better to speak of "nationalisms" rather than "nationalism" because "for every single nationalism which has so far raised its ugly head, nine others are still waiting in its wings."[10]

Nationalism is connected to a people's relationship with their community and country, and it is an irreplaceable and vital part of their identity.[11] This is true in the American understanding of nationalism because the American people are diverse. The understanding of American nationalism is essential to make sense of American politics and political culture because there are multiple versions in America, their definitions as varied as the definitions of patriotism. Nationalism is not a fixed concept but changes over time into multiple versions in response to a contemporary culture; this makes discussion of this term sometimes tricky. Combined with the frequent connections of nationalism to patriotism, it is crucial to have a general understanding of the terms to properly discuss them.[12]

While there are important differences in how nationalism is defined, three major themes emerge from nationalism that frame a proper discussion. First, autonomy stresses the importance of a country's freedom and sovereignty. Second, nationalism stresses national unity and rejects internal divisions. Third, nationalism understands the importance of people sharing a cultural identity

---

[8] Hans Kohn, *Nationalism: Its Meaning and History* (Malabar: Krieger, 1982), 9; Louis Pojman, *Terrorism, Human Rights, and the Case for World Government* (Lanham: Rowman and Littlefield, 2006), 28.

[9] Ernest Gellner, *Nations and Nationalism* (Ithaca: Cornell University Press, 1983), 43.

[10] Gellner, *Nations and Nationalism*, 45.

[11] Pojman, *Terrorism, Human Rights, and the Case for World Government*, 32.

[12] Bart Bonikowski and Paul DiMaggio, "Varieties of American Popular Nationalism," *American Sociological Review* 81 (2016): 949–952, 972.

since they share a homeland.[13] These three themes lay the foundation of nationalism that shows it is more than a shared sentiment among people; it is a dynamic movement inspired by a philosophy centered around the shared concept of a nation.[14]

Nationalism is primarily a political principle that designates the understanding that a person's loyalty should be to the nation-state. In this way, it is primarily a political principle that leads to social cohesion among a people. The American conception of nationalism is somewhat different. Equality is the "cornerstone" of the American system of government, justice, and political understanding. Equality makes America unique among nations because it is the only nation founded upon this ideal.[15] This unique ideal makes America a model nation because its national character is a purer example of a national community centered on ideals rather than ethnicity.[16] Due to nationalism's importance on a homogenous people, it leads to nationalism being a potentially difficult issue because there is no dominant culture in the American melting pot.

The General Understanding
of Cosmopolitanism

Cosmopolitanism is the general idea that each person is a world citizen who is committed to creating a community in the world that collectively seeks out and is committed to shared values.[17] The word "cosmopolitan" comes from the Greek word κοσμοπολίτης coined by Diogenes, a Greek philosopher, when he declared that he was a "citizen of the world."[18] The Stoics built on this concept, giving it a rich history and stressing that being a citizen of the world did not

---

[13] John Hutchinson and Anthony Smith, eds., *Nationalism*, Oxford Readers (Oxford: Oxford University Press, 1994), 4–5.

[14] Anthony Smith, *Ethno-Symbolism and Nationalism: A Cultural Approach* (London: Routledge, 2009), 61.

[15] Liah Greenfeld, *Nationalism: A Short History* (Washington, D.C.: Brookings, 2019), 11.

[16] Greenfeld, *Nationalism*, 59.

[17] Steven Vertovec and Robin Cohen, eds., *Conceiving Cosmopolitanism: Theory, Context, and Practice* (Oxford: Oxford, 2002), 10.

[18] Diogenes Laertius, *Lives of the Eminent Philosophers*, ed. James Miller, trans. Pamela Mensch (Oxford: Oxford University Press, 2018), 288.

mean one had to give up local identifications. The concept of being a world citizen has a rich history and is seen in ancient Greece, Rome, and even Israel and, as such, predates that of nationalism.[19]

There has been a good deal of interest in cosmopolitanism in political philosophy, and there is a more robust discussion of the term and its implications in contemporary philosophy than in recent memory.[20] The root idea of contemporary cosmopolitanism is the idea that each person is a world citizen who understands that he is in an "ethically significant relation to other human beings in general."[21] While ancient cosmopolitanism was concerned with the understanding of freedom, contemporary cosmopolitanism is centered more on the belief in equality and justice. Cosmopolitanism stresses that there is a set of moral principles that apply to all people as co-citizens of the world.[22]

Two main strands of cosmopolitanism emerge. The first strang presents itself as a doctrine primarily concerned about justice. Most theories of cosmopolitanism share a belief in the equality of all people and recognize that this equality should lead to moral obligations to the rest of the world.[23] For cosmopolitans, justice ought to transcend notions of nationality and citizenship. Thus, cosmopolitanism is justice without notions of borders.[24]

---

[19] Gerald Delanty, "Nationalism and Cosmopolitanism: The Paradox of Modernity," in *The SAGE Handbook of Nations and Nationalism*, ed. Gerald Delanty and Krishan Kumar (London: SAGE, 2006), 358; Kok-Chor Tan, *Justice without Borders: Cosmopolitanism, Nationalism and Patriotism* (Cambridge: Cambridge, 2004), 9.

[20] Delanty, "Nationalism and Cosmopolitanism," 357; Julia Driver, "Cosmopolitan Virtue," *Social Theory and Practice* 33, no. 4 (2007): 595; Charles Beitz, "Cosmopolitanism and Global Justice," *The Journal of Ethics* (2005): 11.

[21] Samuel Scheffler, *Boundaries and Allegiances: Problems of Justice and Responsibility in Liberal Thought* (Oxford: Oxford University Press, 2001), 115.

[22] Pojman, *Terrorism, Human Rights, and the Case for World Government*, 28.

[23] Martha Nussbaum, *For Love of Country?* ed. Joshua Cohen (Boston: Beacon, 1996), 14; Bettina Scholz, *The Cosmopolitan Potential of Exclusive Associations: Criteria for Assessing the Advancement of Cosmopolitan Norms* (Lanham: Lexington, 2015), 19–20.

[24] Tan, *Justice without Borders*, 1.

The second strand of cosmopolitanism is primarily concerned about culture and the self.[25] Since moral obligations exist for every person, human beings are the ultimate units of moral concern, which leads to all of humanity mattering equally. This moral status of humanity has a global force that applies to all, making all cultures seemingly relevant.[26] In this way, cosmopolitans stress the importance of the morality of global rights rather than national rights.[27]

While technically not a strand of cosmopolitanism, a recent surge in interest of Marxism is of note in the framing of cosmopolitanism. Of interest here in the framing of cosmopolitanism is the rise of interest in cultural Marxism that seeks a stateless and classless society. While cosmopolitanism seeks to find value in the global world at the expense of the nation, Marxist thought places value in a society devoid of true authority structure in the state. In this way, both Marxism and cosmopolitanism seek to reject the authority of the nation-state that God has clearly established.

Patriotism's Bookends

Nationalism and cosmopolitanism are often seen as opposed philosophies or, at the very least, counterparts of each other.[28] Nationalism is seen primarily as a boundary-making initiative, while cosmopolitanism is primarily seen as a boundary-transcending

---

[25] Scheffler, *Boundaries and Allegiances*, 111.

[26] Thomas Pogge, *World Poverty and Human Rights* (Malden: Polity, 2002), 169. Thomas Pogge goes on to say that this global force "attaches to every living human being equally." Thomas Pogge, "Cosmopolitanism and Sovereignty," *Ethics* 103 (1992): 48. Stephen Vertovec and Robin Cohen argue that the world is a "culturally interpenetrated planet." Vertovec and Cohen, *Conceiving Cosmopolitanism*, 9.

[27] Scholz, *The Cosmopolitan Potential of Exclusive Associations*; Driver, "Cosmopolitan Virtue," 595. This often leads to cosmopolitans' concern with global issues such as poverty. Cosmopolitans' concern with global poverty was highly influenced by Peter Singer's article "Famine, Affluence, and Morality." Peter Singer, *Philosophy and Public Affairs* 1 (1972): 229–243.

[28] Audi, "Nationalism, Patriotism, and Cosmopolitanism in an Age of Globalization," 372.

enterprise.[29] Nationalism seeks to find meaning and purpose around specific people of a country while maintaining their sovereignty is of the utmost concern even in an increasingly global world. Cosmopolitanism, however, forces people to reconsider their nationalistic perspectives and tendencies. It is attractive to some because it allows for more cultural permeability, which is seemingly more valued in a global world than nationalism and offers a solution to globalization, multiculturalism, and nationalism.[30]

If both nationalism and cosmopolitanism serve as bookends to the proper understanding of patriotism, the question is, to what end? Nationalism brings to the forefront the importance of national boundaries and is essential because the world is made up of individual nations with their own specific culture and way of life. A person is born in a country and resides in a country and cannot exist within a vacuum. Nationalism, at the very least, sees the importance of nationality and attachments to those nations where people are born. Cosmopolitanism is attractive because it leads people to seek human flourishing as a central virtue in the world.[31] Nationalism's importance of nations and cosmopolitanism's importance on human flourishing are significant and help frame the discussion regarding patriotism. However, while both help frame the discussion, both leave patriotism as a better alternative to both.

Nationalism seeks to find meaning within a specific country and nationality, while cosmopolitanism seeks to find meaning outside a specific country and nationality. Both ultimately fail because they reject the overarching structure of the world. God has established the nations and their boundaries and the rulers who rule over them.[32] Due to God's structure of creation and His ordaining countries as authorities, it is impossible to ignore their significance. Nationalism can lead to placing one nation above others, which denies their creation by God. On the other side, cosmopolitanism can lead to ignoring the nations that exist to seek global justice and meaning. Ultimately, both of these fail to truly take into

---

[29] Tan, *Justice without Borders*, 13.

[30] Elisabete Silva, "Cosmopolitanism and Patriotism," *Annals of the University of Craiova, Romania* (2008): 151, 157.

[31] Driver, "Cosmopolitan Virtue," 601.

[32] Dt 32:8; Acts 17:26; Dn 5:21; Rm 13:1.

consideration of how God has established the world order, allowing all nations to exist.[33] Patriotism gives people a far better alternative to make sense of the global world by looking at people's proper understanding of a nation and a person's loyalty to it.

The Two General Understandings of Patriotism

Where patriotism stands in political theory remains a critical philosophical issue in need of further investigation due to its being bookended by nationalism and cosmopolitanism. One of the most challenging features of conversation and discussion of patriotism is that it is difficult to understand whether it is talking about the same thing because there can be multiple types and definitions of patriotism.[34] To make a biblical assessment of patriotism, it is crucial to layout a general understanding of patriotism while coming to a specific definition of patriotism to be assessed.

A generally understood definition of patriotism as being a love of one's country is not clear and is, instead, problematic as it does not correctly define what one means by "love" and what duties come with along with its direction toward one's country. Some view patriotism as feelings aimed at the country or symbols of it rather than the people who make up the country, but it is almost impossible

---

[33] Genesis 10; 12:1–3; Ps 22:28; Ex 34:24. Since early in Genesis, God had established nations and continues to allow them to exist. He allows all kings to rule by His sovereign plan as well. What begins to take shape is that God has allowed all countries to exist in their own time. Additionally, when one considers that Christians are to be subjects to their rulers (Rm 13:1; 1 Pt 2:13), one has to take into consideration that countries are important to the created order. Cosmopolitanism denies that natural boundaries, countries, or specific citizenship are important. Nationalism and its insistence on superiority also go against the created order because nationalism believes that other countries, that have been allowed to exist by God, are not valid.

[34] John Kleinig, et al., *The Ethics of Patriotism: A Debate* (Malden: Wiley, 2015), 3. Many see patriotism as something to run from and abhor. Paul Gomberg, "Patriotism Is like Racism," *Ethics* 101 (1990): 144–150. George Kateb argues that patriotism is a mistake. George Kateb, "Is Patriotism a Mistake?" *Social Research* 67 (2000): 901–924. Simon Keller argues for anti-patriotism because of how patriotism can be used for evil. Simon Keller, "Patriotism as Bad Faith," *Ethics* 115 (2004): 563–590.

to see patriotism as a genuinely independent ideal that does not take citizenship into consideration.[35] Primoratz notes the importance of this by stating that a definition of patriotism "cannot provide a full account of its subjects," which causes one to come to different understandings of patriotism.[36] Further, the very word "patriotism" can be used in different ways. Patriotism can be a characteristic of a patriotic person, an emotion of a person who is bursting with pride for his country, and even a position of a person who feels he owes loyalty to his country.[37] The varying uses, thoughts, and definitions of patriotism require one to develop a general understanding of the term to discuss and assess it properly.

Two Major Conceptions
of Patriotism

While there are numerous conceptions of patriotism, they can be divided into two major camps.[38] First, an extreme view, closely associated with nationalism, sees patriotism as a nonnegotiable

---

[35] Elizabeth Theiss-Morse, *Who Counts as an American? The Boundaries of National Identity* (Cambridge: Cambridge, 2009), 25.

[36] Igor Primoratz, "Patriotism: A Two-Tier Account," in *The Ethics of Patriotism: A Debate*, ed. John Kleinig, et al. (Malden: Wiley, 2015), 74.

[37] Audi, "Nationalism, Patriotism, and Cosmopolitanism in an Age of Globalization," 367.

[38] While breaking down patriotism into two strands only may be simplistic, it gives the best opportunity for both a discussion of characteristics and for the proper development of a biblically accessible definition. Depending on the philosopher, patriotism carries many different connotations and can be good, bad, or neutral. For some, patriotism is a virtue, but for others, like Alasdair MacIntyre, state patriotism is a vice. Alasdair MacIntyre, "Is Patriotism a Virtue?" in *Patriotism*, ed. Igor Promratz, (Amherst: Humanity, 2002), 43–58. Leo Tolstoy thought patriotism was an unreasonable belief in the superiority of a country and, as such, was a horrible worldview. Some philosophers stress specific attitudes in regards to patriotism such as loyalty, duty, or love. Andrew Oldequist believes the major component to patriotism is loyalty. Andrew Oldequist, "Loyalties," *Journal of Philosophy* 79 (1982): 173–193. Gomberg stresses that patriotism is like racism. Gomberg, "Patriotism Is like Racism," 144–150. To define "patriotism" as simply "love or loyalty to one's country" might be a reasonable definition, but according to the literature, there is much more that needs to be discussed to come to terms with to properly define patriotism and to discuss the major components of it.

characteristic of citizenship that supports a country regardless of the perceived outcomes. Second, there is a more moderate view of patriotism that sees patriotism as potentially virtuous as long as it is practiced and supported alongside a moral framework. By seeking to understand these camps of patriotism, one can come to terms with the significant issues of patriotism and come to a working definition that will be assessed.

Extreme Patriotism

Patriotism, in its extreme form, can be summed up in the phrase, "[M]y country right or wrong."[39] An extreme—or blind—form of patriotism is often closely associated with nationalism due to its unquestioning loyalty to one's country and people and resistance of criticism to it.[40] Three major characteristics mark extreme patriotism. First, extreme patriots have a belief in the superiority of their own country. Second, extreme patriots have a particular concern for their own country at the expense of others. Third, extreme patriots have an unconstrained promotion of their national good.[41] These major characteristics lead to a blind acceptance of a

---

[39] This phrase has most often been attributed to senator Charles Schurz, a German immigrant to the United States who also became the thirteenth secretary of the interior. However, this is not the full context or the entire quote. In response to the sale of weapons to France, he said to a questioning Senator Sumner, "My country; and my country is the great American Republic. My country right or wrong; if right, to be kept right; and if wrong, to be set right." *The Congressional Globe and Appendix: Second Session Forty-Second Congress*, part II (Washington: Library of Congress, 1872), 1287. A similar quote can be attributed to Stephen Decatur, an American naval officer and hero from the War of 1812. He is quoted as saying, "Our country—in her intercourse with foreign nations may she always be in the right, and always successful, right or wrong." *Niles Weekly Register*, April 20, 1816.

[40] This type of patriotism was termed "pseudo-patriotism" in T. W. Adorno, et al., *The Authoritarian Personality* (New York: Harper and Row, 1950).

[41] Stephen Nathanson, "Patriotism, War, and the Limits of Permissible Partiality," *Journal of Ethics* 13 (2009): 406.

country that focuses on its positives while ignoring the negatives, leading to a rigid attachment to one's country.[42]

Extreme patriotism is often looked at as a vice. George Kateb is critical of this type of patriotism by stating that it is marked by a "readiness, whether reluctant of matter-of-fact, social or zealous, to die and to kill for one's country."[43] While Kateb's criticism may be overly harsh, there is a sense that an extreme form of patriotism that stresses one's country "right or wrong" can lead to adverse outcomes if that devotion leads to potential harm for others.[44] It is here that this type of patriotism can be seen as negative.[45]

Extreme forms of patriotism are guided by emotion and seem to be unconstrained by critical thought because to be critical toward one's country can be seen as being disloyal to the country.[46] Uncritical patriots generally give their country the benefit of every moral doubt by showing an uncritical love and loyalty of their country and are rarely ashamed of it.[47] In Kateb's view, to do so ensures that patriotism is on a "permanent moral holiday."[48]

Extreme patriotism is not always directed at the country but also at one's government. Thus, unqualified support for the current

---

[42] Leisa Martin, "Blind Patriotism or Active Citizenship? How Do Students Interpret the Pledge of Allegiance?" *Action in Teacher Education* 34 (2012): 56.

[43] George Kateb, "Is Patriotism a Mistake?" *Social Research* 67 (2000): 906.

[44] Kateb goes on to argue that patriotism is a mistake "twice over." Ibid., 901.

[45] Carmen Spry and Matthew Hornsey, "The Influence of Blind and Constructive Patriotism on Attitudes toward Multiculturalism and Immigration," *Australian Journal of Psychology* 59 (2007): 151.

[46] Miroslav Nincic and Jennifer Ramos, "The Sources of Patriotism: Survey and Experimental Evidence," *Foreign Policy Analysis* 8 (2012): 377; Robert Schatz, et al., "On the Varieties of National Attachment: Blind versus Constructive Patriotism," *Political Psychology* 20 (1999): 153.

[47] Sean Richey, "Civic Engagement and Patriotism," *Social Science Quarterly* 92 (2011): 1045.

[48] Kateb, "Is Patriotism a Mistake?" 914.

decisions of one's government can be problematic.[49] Excessive emphasis on one's own country without criticism can lead to more opportunities to contradict human rights, which is one of the main criticisms to extreme patriotism. Extreme patriots do not face moral constraints because their support of their country is intimately connected to their personal connection to it. This invariable leads to unquestioning loyalty and resistance to criticism of it despite the morality of actions.

Moderate Patriotism

While the extreme form of patriotism can lead to an unquestioning loyalty, a moderate view seeks to find a middle-ground approach between extreme patriotism and a universalist perspective.[50] Just because patriotism can be used for evil things does not mean it should be discarded all together. This is the motive behind moderate patriots like Marcia Baron and Stephen Nathanson. While the term "moderate" may be misleading since it suggests a more lukewarm approach to the personal attachments of patriotism, it is a form of patriotism that seeks to be supportive of one's country while at the same time recognizing the moral dimensions of doing so.[51] The vast majority of contemporary concepts of patriotism appear as forms of moderate patriotism.[52]

---

[49] Daniel McCleary, et al., "Types of Patriotism as Primary Predictors of Continuing Support for the Iraq War," *Journal of Political and Military Sociology* 37 (2009): 79.

[50] Primoratz, "Patriotism," 82–83.

[51] Stephen Nathanson, "On Deciding Whether a Nation Deserves Our Loyalty," *Public Affairs Quarterly* 4 (1990): 287.

[52] Mitja Sardoč, "The Anatomy of Patriotism," *Anthropological Notebooks* 23 (2017): 46. Examples of types of patriotism that can fall into this camp are Jürgen Habermas's constitutional patriotism, civic patriotism advocated by Cécile Laborde, democratic patriotism advocated by Eamonn Callan, and the patriotism of best tradition advocated by Lawrence Blum. Kwame Appiah even goes so far as to argue for a cosmopolitan patriotism. Jürgen Habermas, ed., "Citizenship and National Identity," in *Between Facts and Norms: Contributions to a Discourse Theory of Law and Democracy* (Cambridge: MIT Press, 1996), 491–516; Cécile Laborde, "From Constitutional to Civic Patriotism," *British Journal of Political Science* 32 (2002): 591–612; Eamonn Callan, "The Better Angels of Our Nature," *The Journal of Political Philosophy* 18 (2010): 249–270;

Moderate patriotism is a patriotism that is not unbridled or blind but instead has restraint. According to Nathanson, moderate patriotism is the only "reasonable and morally acceptable form of patriotism."[53] Moderate patriotism is marked by special affection for one's country but not in a belief in its superiority to other countries. Moderate patriots have a strong desire to see their country flourish, but they do not have a particular concern for it. They have an acknowledgment on certain moral constraints upon the seeking of their country's flourishing and recognize that support for a country is always conditional.[54] Moderate patriotism stresses that a country's support from its citizens should not be uncritical; nor should it be automatic. It is not merely enough that one's country is his own country; moderate patriots expect their country to live up to moral standards to deserve their support. When this fails to happen, a moderate patriot will submit his country to moral criticism.[55]

Moderate patriotism hinges on an understanding of morality that focuses itself on liberal political thought because it understands and recognizes the dangers posed by excessive patriotism.[56] Moderate patriotism is morally opposed to nationalism since it, moderate patriots argue, is self-seeking. At the same time, moderate patriotism is opposed to cosmopolitanism and cosmopolitan concepts of patriotism that deny the importance of citizenship and membership to a specific country.

A morally constrained version of patriotism is attractive to some because it is both limited in the range of actions that a country requires its citizens to support and is conditional on the nature of the country to which loyalty is directed. Since the support of a country is conditional, moderate patriots do not imply that all citizens must

---

Lawrence Blum, "Best Traditions Patriotism: A Commentary on Miller, Wingo and Ben-Porath," *Theory and Research in Education* 5 (2007): 61–68; Kwame Appiah, "Cosmopolitan Patriots," *Critical Inquiry* 23 (1997): 617–639.

[53] Nathanson, "On Deciding Whether a Nation Deserves Our Loyalty," 295.

[54] Stephen Nathanson, "Is Cosmopolitan Anti-Patriotism a Virtue?" in *Patriotism: Philosophical and Political Perspectives*, ed. Aleksander Pavkovic and Igor Primoratz (London: Routledge, 2007), 76.

[55] Primoratz, "Patriotism and Morality," 214.

[56] Stephen Nathanson, "In Defense of Moderate Patriotism," in *Patriotism*, ed. Igor Primoratz (Amherst: Humanity, 2002), 101–102.

be patriotic. That decision falls to whether a country has met the conditional qualities that lead toward a person's patriotism.[57]

Because of moderate patriotism's insistence on a country earning the support of its citizens, Alasdair MacIntyre calls this type of patriotism "emasculated" because it is devoid of any sense of real patriotism that is given to a country because it is one's own.[58] Extreme patriots challenge moderate patriotism because they believe that they concede too much to other countries based upon the conditional support of their country. Cosmopolitans challenge moderate patriotism because if people are of equal value, how can moderate patriots also be partial to their own country?[59] Moderate patriotism is difficult to fully come to terms with based upon the need for clarity of morality. Each country has a particular value system that comes with being a part of the collective group, and as such, each country's sense of morality can be different.

Moderate patriotism's middle-of-the-road position avoids universalism that leaves no room for personal patriotic loyalty and attachment to a country and extreme forms of patriotism that does not acknowledge any moral considerations for supporting a country.[60] However, moderate patriotism does not properly account for different forms of morality. In this way, moderate patriotism fails to live up to its promise of being a virtue because it is based upon subjective versions of morality. If moderate patriotism is to be seen as a duty, or as morally valuable, its proponents must further define its reliance on subjective morality.

----

[57] Nathanson, "In Defense of Moderate Patriotism," 102.

[58] In his classic essay on patriotism, MacIntyre argues that patriotism is a vice. However, his perspective is critical of extreme and moderate forms of patriotism and in favor of a patriotism highly influenced by cosmopolitanism and universal liberal morality. MacIntyre, "Is Patriotism a Virtue?" 43–58. The essay was originally presented as an E. H. Lindley Lecture at the University of Kansas in 1984. For a summary of the history and use of the term "patriotism," see Mary Dietz, "Patriotism: A Brief History of the Term," in *Patriotism*, ed. Igor Primoratz (Amherst: Humanity, 2002), 201–215.

[59] Nathanson, "Patriotism, War, and the Limits of Permissible Partiality," 408.

[60] Primoratz, "Patriotism and Morality," 214.

Major Components of Patriotism

Regardless of the strand of patriotism, patriotism's major components are roughly the same. Patriotism is concerned with some sort of loyalty to one's home country. The degree of loyalty may be to a different degree, can exist for a different reason, and can depend upon a country's worthiness of it. Second, patriotism is concerned with the concept of a homeland. Patriots understand that patriotism's object is a physical place that has a physical location and dimensions. Third, patriotism is concerned with the concept of a country's culture. Whatever makes a country unique to itself is part of the reason that patriots find loyalty in it, which is something that a patriot sees as necessary. These three major components can be found to a varying degree of most patriotic strands and can be found in strands of both nationalism and cosmopolitanism. These three components form the basis for a specific definition of patriotism for the rest of this project and serve as biblically assessable components of patriotism.

Loyalty

Patriotism has "loyalty" as one of its major characteristics. Loyalty is paramount to a proper understanding of patriotism and involves a political act of showing loyalty for a country and its citizens.[61] In this way, patriotism and patriotism's loyalty is always particular to its own. A loyal man, according to Josiah Royce, has a cause, and this cause leads to a willing, practical, and thoroughgoing devotion toward that cause.[62]

It is important to understand that loyalty toward a country—or any major type of loyalty—is not the same thing as commitment because commitment implies that the object of commitment has

---

[61] Polycarp Ikuenobe, "Citizen and Patriotism," *Public Affairs Quarterly* 24 (2010): 298; Ryan LaMothe, "The Problem of Patriotism: A Psychoanalytic and Theological Analysis," *Pastoral Psychology* 58 (2009): 162.

[62] J. Royce, *The Philosophy of Loyalty* (Nashville: Vanderbilt, 1908), 9–10.

worthiness to it.[63] Patriotism's loyalty does not necessarily require that a country be worthy of loyalty, just that the country is one's own, but it does understand that loyalty is given by choice and can be given to another.[64] In other words, patriotism sees loyalty in one's country as necessary, but that does not mean that a patriot will uncritically give a country his loyalty.

Loyalty for a country is similar to other kinds of loyalty and is connected with other ideas about loyalty. One can have a loyalty toward one's parents despite what type of people they are: a person's parents may not be loving or kind, but a child may still feel some sort of loyalty toward them because they are their parents. In this way, patriotic loyalty is similar to filial loyalty but different than loyalty toward something like a political candidate; one cannot decide his country or parent but can choose his level of loyalty to a specific political candidate.[65] In the same way, patriotic loyalty is a serious loyalty in a way that some other loyalties are not.

A critical dimension of any group is an expectation of loyalty. Loyalty to a nation is implied in the practice of patriotism and is almost always marked by it. It involves being loyal as a member of the country: an American to America, a Kenyan to Kenya, and so on.[66] If loyalty is important, then it can demand that one make significant sacrifices toward the object. Patriotic loyalty is loyalty that requires some level of devotion towards one's own country and a willingness to sacrifice one's interests to some degree for one's fellow countrymen. Patriots are motivated by loyalty to

---

[63] Christopher Parker, "Symbolic versus Blind Patriotism," *Political Research Quarterly* 63 (2010): 99. In this way, loyalty toward a country, at least in regards to discussion of patriotism, may be better than duty because duty implies that something is owed regardless of the worthiness of an object.

[64] Keller argues that patriotic loyalty is rooted in seeing a country having certain valuables characteristics that make it worthy of loyalty. Keller, "Patriotism as Bad Faith," 567, 574. While this is an interesting point, it fails to take into consideration that the partiality that comes with being a citizen of a country will always be clouded by seeing it in a particular favorable light.

[65] Keller, "Patriotism as Bad Faith," 568.

[66] Andrew Vincent, "Patriotism and Human Rights: An Argument for Unpatriotic Patriotism," *Journal of Ethics* 13 (2009): 348; Spry and Hornsey, "The Influence of Blind and Constructive Patriotism on Attitudes toward Multiculturalism and Immigration," 156–157; Simon Keller, "Are Patriotism and Universalism Compatible?" *Social Theory and Practice* 33 (2007): 67 .

promote and defend its interest and requires, on some level, putting one's own country's interests before other countries. So patriots express their loyalty of their country by showing greater care and concern for their country and compatriots than they do for other countries.[67] This loyalty to one's country and compatriots is a valuable feeling for patriots because it represents a deep, personal attachment to one's country.[68]

Land

Countries are defined more by their homeland rather than kinship, and there is a strong connection of patriotism to one's homeland or place of residence.[69] Patriotism comes from *patria,* which concerns a person's homeland or fatherland.[70] While attachment to the city is the classic example of patriotism in antiquity, today patriotism is connected to having attachment toward one's country.[71] The *patria* is a specific land with a specific people and a specific way of life.

---

[67] Keller, "Patriotism as Bad Faith," 569; Nathanson, "Patriotism, War, and the Limits of Permissible Partiality," 402; Baron, "Patriotism and 'Liberal' Morality," 63; Charles Jones, *Global Justice: Defending Cosmopolitanism* (Oxford: Oxford University Press, 1999), 112, 115.

[68] Amélie Mummendey, et al., "Nationalism and Patriotism," *British Journal of Social Psychology* 40 (2001): 160.

[69] Roger Scruton, *The Need for Nations* (London: Civitas, 2004), 16.

[70] The roots of the term can be traced back to the Latin *patriota* and the ancient Greek πατριώτης. Both the Latin and Greek terms come from the word for "father," and thus, the term originally implied relationship rather than a specifically political relationship centered on a homeland. The ancient Greeks used the term πατριώτης to refer to the barbarians who possessed a common πατρίς, whereas they used the term πολιται to refer themselves because they possessed a common πολις. On the other hand, for the Romans, the term *patria* implied both the shared interest of politics and kinship of a people who had a common origin. Consequently, from the beginning, the term "patriotism" held two separate and sometimes contradictory conceptions: one representing kinship and the other representing a relationship of common action and choice. Sarah Houser, "Loving Pimlico: Patriotism in the Age of Cosmopolis" (PhD diss., Notre Dame, 2009), 1; Vincent, "Patriotism and Human Rights," 348–349. Also see Deitz, "Patriotism," 201–215.

[71] Liah Greenfeld, *Advanced Introduction to Nationalism* (Cheltenham: Edward Elgar, 2016), 42.

All of these are important to the patriot.[72] To feel strong affection toward one's country is to metaphorically love the land under one's feet because one can only be a patriot of a country in which he identifies. However, to qualify as a patriot, one must do more than simply identify with a country: a patriot must identify a country as one's own because it is one's own homeland.[73]

Patriotism involves an intimate connection between a person and his country. Just as loyalties are particular in that a person has loyalties that are his own, a person can only truly have patriotic attachment toward his own country. While patriotism is generally associated as a basic virtue connected with citizenship, one does not have to be a citizen of the country in which he is patriotic.[74] A patriot does not start off being patriotic, then look for a country to be patriotic. The person who wishes that there was a country worthy of his patriotism is not patriotic even though he would like to be.[75]

Culture

It is impossible to understand patriotism without considering a country's history and legacy. Belonging to a country is based, partly, on a common or shared history, or culture, so a patriot is not restricted to the land only but also to the state, its citizens, and its culture.[76] A shared identity and culture leads to an emotional attachment. Additionally, a country is made up of people with an ambition to be politically self-determining, and this leads to the

---

[72] Igor Primoratz, "Introduction," *Journal of Ethics* 13 (2009): 295.

[73] Simon Keller, "The Case against Patriotism," in *The Ethics of Patriotism: A Debate*, ed. John Kleinig, et al. (Malden: Wiley, 2015), 53, 56.

[74] Mitja Sardoč, "The Anatomy of Patriotism," *Anthropological Notebooks* 23 (2017): 43. Polycarp Ikuenobe argues that one must be a citizen of a country in order to be truly patriotic. Ikuenobe, "Citizen and Patriotism," 297. While citizenship can be a component of patriotic attachment, it is not necessary for it because immigrants can be very patriotic toward their new country even though they may not be citizens. Citizens do, however, have a special obligation toward their fellow citizens. Scruton, *The Need for Nations*, 22.

[75] John Kleinig, "The Virtue in Patriotism," in *The Ethics of Patriotism: A Debate*, ed. John Kleinig, et al. (Malden: Wiley, 2015), 21.

[76] Primoratz, "Patriotism and Morality," 206; Margaret Moore, "Is Patriotism an Associative Duty?" *Journal of Ethics* 13 (2009): 385.

importance of sharing the national culture. While patriots may have different understandings of how to interpret a country's history, there is a nature of believing a country is a project, and despite its perceived evils and wrongs, a shared history brings people together in support of their country. Richard Rorty understands the importance of a shared culture and states there is no such thing as "a nonmythological, nonideological way of telling a country's story."[77] So having a shared culture leads to emotional attachment, and that emotional attachment helps to feed the shared culture.[78]

For people to embrace a patriotic understanding of a shared culture, there must be a belief that the culture has a certain level of value. Martha Nussbaum notes this connection, "In attachment to one's country, there is frequently the thought that this country has valuable things about it, and that it is a good country." Nussbaum goes on to say that national identity can lead to pride, which gives a "special power among the motivations to political actions" of patriots.[79] Patriots tend to have pride in their country because of its shared history but, sometimes, despite it. Whether or not a country is a "good country" is subjective, but it does underscore the importance of having an emotional attachment to a country. A patriot sees value in his country, which helps lead him to support it in some sort of way.[80]

A shared identity and culture of patriots lead them to, at some level, support one another and allow them to develop a sense of being a part of the national whole. The word "patriot" is a word

---

[77] Richard Rorty, *Achieving Our Country: Leftist Thought in Twentieth Century America* (Cambridge: Cambridge University Press, 1998), 11.

[78] David Miller, *On Nationality* (Oxford: Clarendon, 1995), 19, 24–25.

[79] Martha Nussbaum, *Upheavals of Thought: The Intelligence of Emotion* (Cambridge: Cambridge University Press, 2009), 49; Martha Nussbaum, *For Love of Country* (Boston: Beacon, 2002), 3.

[80] Some argue that there is only value in supporting a country if the shared culture is moral and leads to flourishing. Ikuenobe, "Citizen and Patriotism," 301. Jürgen Habermas and Jan-Werner Müller suggest that patriotism does not have to have as its object a specific political entity (such as the country) built on a set of constitutional or political principles. Their understanding of constitutional patriotism also places a strong emphasis on a shared cultural heritage as the basis for patriotic support. Jan-Werner Müller, "On the Origins of Constitutional Patriotism," *Contemporary Political Theory* 5 (2006): 278–296.

linked to the virtues of membership, and as Eamonn Callan notes, this support maintains a part of citizenship education and states it is a basis for patriotism because it helps "connect our very identity to the good of others."[81] Patriots see in compatriots people who are worth supporting because of their shared culture and identity, which brings a certain level of good will inside the country because of the good will toward compatriots. Because of shared culture, patriots endow fellow patriots with an identity that makes it easy for them to disregard the needs and rights of others outside of their group. They do this not because they do not see the moral value of others, but instead, they identify fellow compatriots as being especially worthy of support due to their shared loyalty to a country.[82]

While a country's culture can be subjective due to the way that one can look at it, culture is essential in developing a sense of patriotism because patriotic loyalty is directed not just to an abstract state but also to what the state represents. Thus, while understandings of shared culture may be different, they must be considered at some level to understand what makes compatriots choose to support and show loyalty to a specific country. In this way, a shared culture can be shared at different levels but invariably leads patriots to support their country regardless of whether they share all aspects of its culture.

Toward a Biblically Assessable Definition of "Patriotism"

Patriotism is bookended by nationalism on one side and cosmopolitanism on the other. Nationalism seeks to place a country above all other countries due to its seeming superiority. Cosmopolitanism seeks to erase the importance of a country due to people being citizens of the world. Additionally, there are multiple

---

[81] Eamonn Callan, *Creating Citizens: Political Education and Liberal Democracy* (Oxford: Oxford University Press, 1997), 76.

[82] Houser, "Loving Pimlico," 6. For example, one may have loyalty to one's parents. However, this does not mean that one cannot see the value of other people's parents but leads one to support his own parents first. The attachment within personal relationships prompts people to act on their behalf.

different strands of patriotism that have different themes and concepts. While there are many different conceptions of patriotism, they do share importance with loyalty, land, and culture.

"Patriotism," for this project, is defined as "loyalty to a person's particular country only over any loyalty to other countries that involves a personal identification with its country, culture, and people." While more could be added to this definition, to come to a biblical assessment, one must limit the scope of what is being assessed. This project will show that this definition of patriotism can be assessed biblically and can be maintained by a Christian under specific qualifications. Nationalism's insistence upon the superiority of one culture or nation over all others cannot be maintained biblically, nor can cosmopolitan's insistence that a country's borders do not matter because people are citizens of the world and that means that their native country does not truly matter.[83] Neither of these is tenable to a Christian; therefore, this definition of patriotism is a better alternative.

---

[83] Keller, "The Case against Patriotism," 49.

5

The Apostle Paul as a Test Case
for a Biblically Informed Patriotism

Admittedly, the current political landscape in the United States and much of the world is vastly different from the one found in Scripture. However, that does not mean that a biblically informed notion of patriotism cannot be gleaned from Scripture. Patriotism is loyalty to a person's particular country that involves a personal identification with his country, culture, and people. Building off of this definition, this chapter will posit that the apostle Paul is a test case for a biblically informed patriotism. Paul was a truly multicultural person: he was a Jew, and he was a Roman citizen, but he also had dual citizenship with the important and influential ancient city of Tarsus. Paul became someone who understood a person's role in society and within the culture at large but also became someone who knew how to navigate citizenship through the lens of Scripture. Paul, and what made Paul who he was, will be shown to be a proper basis for a Christian's understanding and practice of patriotism today.

Paul's Cultural Diversity

The apostle Paul was greatly influenced by two capitals: Tarsus, the place of his birth and a center of Greek learning; and Jerusalem, the place of his upbringing and pharisaical education and training. Paul shared dual citizenship with both Rome and Israel. Both of these citizenships were ultimately assigned at birth, and both of these identities become a major theme in the writings and ministry of

Paul.[1] Paul's Jewish, Greek, and Roman character made him a complex individual of the ancient world because of his rich diversity. Paul had to daily navigate his way through the Roman world, much like most Jews would in a day where Rome controlled most of the known world; Paul's sense of being Roman involved various subcultures, including his Jewishness.[2] Paul, a diaspora Jew, was thus a person with a very diverse influence who "lived a life full of paradoxes."[3]

Paul's multicultural identity and his dual citizenship were a part of his background and upbringing that helped mold him into the person he eventually became. His shared identities allowed him to become very aware of politics and culture and helped shape the way that he saw the world. In this way, Paul was of Tarsus, of Rome, and of Jerusalem and, with that, had a host of life experiences that shaped him. Paul's "lifelong preoccupation with Gentiles and his participation in wider Greco-Roman culture are the major points of continuity between his past life in Judaism as a Pharisee" and the life he lived as an apostle.[4] Each part of Paul's Greco-Roman character, merged with his Jewish ancestry, made him an exciting test case of how to look at a person's sense of patriotic loyalty because he was, in a sense, a person who walked in multiple worlds.

---

[1] Paul claimed he was from Tarsus in Acts 21:39 and described his Jewish upbringing in detail in Philippians 3:6–7. These texts will be discussed in more detail.

[2] J. Albert Harrill, *Paul the Apostle: His Life and Legacy in Their Roman Context* (Cambridge: Cambridge University Press, 2012), 79. While beyond the scope of this project, it is essential to note the missiological implications of Paul's multicultural identity and dual citizenship. Judy Diehl notes this importance and argues that "it is apparent that the combination of Paul's Jewish background and his Roman citizenship helped him advance the gospel message across Asia Minor." Judy Diehl, "Empire and Epistles: Anti-Roman Rhetoric in the New Testament Epistles," *Currents in Biblical Research* 10 (2012): 222.

[3] Stanley Porter, *Paul: Jew, Greek, and Roman* (Leiden: Brill, 2008), 3; Harrill, *Paul the Apostle*, 23.

[4] Harrill, *Paul the Apostle*, 31.

Paul of Tarsus

Tarsus was the birthplace and hometown of Paul and the capital and chief city of the Roman province of Cilicia in Asia Minor since at least 67 BC.[5] Tarsus is mentioned only five times in the Bible and only mentioned in the book of Acts. After Paul's conversion, the Lord directed Ananias to visit Saul and referred to him as "a man of Tarsus named Saul" (Acts 9:11). During this residence back in his home territory, Paul seemingly continued his witness and ministry for Christ. When Paul returned to Jerusalem and a scheme against his life was exposed, the Christian leaders sent him back to Tarsus (9:30). When Barnabas was serving in Syrian Antioch and needed help, he went to Tarsus to get Saul to work with him (11:25). He was there until Barnabas brought him back to Antioch (11:25f.). The period between Paul's sailing to Tarsus in Acts 9:30 and Barnabas's bringing him to Antioch in Acts 11:25 covered some ten years or so. Neither Paul's writings nor Acts gives an account of this period and is often referred to as Paul's "silent years."[6] Lastly, Paul identified himself as a "Jew, from Tarsus in Cilicia, a citizen of no obscure city" (21:39).[7]

Indeed, Tarsus was no obscure city but an incredibly important city of the day. Tarsus was an intellectual center famous for its philosophy and was the seat of a famous university that was "higher than even that of Athens and Alexandria," two of the most respected and known universities of the day.[8] This intellectual nature of Tarsus had to have had a strong influence on the young Paul. Paul "came out of a classical centre of international intercourse and his home itself was for him as a child a microcosmos, in which the forces of the great ancient cosmos of the Mediterranean world

---

[5] Promise Godwin, "Tarsus and Jerusalem: The Interplay of Knowledge and Spirituality Reading Acts 17:22–28 as a Theological Response to the Quest for Gospel," *Journal for Biblical Theology* 3 (2020): 51.

[6] John Polhill, *Acts*, The New American Commentary (Nashville: Broadman & Holman Publishers, 1992), 244.

[7] *Baker Encyclopedia of the Bible* (1988), s.v. "Tarsus."

[8] Godwin, "Tarsus and Jerusalem," 51; Richard Wallace and Wynne Williams, *The Three Worlds of Paul of Tarsus* (New York: Routledge, 1998), 125, 133.

were all represented."[9] Although Paul did not explicitly say that he attended this university, it has often been suggested that he studied there.[10]

Tarsus, a city seemingly well-governed and prosperous, stood on the "frontier of east and west and its citizens were prepared to function in both."[11] It is not ironic then that Paul, though a Jew by birth, was considered the apostle to the Gentiles. While a Jew, Paul lived much of his life within a larger context: in Tarsus, he lived within the larger Greco-Roman world that was influenced by the microcosmos of both Hellenism and Roman culture.[12] While Paul was from Tarsus and raised there, very little is known on how one could become a citizen of Tarsus, and it seems to be unlikely that a Jew born in Tarsus would be a citizen. Additionally, it is certainly not the case that Paul's Roman citizenship would have automatically given him Tarsian citizenship.[13] However, his upbringing in this multicultural Tarsus set the stage for his understanding of citizenship because he understood how to walk in diverse worlds and cultures simultaneously.

Paul the Jew

While much of Paul's Tarsian influence has to be speculated, much more is known about his Jewish influence. In Acts 22:3, Paul stressed that although he was born in Tarsus, he was educated in Jerusalem at the feet of Gamaliel, a significant Jewish teacher and, according to Philippians 3:20–21, had advanced very highly within

---

[9] Adolf Deissmann, *Paul: A Study in Social and Religious History*, trans. William Wilson (New York: Harper, 1957), 34.

[10] *Baker Encyclopedia of the Bible* (1988), s.v. "Tarsus." Stanley Porter notes that it does seem as if Paul had extensive Greek training that would have been available to him in Tarsus at the university. He wrote his letters in Greek; he signed the letters in Greek; he cited the Greek Septuagint widely; and he used and expanded upon Greco-Roman letter form. All of these point to Paul being trained classically and seem to point to him being trained in Tarsus. Porter, *Jew, Greek, and Roman*, 2.

[11] J. Murphy-O'Conner, *Paul: A Critical Life* (Oxford: Clarendon, 1996), 35.

[12] Porter, *Jew, Greek, and Roman*, 2.

[13] Wallace and Williams, *The Three Worlds of Paul of Tarsus*, 142.

the Jewish culture. Paul, in Galatians 2:15, acknowledged the fact that he was a Jew by heritage and birth and had a significant advantage over those who were mere "Gentile sinners." From the Jewish perspective, Gentiles were sinners simply because they were born Gentiles. On the other hand, those who were Jews by birth were on an altogether different level because they were soteriologically privileged in that they had already received the law of God and circumcision, which were the signs of the covenant.[14] Paul affirmed much pride in his Jewish nature and lineage and took his ancestry very seriously.[15] Paul largely remained a Jew after becoming a Christian in spite of his speaking out against the Old Testament law.[16] As a result of Paul's Jewish upbringing, his gospel remained heavily influenced by his understanding of the Old Testament, and he "lived, thought, worked, and read Scripture as a self-identified Jew."[17]

Philippians 3:5–6

Paul's Jewish self-identification is most clearly seen in Philippians 3:5–6 that states that he was "circumcised on the eighth day, of the people of Israel, of the tribe of Benjamin, a Hebrew of Hebrews; as to the law, a Pharisee; as to zeal, a persecutor of the church; as to righteousness under the law, blameless."[18] Paul stressed his membership in the nation of Israel to the particular tribe of Benjamin and was brought up in a family who was strictly observant of Jewish culture. Paul's being a Pharisee in relation to the law is furthered in the assertion about his blamelessness in regard to his own personal righteousness under the law.[19] Here, Paul was challenging those

---

[14] Timothy George, *Galatians*, The New American Commentary (Nashville: Broadman & Holman, 1994), 188–189.

[15] Ryan Schellenberg, "Seed of Abraham (Friesen?): Universality and Ethnicity in Paul," *Direction* 44 (2015): 18.

[16] Deissmann, *Paul*, 96.

[17] Gordon Zerbe, "Citizenship and Politics According to Philippians," *Direction* 38 (2009): 194.

[18] Unless otherwise specified, all Bible references in this paper are to the English Standard Version, (ESV) (Wheaton: Crossway, 2001).

[19] Peter O'Brien, *The Epistle to the Philippians*, New International Greek Testament Commentary (Grand Rapids: Eerdmans, 1991), 369.

who would privilege their Roman citizenship over their fellow believers in Philippi, and his description of his own inherited status and personal achievements in Judaism would have resonated in his Roman setting, where the display of one's honors was familiar. Paul's list is in the form of a Roman *cursus honorum.* These honor inscriptions were popular and usually done with a chisel, hammer, and in stone, so they were necessarily brief. [20] The *cursus honorum* existed as the pecking order of power and dignity in the Roman world. Broadly speaking, the Romans divided society into two groups concerning honor: the *honestiores*, or privileged and honorable strata of society, and the *humiliores*, who did not qualify for reasons of their birth or lack of wealth. [21] Paul's list in this *cursus honorum* was distinctly Jewish and helped him make a case for being a prominent Jew, but was made in a distinctly Roman format. [22]

"Circumcised on the Eighth Day"

Circumcision stands at the head of Paul's list: this was a sign that Paul belonged to the covenant people of God with all the rights and privileges that this included. That Paul had been circumcised, on the eighth day, according to the terms of God's covenant with Abraham, meant he was in strict conformity with the law. [23] Therefore, Paul was not like a proselyte or convert from the Gentile world who would have been circumcised when he was converted; adult circumcision would have been looked at as a "second-rate circumcision." [24] Paul here was stressing not only that he was a Jew but that he was brought up in a family who was meticulous in

---

[20] Joseph Hellerman, *Reconstructing Honor in Roman Philippi: Carmen Christ as Cursus Pudorum*, Society for New Testament Studies Monograph Series 132, (Cambridge: Cambridge University Press, 2005), 123. Joseph Hellerman, *Philippians*, Exegetical Guide to the New Testament (Nashville: Broadman, 2015), 176–177.

[21] Ben Witherington III, *Conflict and Community in CorinthCorinthians* (Grand Rapids: Eerdmans, 1995), 259–260.

[22] Hellerman, *Philippians*, 176.

[23] Gn 17:12; Lv 12:3; Lk 1:59; 2:21.

[24] Hellerman, *Philippians*, 176.

fulfilling all the requirements of the law.[25] The point Paul was making was that not only was he circumcised but that he was circumcised as a Jewish boy in a Jewish home where his family was deeply committed to giving Paul an upright Jewish upbringing.

"Of the People of Israel"

Paul stressed that he was of the people of Israel. This set him apart from Gentiles. Claiming to be of the people of Israel means that Paul was claiming blood kinship and not just simple membership, since the people in Israel could include nonethnic Jews.[26] Against the possibility that he was the child of proselytes, Paul referenced his direct Israelite ancestry by being a member of the people of Israel. When Paul used the term "Israel," he meant a term of special significance for his countrymen. By contrast, the name "Jew" was uttered by Gentiles, often in a somewhat derogatory manner. Thus, "Israel" was a designation that would draw attention to the privileges of God's people. Having been born into the chosen race of the Israelite nation, Paul inherited all the privileges of the national covenant community.[27]

"Of the Tribe of Benjamin"

Paul not only stressed that he was of the people of Israel but he also narrowed down his focus to the tribe of Benjamin. Some Israelites could not provide proof of their genealogy, but this was not the case for Paul: he was of the tribe of Benjamin, whose land included Jerusalem.[28] Being from the tribe of Benjamin gave Paul a privileged ancestry. Paul remained true to that heritage and stressed the correct pedigree that he possessed showing he was able to trace

---

[25] O'Brien, *The Epistle to the Philippians*, 369–370; I-Jin Loh and Eugene Albert Nida, *A Handbook on Paul's Letter to the Philippians*, UBS Handbook Series (New York: United Bible Societies, 1995), 95.

[26] Hellerman, *Philippians*, 177.

[27] O'Brien, *The Epistle to the Philippians*, 370.

[28] Murphy-O'Conner, *Paul*, 36–37.

his lineage from a vital tribe to Israel.[29] Paul seemed to have attached some particular importance to his own membership in the tribe of Benjamin, as he mentioned it also in Romans 11:1. The tribe of Benjamin gave Israel its first king (1 Sm 9:1–2) and remained loyal to the house of David even after the division of the monarchy (1 Kgs 12:21), so it stood high in Jewish culture. It was regarded as a special honor to belong to it, so to assert he was of this tribe shows that Paul was able to trace his descent from this highly regarded tribe in Israel.[30] Paul's claim of being from the tribe of Benjamin meant that he was one of "Israel's elite" and of "its highest aristocracy."[31] Paul was claiming his identity was one of a "true" Israelite.

"A Hebrew of Hebrews"

Paul stressed that he was of the people of Israel, but more than that, Paul further stressed that he was a Hebrew. In Acts 6:1, the term Ἐβραῖοι refers to Jews who normally spoke Aramaic with one another even though they attended synagogues where the service was spoken in Hebrew. The Hellenists in Paul's day, by contrast, spoke only Greek. Paul spoke Hebrew, and according to Luke in Acts 26:14, Paul even heard the heavenly voice on the Damascus road in Hebrew. In claiming to be a "Hebrew of Hebrews," Paul was claiming that his parents, who had brought him up to speak both Hebrew and Aramaic, avoided assimilation to Gentile customs and culture in their Tarsian setting. Here, Paul insisted that he was a "Hebrew" and was also insisting that his parents were Hebrews before him and that his family was rigorously observant of the Jewish culture and law. Additionally, Paul was claiming that he was

---

[29] Richard Melick, *Philippians, Colossians, Philemon*, The New American Commentary (Nashville: Broadman & Holman, 1991), 129; Cheol-Won Yoon, "Paul's Citizenship and Its Function in the Narratives of Acts" (PhD diss., University of Sheffield, 1996), 53.

[30] O'Brien, *The Epistle to the Philippians*, 370–371.

[31] William Hendriksen, *Philippians*, New Testament Commentary (Grand Rapids: Baker, 1962), 156.

a Hebrew and not a Hellenist, even though he was a Diaspora Jew and was thus the "purest of the pure."[32]

"A Pharisee"

Paul had already claimed to be a Pharisee and even a son of the Pharisees (Acts 23:6). Further, there he spoke to the Pharisees and referred to them as "brothers." Claiming to be a Pharisee, Paul certainly exhibited the major characteristics of Pharisees that are found in the New Testament. He would have known the Scriptures (Mt 23:2) and considered himself righteous (Mt 5:20); Paul would have obeyed the pharisaic interpretation of the law (Mk 2:24; Acts 26:5); he would have tithed (Lk 18:12); Paul would have fasted (Mt 9:14) and been diligent in his prayers (Mk 12:40). Before becoming a Christian, he would have been a separatist, which is what the name "Pharisee" implies.[33]

Paul's approach to the law of Moses was that of a Pharisee, and this statement was in keeping with Acts 22:3, where he claimed that he was "educated at the feet of Gamaliel," who was the leading Pharisee of the day (cf. Acts 5:34). As a disciple of the great Gamaliel (Acts 5:34; 22:3), he set himself to be the most zealous of all Pharisees who kept the law (Gal 1:14). The term Φαρισαῖος occurs ninety-nine times in the New Testament, and the reference here in Philippians 3:5 is the only reference outside of the Gospels and Acts. Although Paul was not the first member of his family to be a Pharisee, he was committed to being one. Paul had set himself apart as a Pharisee and had given himself to the faithful service of the law in order to walk in the way of separation, holiness, and righteousness.[34]

---

[32] O'Brien, *Epistle to the Philippians*, 371–372; Hendriksen, *Philippians*, 158.

[33] Charles Ryrie, *Biblical Theology of the New Testament* (Dubuque: ECS Ministries, 2005), 142.

[34] O'Brien, *The Epistle to the Philippians*, 372–374.

"Blameless"

These personal characteristics were important to Paul, but there was more: as a measure of his great love and zeal for the law and Old Testament traditions, which Paul understood as a true zeal for God, he persecuted the church. Finally, the culmination of his personal achievements lay in his meticulous observance of the Old Testament law, as interpreted along his Pharisaic lines: with regard to that righteousness rooted in the Old Testament law, he claimed that he was "blameless."[35] Paul's point was that he was outwardly blameless and had never been accused of breaking any of the law. Therefore, Paul showed himself to be blameless. This does not cancel out Paul's personal testimony of sinfulness in Romans 7:7–12, which shows that Paul knew his inner spiritual condition. Inwardly he was sinful, but publicly he was apparently above reproach and was able to claim it. Outwardly, Paul's conduct in regards to his Jewish makeup was irreproachable.[36] These characteristics of Paul's personal heredity and achievement show that Paul's accepting Christ did not occur because he was "marginally" Jewish. No, Paul had not failed in his own religion but was proficient. Rather, Paul had seen a much better way and had chosen to follow it.[37]

What to Make of Paul the Jew?

Paul and his characteristics and qualifications made him, in the words of Joseph Hellerman, "quintessentially Jewish."[38] In Philippians 3:5–6, Paul was claiming to have advanced in the religion and culture of his ancestors far beyond many of his own age, and also, maybe, more importantly, he was claiming that he was not of "mixed stock" like so many Jews in his day who were living in Palestine.[39] In this way, Paul stressed his

---

[35] O'Brien, *The Epistle to the Philippians*, 374.

[36] Hendriksen, *Philippians*, 160.

[37] Melick, *Philippians, Colossians, Philemon*, 130.

[38] Hellerman, *Reconstructing Honor in Roman Philippi*, 159.

[39] Hendriksen, *Philippians*, 156, 159.

pure Jewish descent, and maintains his Jewish language and customs and manner of life; he is no Hellenist or Graecised Jew, and, born of Pharisaic parents, he is also educated in Jerusalem in the Law and morals of his fathers, and in Hebrew, his mother tongue. He can, therefore, trace his genealogy as a full-blooded Jew.[40]

As such, Paul had a relationship with Palestine in a way that the average Hellenist did not.[41]

Paul the Roman

Paul's Roman citizenship was only mentioned in the book of Acts in 16:37–38; 22:25–29. And while the writings of Paul never directly mentioned his Roman citizenship, it was never questioned in Scripture.[42] While there is much speculation as to how Paul's family had gained citizenship, there has not been much concrete information to posit a legitimate source of their citizenship.[43] In Acts 22:28, Paul claimed that he was a Roman citizen by birth. This is significant because in claiming birthright citizenship, Paul was claiming that he was no Johnny-come-lately to citizenship status.

---

[40] Jac Müller, *The Epistles of Paul to the Philippians and to Philemon*, New International Commentary on the New Testament (Grand Rapids: Eerdmans, 1978), 110.

[41] Murphy-O'Conner, *Paul: A Critical Life*, 36.

[42] This is not to say that scholars have not doubted Luke's account of Paul being a Roman citizen. There are numerous scholars that have doubted the sincerity of Paul's Roman citizenship: J. C Lentz Jr., *Luke's Portrait of Paul* (Cambridge: Cambridge University Press, 1993), 43–51; P. Vielhauer, "On the 'Paulinism' of Acts," in *Studies in Luke-Acts*, ed. Leander Keck and J. Louis Martyn (Philadelphia: Fortress, 1966), 33–50; Ernst Haenchen, *The Acts of the Apostles: A Commentary*, trans. B. Noble (Philadelphia: Westminster Press 1971), 112–116. These scholars are unconvincing and wrongly make the claim that either Luke was embellishing the claim of Paul's citizenship or outright creating a fictional narrative. Luke, writing under the leadership of the Holy Spirit, truthfully wrote that Paul was a Roman citizen because he actually was. If such a large part of the book of Acts is centered around the notion of Paul's Roman citizenship, it makes sense that it must be historical.

[43] I. Howard Marshall, *Acts*, Tyndale New Testament Commentaries (Downers Grove: InterVarsity, 2008), 379.

This stands in sharp contrast to Lysias's comment that he had purchased his Roman citizenship. Citizenship was often granted for the performance of some service to the state or for outstanding military service. Slaves of a citizen who were freed on the basis of service to their owners were also granted citizenship. Additionally, when towns were given the status of colonies, they were granted citizenship; however, the individual purchase of the rights of citizenship would have been looked on suspiciously.[44] It is possible that Lysias was a bit sarcastic in his tone when he referred to paying a "big price" for his citizenship; the suggestion being perhaps if Paul was also a citizen, that "now it seems that just anyone can afford it." However, this was not the case: Paul did not purchase his citizenship; he was born into it.[45]

The readers are not informed if there was any documentary evidence given that proved Paul's citizenship. The Roman tribune simply verified it by a simple question to Paul, which he answered positively. It stands to reason that because most citizens did not travel far from their hometown, they would not normally carry with them any sort of proof of citizenship. Regardless of how it was proven, if Paul was born a Roman citizen, then he inherited it from his father. How Paul's family received Roman citizenship is unclear and open to speculation, but it would have required significant help from the Roman government, so it would seem that it was given to him for some valuable service rendered to the Roman Empire.[46]

In both Acts 16 and 22, it was only after Paul had been beaten or arrested that he was public in his claim of Roman citizenship. Against these contexts, it seems that Paul only went to claim his Roman citizenship when it suited him.[47] In Acts 16, Paul clearly had the upper hand in the matter. He and Silas were both Roman citizens who had been publicly beaten and thrown into prison, and all that without a trial. To arrest a Roman citizen without a trial was an illegal procedure. So, the authorities had scourged and

---

[44] Polhill, *Acts*, 465.

[45] Polhill, *Acts*, 465.

[46] Bruce, *Commentary on the Book of the Acts*, 378, 446; Godwin, "Tarsus and Jerusalem," 47.

[47] Christopher Bryan, *Render to Caesar: Jesus, the Early Church, and the Roman Superpower* (Oxford: Oxford University Press, 2005), 103.

imprisoned two Roman citizens with no formal declaration of guilt, and that was beyond their authority. In this case, the civil magistrates were unaware that Paul and Silas were Roman citizens.[48] In both texts, Paul's claim of Roman citizenship came as a climatic feature of the narrative as a surprise and shock, out of the blue and at the last possible minute.[49] It is possible that Paul did not want to take advantage of being a Roman citizen except in extreme emergencies saving it as some sort of "trump card" in order to escape more violent aspects of punishment.[50] Regardless, that Paul suffered much *before* he publicly declared his Roman citizenship shows that he was very willing to suffer for his faith. Brian Rapske more accurately observes that in the contexts of Acts, Paul's self-disclosure indicated that "he has some confidence that his Roman citizenship may make a difference in his treatment, its manner suggests that Paul is still prepared to suffer or even die without complaint (cf. Acts 21:13) if it is disregarded."[51]

Regardless of how Paul's family received Roman citizenship, it shows that Paul was not of normal circumstances socially and politically because his citizenship put him in a high social sphere and good moral standing. In fact, Paul was the only apostle who had Roman citizenship, and more than that, only approximately one percent of the Mediterranean population had Roman citizenship during Paul's time.[52] Since such a large part of the book of Acts centers around Paul's citizenship, it is safe to say that it played a significant role in understanding the life of Paul. Paul's claiming to be a Roman citizen and being protected by it

---

[48] Polhill, *Acts*, 357.

[49] Daniel Christensen, "Roman Citizenship as a Climatic Narrative Element: Paul's Roman Citizenship in Acts 16 and 22 Compared with Cicero's *Against Verres*," *Conversations with the Biblical World* 38 (2018): 64; Harrill, *Paul the Apostle*, 99.

[50] Marshall, *Acts*, 378; Philip Esler also calls Luke's use of Paul's citizenship as a "trump card," noting Luke's "apparent delight" in playing it at the last minute. Philip Esler, *Community and Gospel in Luke-Acts: The Social and Political Motivations of Lucan Theology* (Cambridge: Cambridge University Press, 1987), 210.

[51] Brian Rapske, *The Book of Acts in Its First-Century Setting: The Book of Acts and Paul in Roman Custody* (Grand Rapids; Eerdmans, 1994), 143.

[52] Harrill, *Paul the Apostle*, 98.

gives clear evidence that a Christian does not necessarily need to reject the entire notion of citizenship or empire but can, on occasion at least, claim to be a part of it while using it for protection that comes from God.[53] Paul's multicultural background made him comfortable with his Roman citizenship. Politically, Paul was Roman; religiously, he was Christian, although heavily influenced by his former life in Judaism.[54] Interestingly, since Paul was a Roman citizen, why did he not find it appropriate to confront it in the same way that he did with his Jewish background? In Philippians 3, right after making a case for his Jewish lineage, he counted it as "rubbish," which was something Paul never did with his Roman citizenship.

Paul and Empire

It is safe to say that the apostle Paul lived, ministered, and wrote in a deeply political culture. Roman imperial ritual and propaganda filled Paul's environment, and both were important elements of Roman culture.[55] While much has been written on Paul's thoughts about the Roman Empire, his political position in regard to the empire has not been clarified, and there is no clear consensus of what Paul thought of the empire.[56] However, acknowledging the tension between the Roman Empire and the young Christian faith is crucial to understanding Paul and his corpus, including the ambiguity that arises among many Pauline scholars.[57]

The New Perspective on Paul

Most of the tension in understanding Paul's thoughts on the Roman Empire stems from the "new perspective on Paul" (NPP). The NPP

---

[53] Bryan, *Render to Caesar*, 103.

[54] Zerbe, "Citizenship and Politics According to Philippians," 194.

[55] Neil Elliott, "The Apostle Paul's Self-Presentation as Anti-Imperial Performance," in *Paul and the Roman Imperial Order*, ed. Richard Horsley (Harrisburg: Trinity Press, 2004), 67.

[56] Marshall, *Acts*, 157.

[57] Jeremy Punt, "Paul's *Imperium:* The Push and Pull of Empire, and the Pauline Letters," *Religion and Theology* 23 (2016): 361.

is a term coined by James Dunn to represent a new approach to the interpretation of Paul's writings and was posited in the Manson Memorial Lecture he delivered at the University of Manchester in 1982.[58] This novel approach was set off by the publication in 1977 of E. P. Sanders's influential book, *Paul and Palestinian Judaism*—a book that has proved to be a watershed in the study of Paul. Sanders's aim was to compare Palestinian Judaism with Pauline Christianity.[59] The NPP is difficult to define since it is not a strict school of thought with established boundaries. For example, if one compares the works of Sanders, Dunn, and N. T. Wright, one will find many issues upon which they differ (e.g., Paul and the law, the faithfulness of Jesus, etc.).[60] Additionally, much of the issue within the NPP is centered around a newfound critique of imperialism that came from European nation-state building in the nineteenth and early twentieth centuries and the notion of the "colonized" and the "colonizers." Despite the growing interest in looking at imperialism connected with Pauline studies, the problem with looking at the Roman Empire through these lenses is that they are not directly applicable to antiquity.[61]

The NPP wrongly assumes much about the political nature of the Roman Empire. Denny Burk's critical analysis of the NPP is helpful in fleshing out some of the deficiencies of this perspective. First, the NPP assumes that the Imperial Cult was pervasive in Roman culture while it was not. Second, it sees Paul's theology as both theo-political and anti-imperial. Third, Paul's theology must then confront all imperial systems.[62] By assuming too much, the NPP views Paul through the lens of an emperor cult and sees it as

---

[58] James Dunn, "The New Perspective on Paul," *BJRL* 65 (1982): 95–112.

[59] Colin Kruse, *Paul's Letter to the Romans*, The Pillar New Testament Commentary (Grand Rapids: Eerdmans, 2012), 14.

[60] Michael F. Bird, *The Saving Righteousness of God: Studies on Paul, Justification and the New Perspective* (Eugene: Wipf and Stock, 2007), 88.

[61] Punt, "Paul's *Imperium*," 339; Harrill, *Paul the Apostle*, 78.

[62] Denny Burk, "Is Paul's Gospel Counterimperial? Evaluating the Prospects of the 'Fresh Perspective' for Evangelical Theology," *JETS* 51 (2008): 311. To be fair, Burk's assessment comes from Wright's own treatment of the subject here: N. T. Wright, "A Fresh Perspective on Paul?" *Bulletin of the John Rylands Library* 83 (2001): 21–39.

the hermeneutical backdrop for the proper interpretation of Paul and his writing; this is a flawed method.[63] Due to this flawed method, the NPP makes several errors.[64] First, it attempts to "force" the finding of parallels in the biblical literature, but any first-century writer dealing with issues of authority would almost have to use language drawn from Roman sources.[65] Second, it forces deductions based upon assumptions. Third, it requires proof texting, selecting specific verses or texts out of context from the entire Pauline corpus to force an agenda. Fourth, it appeals to Paul using "coded" messages in his writings as if he were seeking to offer imperial criticisms in a way that would slip by the Roman authorities. These flaws are tragic and attempt to see Paul as a twenty-first-century critic of the political system rather than a first-century citizen of the Roman Empire who wrote to first-century people living within it.[66]

---

[63] Burk, "Is Paul's Gospel Counterimperial?" 326.

[64] Seyoon Kim, *Christ and Caesar: The Gospel and the Roman Empire in the Writings of Paul and Luke* (Grand Rapids: Eerdmans, 2008), 28–33.

[65] Peter Oakes, "Re-Mapping the Universe: Paul and the Emperor in 1 Thessalonians and Philippians," *JSNT* 27 (2005): 309. It is fair to say that some of Paul's gospel-centered language does parallel some of the Roman imperial language. For example, κύριος, πίστις, εἰρήνη, and other Greek words have a theological use in the New Testament while also having use in the imperial world. However, just because they were not strictly technical Christian words does not mean that they had to have a purely political use when Paul used them. Michael Bird, *An Anomalous Jew: Paul among Jews, Greeks, and Romans* (Grand Rapids: Eerdmans, 2016), 207–208. For more on the use of parallel political terms, see the chart in Michael Gorman, *Apostle of the Crucified Lord: A Theological Introduction to Paul and His Letters* (Grand Rapids: Eerdmans, 2004), 108–109; also see Dieter Georgi, *Theocracy in Paul's Praxis and Theology*, trans., D. E. Green (Minneapolis: Fortress, 1991), 82. However, for all of the NPP, there is a flaw that necessitates that a shared language system has a political agenda when it is used. This is untrue and a glaring weakness in the NPP. For the dangers of forcing parallels, see Samuel Sandmel, "Parallelomania," *Journal of Biblical Literature* 81 (1962): 1–13.

[66] To be more clear: while it is difficult to look at Pauline theology by completely disregarding the NPP, it must be looked at through an extremely critical eye. The stance of this book is that Paul wrote exactly what he meant and meant exactly what he said. While, at times, NPP scholars will be used, they will only be used in ways that deal with what Paul actually said and not what the NPP wants to imply that he meant.

How Did Paul Actually See the Imperial Cult?

The Imperial Cult had become well established all over the eastern Mediterranean world before the birth of Christ, and examples of the ruler cult abound in Greece. After Julius Caesar refounded the city of Corinth in 44 BC, following its destruction a century earlier, a grateful people introduced the worship of the deified Caesar and built a temple of Octavia, sister of Augustus, in Corinth, which became the center of the Imperial Cult in the city.[67] The Imperial Cult was not just a way for the Roman government to gain the loyalty of its people. By participation in the cult, Romans and provincials demonstrated their own relationship to the emperor, who was seen as both man and god. In this way, they were looked at as "buttering up the boss." Additionally, by participation in the Imperial Cult, they advanced their own political and social standing in the Roman community.[68]

Was Paul Genuinely Anti-Roman?

To be sure, the Imperial Cult was an important element of Roman culture, and there was some sort of expression of it in almost every town in the Roman Empire.[69] Roman power was clearly represented in the figure of the emperor, and the Imperial Cult was central to the maintenance of the power relationship within the empire. Religion, politics, and economics were all intertwined within this concept. It is safe to say that the union between religion and government reached its climax in the Imperial Cult.[70] Therefore, the resistance of church members to any expression of homage or worship to the emperor would be dangerous, and the pagans and many synagogue members would soon alert the respective authorities to such treasonable behavior. Furthermore, this deification of the emperor

---

[67] Howard Frederic Vos, *Nelson's New Illustrated Bible Manners and Customs: How the People of the Bible Really Lived* (Nashville: Nelson, 1999), 549.

[68] Vos, *Nelson's New Illustrated Bible Manners and Customs, 549.*

[69] Oakes, "Re-Mapping the Universe," 306–307.

[70] Green, *The Letters to the Thessalonians,* 38–39.

was characteristic of what was fundamentally wrong with Roman rule: it claimed absolute power over the people.[71]

The role of the Imperial Cult was a well-known part of the Greco-Roman world, and while the emperor cult was firmly established within the New Testament world and to the readers of Paul, to ascribe to its inhabitants a preoccupation with it is untrue.[72] The cult confounded expectations about the relationship between politics, power, and religions and was essentially a political issue because it was either exploited by the Roman state for control of the people or because Roman citizens made political issues in response to it.[73]

The role of emperor worship should not be underestimated in the first-century Roman world, but neither should it be overemphasized.[74] Paul wrote to the churches not unconcerned about the political situation that his readers found themselves in, but he was not as deeply concerned with it as some would claim. Paul deeply cared for the church and wanted the church to thrive in the midst of the Roman political situation. As a Roman citizen, he no doubt found himself specially situated to bridge the gap between his readers and the empire, but he was far more concerned about their faith in Christ and their faithfulness to Him in the midst of a politically tense situation. In this way, although Paul understood the political realm, he was attempting not to circumvent the imperial rule but rather was attempting to urge biblical fidelity. In this way, for Paul, the Imperial Cult was simply another facet of Roman religion and culture that he needed to navigate and lead the people through.[75]

---

[71] Mark Bredin, *Jesus, Revolutionary of Peace: A Nonviolent Christology in the Book of Revelation* (Milton Keynes: Paternoster, 2003), 136.

[72] Anders Peterson, "Imperial Politics in Paul: Scholarly Phantom or Actual Textual Phenomenon?" in *People under Power: Early Jewish and Christian Responses to the Roman Empire*, ed. Outi Lehtipuu and Michael Labahn (Amsterdam: Amsterdam University Press, 2015), 109.

[73] Simon Price, *Rituals and Power: The Romans Imperial Cult in Asia Minor* (Cambridge: Cambridge University Press, 1984), 1, 16.

[74] Punt, "Paul's *Imperium*," 3.

[75] Bird, *An Anomalous Jew*, 212.

Paul and Romans 13

When it comes to what Paul wrote about politics and empire, one of the most influential and texts is Romans 13:1–7. It stands as one of the most significant texts regarding the relationship between Paul and the surrounding Roman society the early church found itself in and serves as the only direct discussion or instruction on the relationship between the church and the state and also of how to deal with resistance within the Roman Empire.[76] However, for all of its importance, Romans 13:1–7 is one of the most hotly debated passages in all of the Pauline corpus in regards to Paul's thoughts on politics, if not to his theology as a whole.[77] There has been a very wide divergence of opinion about the way this passage is to be understood, which is strengthened by the fact that there is nothing else quite like it anywhere else in Paul's writings.[78]

The "Hidden" or "Visible"
Meaning of Romans 13

One of the difficulties in assessing the literature of what Paul meant when he wrote this text was whether he was expressing Roman endorsement or a hidden critique. As already discussed, one of the

---

[76] Peterson, "Imperial Politics in Paul," 120; Erik Borggren, "Romans 13:1–7 and Philippians 3:17–21: Paul's Call to True Citizenship and to *Gaman*," *The Covenant Quarterly* 73 (2015): 26; Marshall, *Acts*, 163; Harrill, *Paul the Apostle*, 91.

[77] Christoph Stenschke, "Paul's Jewish Gospel and the Claims of Rome in Paul's Epistle to Romans," *Neotestamentica* 46 (2012): 359; Harrison, *Paul and the Imperial Authorities at Thessalonica and Rome*, 271. Although this passage in Romans is often spoken of as one in which Paul discussed the relation of the church to the "state," it is important to see there is no mention in it of the "state." Joseph Fitzmyer argues this view reflects a modern problem that came to the forefront in the period of the Second World War in response to tyrants such as Hitler and Mussolini. Additionally, there is no mention of "Rome" in this text, which is interesting considering the important and oppressive civil authority in the world at the time. Joseph Fitzmyer, *Romans: A New Translation with Introduction and Commentary*, Anchor Yale Bible (New Haven: Yale University Press, 2008), 662.

[78] Leon Morris, *The Epistle to the Romans*, The Pillar New Testament Commentary (Grand Rapids; Eerdmans, 1988), 457.

major components of the NPP was the belief in coding or using language that, on more in-depth inspection, meant something not seen in the text. In this way, Paul wrote coded messages within his writings and, in some cases, even wrote "hidden transcripts" in particular passages like Romans 13.[79] These "hidden transcripts" are believed to tell a different story than the surface one Paul wrote and pose a challenge to the proper interpretation of the texts.

Due to these interpretations, one must wonder what Paul did actually mean. Did he offer a blanket statement of support to the governing authorities, or did he mean something inherently different? Indeed, some even argue that Paul was offering a statement of counterfeit praise and support.[80] Regardless of what the NPP thinks about coded messages in the Pauline corpus, the most faithful way to interpret Romans 13 is to look at the plain language of the text. Deferring to coded messages and hidden transcripts lead to wrong interpretations and have fed the desire of many to present a Paul who was extremely critical of the Roman Empire and, as a result, also critical of contemporary politics.[81] This is unhelpful and harmful to areas of theology, especially in this area of political theology. Even noted advocate of NPP, Wright stresses that people must not attempt to force the meaning of coded messages in the writings of Paul when he states people must not be so "keen on coded meanings that we miss the main thrust of the text."[82] Paul wrote what he meant in Romans 13 and meant what he wrote. Douglas Moo states this plainly: "[I]t is only slight exaggeration to say that the history of interpretation of Romans 13:1–7 is the history of attempts to avoid what seems to be its plain meaning."[83] Reading the plain meaning is the best and most favorable way to read and interpret this text because it allows the text to speak for itself in

---

[79] The concept of hidden transcripts has been bolstered by the work of J. C. Scott, *Domination and the Arts of Resistance: Hidden Transcripts* (New Haven: Yale University Press, 1990). For more, see Harrison, *Paul and the Imperial Authorities at Thessalonica and Rome*.

[80] Harrill, *Paul the Apostle*, 92.

[81] Ed Mackenzie, "The Quest for the Political Paul: Assessing the Apostle's Approach to Empire," *EJT* 20 (2011): 41.

[82] Wright, "A Fresh Perspective on Paul?" 37.

[83] Douglas Moo, *The Epistle to the Romans,* New International Commentary of the New Testament (Grand Rapids: Eerdmans, 1996), 806.

regards to Paul and to Paul's theological message to the church. In this way, Paul wrote as a Roman citizen inspired by the Holy Spirit to the church at Rome, and furthermore, he has much to say to contemporary readers in regards to politics.

Romans 13:1–7 as the Lens in which
to See the Patriotism of Paul

Romans 13:1–7 is the clearest lens that we have to see the political theology of Paul. It is clear from the plain meaning of the text that Paul was not writing from an anti-imperial stance but was writing so that believers in Rome would know how to navigate the political situation of their day. While not necessarily a political theology of the state, Romans 13:1–7 can be seen as a Pauline response to the pressures from Rome.[84] It may be that Paul took up this issue of writing about the government, which he had not examined in any of his other letters because he was writing specifically to the Christians of Rome, the capital of the empire at the time. The church in Rome would have been a group that would have been mindful of imperial authority.[85] The imperial authority that existed already had Paul imprisoned for the gospel; however, Paul continued to posit that Christians must see governing authorities as God's servants in rewarding good and punishing evil. This was not an ironic statement of behalf of Paul but serves as a way to show the importance of proper submission to authority that has been placed over believers by God Himself.[86]

"Let Every Person Be Subject to the
Governing Authorities . . . One Must Be in Subjection"

That Paul began this section by suggesting that every person, not just Christians, should be subject to the governing authorities is

---

[84] David Horrell, "The Peaceable, Tolerant Community and the Legitimate Role of the State: Ethics and Ethical Dilemmas in Romans 12:1–15:13," *Review and Expositor* 100 (2003): 85.

[85] Fitzmyer, *Romans*, 662.

[86] Horrell, "The Peaceable, Tolerant Community and the Legitimate Role of the State," 87.

important because he was stating that no one is above the command to be subject to the state. Paul used ὑποτασσέσθω ("be subject") to indicate submission to government as an expression of the believer's relationship to God, who has established the governing authorities Himself.[87] Christians are called to submission here but not necessarily to obedience. While submission may well include obedience, at least on some occasions, we should observe the context of what Paul said. While the word may be used in the reaction to authoritative commands, it is also used of Christians being subject to one another (1 Cor 16:16), where it refers not to being subject to authority but mutual submission. In this context, Paul was not advocating that Christians blindly obey the governing authorities; he was simply looking for the proper recognition of the authorities that exist within the government. Christians recognize they are under governmental authority in the same way they recognize that their brother is also Christ's representative.[88]

By stating all authorities that exist have been established by God, Paul was drawing upon the Old Testament teaching that God is sovereign over the rise and fall of earthly rulers and was keeping with the Old Testament attitude to the powers of its day.[89] Regardless of whether a ruler is good or bad, the Old Testament affirms that God ultimately rules over them all.[90] All governing authority is ultimately placed upon the earth by God; therefore, according to Paul, people must submit to them by honoring their authority in a way that is fitting to their position.[91] Additionally, by appealing to God's sovereignty in giving earthly rulers their authority, Paul was clearly not revealing any sort of overt ideological critique of the Roman rulers, so he must have been motivated by something other than an anti-imperial agenda. Paul, as

---

[87] Fitzmyer, *Romans*, 665–666.

[88] Morris, *The Epistle to the Romans*, 461.

[89] John Goldingay, *Old Testament Theology: Israel's Life* (Downers Grove: InterVarsity, 2009), 539.

[90] For example, Proverbs 8:15–16; 21:1; Jeremiah 27:5–7; and Daniel 2:21 all indicate that God has sovereignly established rulers to exist; even the way in which they rule are all due to the sovereign plan of God.

[91] Jesus also recognized that governing authority comes from God. In John 19:11, Jesus said he would have no power at all if it had not been given to Him from above.

a citizen and a Christian, recognized that the government that existed did so because of God Himself; therefore, he could not have been a total political revolutionary because to do so would mean that he would be against the very authority of God (v. 2). Thus, proper Christian submission to the government is actually proper Christian submission to God.

*"Therefore Whoever Resists the Authorities
Resists What God Has Appointed"*

Undoubtedly, Paul did not believe that Christians must always agree with or obey their government in all things. But as a general rule, even within the pagan Roman Empire, Paul expected Christians to be model citizens. This would not mean that Christians should not attempt to work for positive and lasting change by evangelizing and seeking justice. However, Paul's audience did not have all the same options for political transformation available in most modern democracies.[92] Regardless, Paul did not say Christians should be subject to the governing authorities as long as the authority is just or meets some sort of prescribed qualifications.

Paul was saying that the Christian is not justified in refusing obedience to the state simply because he may doubt the legal standing of the government or simply does not like it. It is important to remember that to rebel against the authority of the state is a serious matter because it means to rebel against what God has instituted Himself. However, if the state surpasses its lawful function, or if it directs citizens to actions that are wrong, then that is another matter. The government sometimes oversteps its rightful domain, and when this happens, the believer will find it difficult to obey the government.[93] Jesus said that Christians must render to Caesar only the things that are his because they are to render to God what is God's (Mk 12:17). Additionally, Christians have always understood that "[w]e must obey God rather than men" (Acts 5:29) in times where obeying the authority in place puts them at odds with being obedient to God. As John Stott rightfully noted, "If the

---

[92] Craig Keener, *Romans*, New Covenant Commentary Series (Eugene: Cascade Books, 2009), 154.

[93] Mounce, *Romans*, 244.

authority concerned misuses its God-given power to command what he forbids or forbid what he commands, then the Christian's duty is to disobey the human authority in order to obey God's."[94] So, while Paul did not say this explicitly, that is the reasonable conclusion from his view of the state's God-given authority, which is the only authority that it has.[95]

"Rulers Are Not a Terror to Good Conduct, but to Bad . . . for He is God's Servant for Your Good" (Romans 13:3)

Not only has God established the governing authorities and given them their authority but Paul also wanted his readers to understand they play an important role within the state. The state exists in order to deal with bad conduct and to be a servant of good for the people. In this way, rulers are not a terror to those who do good but to those who do bad. Paul wanted the church to know it would be a dangerous thing to set oneself in resistance to the divinely ordered process of government. Therefore, those who rule pose no serious threat to those whose lives are marked with good deeds; only the one who does evil should fear God-mandated authority.[96] This is significant because it seems that Paul's point was that Christian submission to duly constituted authority is a divinely instituted good. The governing authorities may not always do what is right in Christians' eyes, but that does not negate their authority coming from God. Paul wanted his readers to be law-abiding citizens, and he wrote in order to assure them that they will be commended if they do what is right.[97]

"He Does Not Bear the Sword in Vain"

Continuing the theme that the government is actually a servant of the people, Paul brought up the mandate for the state to be a servant of justice. Just as good citizens have no reason to fear the

---

[94] John Stott, *The Spirit, the Church and the World: The Message of Acts* (Downers Grove: InterVarsity Press, 1990), 116.

[95] Morris, *The Epistle to the Romans*, 461–462.

[96] Mounce, *Romans*, 244.

[97] Morris, *The Epistle to the Romans*, 463.

government, Paul brought up the issue of how the government or state has the authority to punish wrongdoers. The state serves as the agent of God for the punishment of the wrongdoers, and in this way, the state "does not bear the sword in vain." The sword is a symbol of the power delegated to governing authorities to enforce law and order and acceptable conduct.[98] Romans 13:4 gives the biblical basis for the use of force by the government for the protection of law and order. This important power to punish has been given to the state by God and again enforces the theme that to disobey the laws of the land, except where they contravene the expressed will of God, is to violate the authority of God Himself.[99]

"For this Reason You Pay Taxes"

Paul took it for granted that his Roman audience paid taxes. In this way, citizens need to give the state more than simple goodwill. Citizens must pay taxes, which are not just an arbitrary imposing by the state; rather, taxes are the means of carrying on responsible government because the state, even though established by God, could not exist without taxes. Since these authorities are God's

---

[98] The term "bearing the sword" has been interpreted in various ways. Jon Isaak argues that the "sword" here refers to some sort of small dagger used by the police force to ensure that people complied with their orders; however, he does not think that this implies the right to inflict capital punishment. Jon Isaak, "The Christian Community and Political Responsibility: Romans 13:1–7," *Direction* 32 (2003): 42. Robert Jewett identifies it as a military sword carried by law enforcement officers who were trained soldiers who helped to keep the peace. Additionally, Jewett claims that there is evidence in the papyri from the time period that refers to police officers as "sword bearers," adding that Paul's readers had little protection from the power of the state and would have clearly understood the fate of various evildoers. Robert Jewett, *Romans: A Commentary*, Hermeneia (Minneapolis: Fortress, 2007), 785. Troels Engberg-Pedersen supports the view that Paul's reference to "bearing the sword" implied that the state had the right to inflict capital punishment as Nero served as the ultimate sovereign mediator of life and death for all his subjects. Troels Engberg-Pedersen, "Paul's Stoicizing Politics in Romans 12–13: The Role of 13:1–10 in the Argument," *JSNT* 29 (2006): 167. Additionally, the fact that references to the "sword" in the New Testament frequently imply violent death (Rm 8:35; Acts 12:2; 16:27; Heb 11:34, 37) connects "bearing the sword" to state authority to inflict capital punishment. Kruse, *Paul's Letter to the Romans*, 496–497.

[99] Mounce, *Romans*, 244–245.

servants for the public good, taxes must be paid.[100] Paying taxes, apart from being something a good citizen does, is something a Christian does as a means of being subject to the governing authorities. Additionally, it is also a way to be subject to those who are servants of God who devote their time and energies to governing. The governing authorities are "God's servants" in the sense that their authority has been granted to them by God in an effort to maintain law and order.[101]

"The Authorities are Ministers of God"

For the third time in this short text, Paul stressed the entrusted nature of all civil authority coming from God. The word Paul used here to describe the state authorities as "ministers" (λειτουργοί) was a common term for public officials and those who carried out public service to the state. The word in itself is not technically a theological term, even though Paul used it to describe himself in Romans 15:16, but it does give a theological significance in that the state is a minister "of God." Ironically, the Roman authorities thought themselves public servants of Rome but, in actuality, were servants of God and, as a result, were worthy of paying taxes.[102]

"Respect to Whom Respect is Owed,
Honor to Whom Honor is Owed"

Because civil authorities are placed in a higher rank in society, they command due recognition, and the Christian is called on to respect them. In this way, Paul called on the believers to respect and honor those who are leaders in civil and political society because they are servants of God who help to properly manage the state.[103] The benefits that come from this properly managed state place the Christian under a duty to abide by the accepted regulations and rule that come from the authority of God delegated to those who rule.[104]

---

[100] Morris, *The Epistle to the Romans*, 465–466.
[101] Mounce, *Romans*, 245.
[102] Barrett, *The Epistle to the Romans*, 227–228.
[103] Fitzmyer, *Romans*, 670.
[104] Mounce, *Romans*, 245.

Paul used "respect" and "honor" to move away from the realm of taxes in order to indicate proper regard for those in high places. Paul used the terms to stress the proper attitude one should have toward the state, and he was also saying that Christians should have a respectful attitude toward those in high places. Christians do not have honor and respect for authorities simply because of their power or influence but because God has made them His ministers, and their honorable work should provide them a certain level of dignity.[105]

Romans 13:1–7 and Pauline Politics

Paul was neither a political radical nor was he was uninterested in the affairs of the Roman Empire and unconcerned with patriotism. However, looking at Romans 13:1–7 helps us frame the discussion of what Paul's sense of patriotism would be in a number of ways. First, Paul saw the state as a legitimate authority over believers. This cannot be understated. Three times in Romans 13:1–7, he connected the state's authority to God Himself, so a believer must see the authority of the state as being connected to God's own authority. If God is the one who is giving the authority, it must, in some sense, be just. Stanley Porter points out this important connection by showing Christians must willingly submit to the authorities on the assumption that they are just. Additionally, if the rulers' authority comes from God, they must rule in a way that is consistent with God's justice.

Second, it is important to stress that Paul was not anti-empire. There is nothing in this text to indicate that he was anti-imperial or intentionally trying to disrupt the Roman order that existed, and it serves as an Achilles' heel for any anti-imperial reading of Paul.[106] Romans 13:1–7 and the lack of a specific critique of the empire is surprising if Paul intended to criticize the Roman Empire because Paul had no problem in clearly stating what he meant.[107] Paul could not have been against the Roman government and, at the same time, posit that they were servants of God, so the argument that Paul was anti-imperial simply does not hold. Paul did

---

¹⁰⁵ Morris, *The Epistle to the Romans*, 466–467.
¹⁰⁶ Kim, *Christ and Caesar*, 36.
¹⁰⁷ Mackenzie, "The Quest for the Political Paul," 45.

not see Rome as the chief enemy to overcome; he saw the powers at work to be far subtler. Thus, Paul was not hostile toward Rome.[108] Since Paul was not hostile toward the state, a case can be built that he would at least be open to the notion of patriotism.

Third, although Paul was not anti-empire, it does not follow that he was pro-empire. To be sure, Paul was giving a respectful gesture to the Roman empire, but he was not wholeheartedly endorsing them in all things. Romans 13:1–7 points the way to a critical patriotism because it recognizes that states exist because of God Himself, and the authority they have comes from Him. Therefore, some level of support must be given. However, the believer recognizes that it is ultimately God who gives all authority to the state, and because of that, the state is limited in its scope. The state is not the most important thing in culture even if it is significant, and a Christian knows where the supreme importance lies: God Himself.

Fourth, Romans 13:1–7 shows that Paul was not apolitical even if he was not consumed with political notions of activism.[109] While Paul did not write a political treatise, nor should Romans 13:1–7 be seen as one, it would be a stretch to say that Paul was unconcerned with politics. While Romans 13:1–7 is not a political treatise, it stands as a text with significant importance as a way to show how the church was to live its political life. He clearly knew that the church was going to have to find their proper place within the political world in which they found themselves. For Paul, politics was simply a part of life in which a Christian was going to have to be found faithful.

Fifth, Romans 13:1–7 shows being faithful to Christ would require that a Christian must navigate the tension that existed between the spiritual and political world. While Peter Oakes argues that Rome was barely aware of Christianity in Paul's day, he also notes that in some sense, "Rome conflicts with Christianity and Christianity conflicts with Rome."[110] In other words, Paul wrote

---

[108] Zerbe, "Citizenship and Politics According to Philippians," 204.

[109] This point is made strongly by Michael Bird in *An Anomalous Jew*, 214.

[110] Oakes, "Re-Mapping the Universe," 305, 316. Anders Peterson also finds it unlikely that Rome would have paid much attention to a "marginal

Romans 13:1–7 knowing that the believers were going to find themselves existing in two kingdoms: one of God and one of Rome. The nature of living in both of these kingdoms simultaneously is an important factor in dealing with politics and stresses the need for understanding the nature of both. Both Augustine and Luther built theological frameworks to deal with living within these two kingdoms, but both also understood the supremacy of one over the other.[111] Paul, in the entire book of Romans, as well as his entire corpus, was far more concerned with God's kingdom but knew that the majority of believers were not able to escape the kingdom of Rome, so they had better be prepared to live and exist in both.

Romans 13:1–7 helps make the case that Paul was a concerned Christian citizen who wanted Christians to see their proper role in a structured society. He understood the nature of power and authority because he understood the authority of God in all things, and this extended to the state, who used their God-given authority to structure society. While Paul did not necessarily see the kingdom of God at odds with the kingdom of Rome, he did understand that the gospel had world-changing implications, and those implications would come into eventual conflict with any

---

movement" such as Christianity at this time and instead would have seen it as only a minor matter. Peterson, "Imperial Politics in Paul," 108.

[111] Augustine developed his concept of theology of the two cities in his *City of God*. Chapters 11–14 deal with the origins of the two cities, chapters 15–18 deal with growth of the two cities, while chapters 19–22 deal with the eventual ends of the two cities. For Augustine, Christians are citizens of the heavenly city while everyone else are citizens of the worldly city that is doomed for destruction, and the Christian is a simply a sojourner in this world on his way to his eternal home. Luther, and many in Reformed circles, build on this concept in the two-kingdom theology that states God has both a common and redemptive rule in the world. God uses the common rule to preserve the world and ordains the government and other social institutions to play their part, while He uses His redemptive rule to build the church. For an introduction of Luther's conception of this doctrine, see William Wright, *Martin Luther's Understanding of God's Two Kingdoms: A Response to the Challenge of Skepticism* (Grand Rapids: Baker, 2010). For a contemporary conception, see David VanDrunen, *Natural Law and the Two Kingdoms: A Study in the Development of Reformed Social Thought* (Grand Rapids: Eerdmans, 2010); David VanDrunen, *Living in God's Two Kingdoms: A Biblical Vision for Christianity and Culture* (Wheaton: Crossway, 2010).

holder of power.[112] In the face of potential conflict and in light of being dual citizens (of the kingdom of God and the kingdom of Rome), Paul set the stage for a critical sense of patriotism that understands the allegiance and loyalty that one must have for each kingdom. In light of who Paul was as a person and what he wrote as a theologian in Romans 13:1–7, one can make the case that he would have had a sense of patriotism that all Christians should emulate.

Paul the Patriot

If Paul serves as a model for a biblical understanding of patriotism, it must be seen as a subtle one. Paul was obviously influenced by his multicultural makeup and also by his citizenship of both Rome and of Israel. So how would Paul look at patriotism as defined by a loyalty toward one's country, people, and culture? Glimpses of Paul's patriotism are frequently seen in his writings, especially in connection with his understanding of Israel and his view of the church. Paul understood the nature and role of the state but also understood a Christian's role as a citizen, and by looking at his writings, one can flesh out his sense of patriotism.

Paul's Sense of Patriotic Loyalty to One's Country: Acts 17:26

Paul clearly understood that God had not only established the nation of Israel but had also established every human nation. Harkening back to Genesis 1:28, Paul added some nuance to his understanding of the establishment of all nations by stating they all come "from one man," referring to Adam and the emphasis it plays on the nature of all mankind's relationship to God. According to Paul, though there are many nations throughout the world, all are one in their common ancestry and in their relationship to their Creator. Here, Paul proclaimed that God was not just the God of Israel but the sovereign Lord of all mankind.[113] God has both the history and the geography of all nations firmly in His own control, and Paul pointed

---

[112] Oakes, "Re-Mapping the Universe," 315.
[113] Polhill, *Acts*, 374.

to God's providence in creation in establishing the boundaries of all nations showing His lordship and providence over all of history.[114] Much like Paul argued in Romans 1:18–20 and in his speech at Lystra (14:17), God had clearly made Himself known in some sense by the works of His creation.

Additionally, this text also shows that nationalism must be rejected. The Athenians prided themselves on being autochthonous or sprung directly from their native soil, but Paul showed this pride was foolish because all of mankind was from one joint and shared origin: they were all created by God and were given the entire earth to dwell in.[115] Paul countered all notions of ethnic exclusivity with this statement about the human race being one in its origins. Paul used the term εθνος here, and one could question does it mean "nations," or does it mean "races"? Either is possible, but in either case, the point is the same: all nations, despite their ethnicity, came from one human.[116] Regardless, Paul was claiming that it is this one global humanity as a whole who is to rule over, to care for, and to enjoy all of God's creation. Thus, there is a shared responsibility and privilege shared by every nation in God's creation. Yet God has also destined special times and places for all nations within his purpose; therefore, according to Paul, there is a plan for all nations and races.[117] Since God has established all nations and their boundaries, each nation has the understanding that God has a plan and purpose for them. Additionally, because each nation is established by God, each citizen of each nation can exhibit a sense of patriotism for his land because it is a gracious gift from God.[118]

---

[114] Stott, *The Spirit, the Church and the World: The Message of Acts*, 286.

[115] Bruce, *Commentary on the Book of the Acts*, 357–358.

[116] Ben Witherington III, *The Acts of the Apostles: A Socio-Rhetorical Commentary* (Grand Rapids: Eerdmans, 1998), 527–528.

[117] David Peterson, *The Acts of the Apostles*, The Pillar New Testament Commentary (Grand Rapids; Eerdmans, 2009), 497.

[118] Ryan Schellenberg notes, "Paul is claiming for Jewish and Gentile believers a shared ancestry, a claim that makes it difficult to sustain the notion that Paul's emphasis on unity in Christ results in a radical devaluation of ethnicity or kinship." In other words, Paul was stressing both a shared ancestry while also maintaining the importance of national diversity. Schellenberg, "Seed of Abraham (Friesen?)," 21.

Paul's Sense of Patriotic Loyalty to His People:
Romans 9:1–5

Paul's clearest picture of patriotism came in his response to the people he saw as his own: the Jews. Paul's mission to the Gentiles was largely responsible for the Christian church becoming predominantly Gentile, so his personal involvement raised problems for him regarding the members of his former religion. Throughout the book of Romans, Paul had been concerned to teach about God as the source of human justification and salvation, but now his main concern would be instead with God who has granted special privileges to the Jews and called them to be His people, but who now calls the Gentiles to faith. Paul spoke out as a Christian without any resentment against his fellow Jews, a group that may have caused him much trouble. Paul here spoke too as a Jew and not a random apostate without sympathy for his fellow brothers. Instead, Paul was deeply pained and hurt at the thought of Israel's failure to accept the gospel he had preached. Paul made it clear that Israel's failure to accept his message of salvation by God in Christ was a cause of constant sorrow and pain to him.[119]

Paul went to great pains to let his readers know how greatly troubled he was about his Jewish kinsmen. Were Paul to forget his Jewish roots and not feel sorrow for the spiritual state of his fellow countrymen, how could he be called the apostle to the Gentiles? Paul cared for his people so deeply and was so burdened for his Jewish family that he could have almost wished himself cursed by God and taken their curse upon him and thus be cut off from Christ if it could somehow help his kinsmen.[120] Paul's willingness to undergo being cursed on behalf of his countrymen is clear evidence of his concern for his people.[121]

Not only did Paul refer to his fellow Jews as kinsmen, but he also referred to them as "brothers." Normally, Paul would use ἀδελφός to refer to his fellow Christian brothers, but now he used it for members of his former religion.[122] It is important to note this is

---

[119] Fitzmyer, *Romans*, 541–543; Morris, *The Epistle to the Romans*, 345.

[120] Mounce, *Romans*, 195; Osborne, *Romans*, 237.

[121] Morris, *The Epistle to the Romans*, 347.

[122] 1 Cor 10:1; 12:1; 15:1; 2 Cor 1:8; 8:1; Gal 1;11; Phil 1:12.

the only place Paul used the term "brother" for the Jews, showing that he recognized that they are still fellow members of God's chosen people in spite of their failure to accept his gospel.[123] Additionally, by calling them brothers, he was also showing that he still regarded himself as a faithful Jew. In this way, Paul was not a casual passerby but a person who deeply identified with the nation of Israel. Additionally, by calling his kinsmen "Israelites," he was using a term that means they are not simply members of a national or racial group but members of the people of God. This term is more than the more common ethnic or political designation of "Jews." Paul only used "Israelite" in three places (here in 9:4; Rom 11:1; 2 Cor 11:22), but in each case, it was used to signify something of the blessedness of being God's covenant people.[124]

Paul's Sense of Patriotic Loyalty to the Culture:
Philippians 2:9–11 and 3:20–21

While Paul clearly understood the role of government, it is important to note that he also clearly understood the notion of citizenship. Paul saw the Christian as one who had to navigate the immediate culture, and for many of his readers, that culture necessitated they understand how to view the Roman Empire. Philippians offers a true sense of the Pauline nature of loyalty toward culture because it looks forward to the coming kingdom. Looking through an eschatological lens, Paul showed that while Rome (and the state in general) has a level of authority, Jesus is the coming κύριος and also is the ruler of the only eternal kingdom. This lens helps the believer understand that his sense of patriotic loyalty to a state must always be tempered by the kingdom of God.

Philippians 2:9–11

The immediate context for Paul's letter to the Philippians provides an important reason for the view that the name Lord is the name that God gave Jesus. In a Roman colony, the Philippians would hear the

---

[123] Osborne, *Romans*, 237; Fitzmyer, *Romans*, 545.

[124] Morris, *The Epistle to the Romans*, 346, 348; Kruse, *Paul's Letter to the Romans*, 370.

claim that "Jesus is Lord" as a counterclaim to the declaration of the Roman Empire that "Caesar is Lord."[125] In this way, Paul claimed Jesus as Lord in language that both reflects and undermines the claim that Caesar is Lord.[126] "Bowing the knee" is a common idiom for doing homage, sometimes in prayer, but always in recognition of the authority of the god or person before whom one is kneeling.[127] Here, Paul used the term to declare the adoration is in honor of the exalted Christ, and it describes the act of reverence that is paid directly to the Son and "to the glory of God the Father."[128]

Does Paul calling Jesus Lord challenge and ultimately overturn the supreme lordship of the Roman emperor? "Lord" was an epithet common of all deities in the ancient Mediterranean world and was not unique to Roman emperor worship. Additionally, in Rome's fundamentally hierarchical society, κύριος saw regular use in the daily speech of slaves to masters, commoners to nobles, and even soldiers to commanders. In fact, virtually all ancient people spoke this way to people in higher social circles.[129] Paul calling his Messiah Jesus "Lord" does not necessarily prove anything about an anti-imperial stance to Rome but does show that at the end of all things, both Christians and their "lord Caesar" will join with all others to declare that κύριος is none other than Jesus Christ.[130] So, for Paul to use this term for Jesus meant that he was stating that Jesus was Lord and not Caesar.[131]

Jesus being highly exalted figuratively points to Jesus being placed in a position of highest honor and power. Paul here was stressing that nothing is higher than Jesus, who is supreme over everything and is given the name above every name, and ultimately,

---

[125] Richard Horsley, ed., *Paul and Empire: Religion and Power in Roman Imperial Society* (Harrisburg: Trinity Press, 1987), 140–141.

[126] G. Walter Hansen, *The Letter to the Philippians*, The Pillar New Testament Commentary (Grand Rapids: Eerdmans, 2009), 163; Wright, *Paul in Fresh Perspective*, 72–74, 93.

[127] Gordon Fee, *Philippians*, The IVP New Testament Commentary Series (Westmont: InterVarsity, 1999), 100.

[128] O'Brien, *The Epistle to the Philippians*, 240.

[129] Harrill, *Paul the Apostle*, 88.

[130] Fee, *Philippians*, 100–101.

[131] James Harrison, "Paul and the Imperial Gospel at Thessaloniki," *JSNT* 25 (2002): 78; Kim, *Christ and Caesar*, 15.

everyone will bow to Him. In other words, this expression emphasizes Jesus's unique authority.[132] Additionally, Paul stated the second portion of the exaltation is that God "bestowed on him the name that is above every name." The name which is above all other names is, of course, the name of God, and so here Paul was referring to the name κύριος, and not Jesus, with it here being the LXX equivalent to "Yahweh."[133] In this way, Paul recognized that Jesus is the ultimate sovereign ruler who should occupy the place of the highest honor for all believers. While the state (or ruler) has a natural level of authority, it fails in comparison to Jesus, who is the one true κύριος.

Philippians 3:20–21

Paul specifically contrasted the earthly with the heavenly in Philippians 3:20 by stating that a Christian's "citizenship is in heaven." This metaphor would have had a rich meaning to the Philippians, who were proud of their Roman citizenship, so when Paul said that they belonged to special citizenship, he spoke directly to them.[134] The noun used here for "citizenship" is πολίτευμα and appears nowhere else in the New Testament, so it seems Paul used it to describe the fact that Christians are, at best, temporary resident aliens here on the earth while their true citizenship is in heaven.[135] Again, Paul was writing to Christians in a proud city in regards to its relation to Rome and telling the Philippians they belong to a heavenly commonwealth. This meant they were its citizens, and they needed to reflect its character by understanding that the Christian's commonwealth and ruling principles and constitutive

---

[132] O'Brien, *The Epistle to the Philippians*, 235–236.

[133] Ben Witherington III, *Paul's Letter to the Philippians: A Socio-Rhetorical Commentary* (Grand Rapids: Eerdmans Company, 2011), 152.

[134] Ancient Greek and Roman societies were organized around their cities. The size of the city was a source of great pride for citizens, and their loyalty to the city was clear to all who lived there. James Jeffers, *The Greco-Roman World of the New Testament Era: Exploring the Background of Early Christianity* (Downers Grove: InterVarsity, 1999), 57.

[135] Loh and Nida, *A Handbook on Paul's Letter to the Philippians*, 118.

government come from Christ, who is reigning from heaven, not from the emperor, who is ruling from Rome.[136]

The political overtones continue in verse 21. The Philippians awaited the coming Savior who granted citizenship and who would come with power sufficient to subject everything to Him, including Christians' earthy bodies. The Philippians would logically associate all earthly subduing power with a Roman emperor, but the true power, according to Paul, was unique to Christ.[137] Christ is able not only to transform the body but "to subject" (καὶ ὑποτάξαι) the entire universe (τὰ πάντα) to Himself. Christians await this coming universal subjection of all things under God's control, knowing it does not matter what the current political situation may be. Hansen points this out well:

> No matter how glorious Caesar is or how great the power of his rule over all things in his empire, Caesar is no match for the Savior and Lord from heaven. Writing from a Roman prison to a Roman colony, Paul spells out a greater vision of the future than any Caesar could ever accomplish.[138]

Paul stated that Christians are to be subject to the governing authorities against this coming future universal subjection of all things to Christ. While Paul recognized and accepted earthly governmental authority because it comes from God, he also knew that all earthly governmental power is, at best, temporary. This authority is not absolute; nor is it final. Against this understanding, Paul wrote Philippians 3:20–21 with tears (3:18), watching those who set their minds on earthly things, watching Caesar attempting to bring all things under his control. Paul did not allow the false saviors of the empire to overshadow Jesus, who will come from heaven to exercise his absolute and sovereign power over all things and even transform His people into glory.[139]

---

[136] O'Brien, *The Epistle to the Philippians*, 461; Witherington, *Paul's Letter to the Philippians*, 217.

[137] Melick, *Philippians, Colossians, Philemon*, 143–144.

[138] Hansen, *The Letter to the Philippians*, 272.

[139] Hansen, *The Letter to the Philippians*, 276.

By stressing the coming kingdom and reign of Jesus, Paul was making the clear point that Jesus is the one who will reign forever. Jesus's kingdom is the one eternal kingdom, not Rome. While the Philippians had a patriotic sense of pride in their city, Paul wanted that sense to be tempered by the understanding that the real pride needed to be focused on their citizenship that resides in heaven. This heavenly citizenship should change everything for a Christian because it shows that there is a highly patriotic loyalty that must be exhibited. Ultimately, loyalty to Christ and His kingdom overshadows the loyalty to Rome because it is the one that will be eternal for a Christian.

Concluding Thoughts on
Pauline Patriotism

Paul had a clear understanding of both the state and of citizenship, and he wrote with a clear sense of purpose in leading his readers to be able to navigate both. Writing as a Roman citizen, Paul had a clear picture of what it meant to be Roman, but as an apostle, he had a clear picture of what it meant to be a Christian living in Rome. Paul knew what it meant to be a Roman was more than merely a citizen because it was balanced with his life as a Jew within the larger Roman world.[140] By balancing both of these and his time in Tarsus and Rome, Paul was able to write to his audience, encouraging them to live in tension with the state while being faithful to Christ. James Jeffers notes this tension:

> Since most of his readers would not have been Roman citizens, they would have understood what it was like to live as foreigners in an earthly city. Paul may have been telling them that citizenship, the identification that should truly matter to them, is citizenship in the kingdom of heaven.[141]

Thus, Paul spoke to this tension, making it clear that one could be both a faithful citizen and Christian. Further, by being both a faithful citizen and a Christian, one could be a faithful patriot.

---

[140] Porter, *Paul*, 3–4.
[141] Jeffers, *The Greco-Roman World of the New Testament Era*, 209.

Paul's sense of patriotism was rooted in his understanding of the gospel. First, it understood that God was the one who established all earthly powers, thereby giving all of them validity. In this way, a faithful Christian must be "subject" to the authorities over them. Second, Paul made it clear that all states were allowed to have specified national boundaries. This allows all nations to coexist and be a part of God's call to rule the world. Third, Paul understood that the power of all states is limited and finite. Ultimately, Paul looked at all states through the lens of the second coming of Christ, knowing that He will be the final ruler of all things, and the states that Christians are subject to now will one day be subjected to Him. In this way, Christians know the proper place of all states is one that is under Christ. Paul would have been a productive citizen because he had a proper understanding of the role of the state, but more importantly, he had a proper understanding of the lordship of Christ that both gave nations their authority but also placed them under His own divine authority. In the same way Paul's readers had to navigate the political realm, so too must contemporary Christians today. All are residents of this earth and are subject to earthly authorities. Therefore, all Christians, just like Paul, must seek to model a proper sense of patriotism toward their nation, showing a proper sense of loyalty to the land, people, and culture.

6

Pastoral Implications of a Biblical Understanding of Patriotism

In a diverse and divisive America, Christians must have a biblical understanding of patriotism. A person can be a Christian and patriotic as long as there is a biblical framework for the Christian to live out his understanding of patriotism in his context. Additionally, it has been shown that Paul exhibited a great understanding of a Christian's obligation toward a state while also understanding that his loyalty was ultimately due to his Savior. In this way, Paul serves as a test case for how a patriotic Christian lives in a secular culture hostile to a biblical worldview.

While American Christians may be patriotic, is it just that simple? Are there restrictions and warnings that must be associated with a proper understanding of patriotism? Further, many Americans have so intimately connected their understanding of patriotism to the very act of worship in the church through the heavy presence of the American flag in the church and the use of patriotic liturgy. Is this acceptable, or is it something too closely akin to idolatry? This chapter will seek to give some pastoral implications of a proper sense of patriotism by looking specifically at the issue of whether the American flag should be present in the church and whether patriotic songs are appropriate in worship. These are two of the essential issues concerning a proper understanding of how a Christian can be faithful to Scripture while also being patriotic.

Mark 11 and Jesus's Cleansing of the Temple:
The Need for the Nations in the Church

The temple in Jerusalem was the heart of Israel's spiritual life and the focus of its national identity and character and had become a patriotic symbol of religion for the nation.[1] The temple erected by the exiles on their return from Babylon had stood for about five hundred years. When Herod the Great became king of Judea, the temple had fallen into disrepair, and he, wanting to gain the favor of the Jews, rebuilt it.[2] The temple that Herod built had an enormous and impressive structure that spread out over thirty-five acres, which made it the largest temple in the ancient world.[3] The temple's significance stands out not only in its enormous size but also in its large proportion of the city: the temple occupied around twenty-five percent of the city of Jerusalem. Not only that, Jerusalem was different from many other cities of its day because it was made up of one single temple and did not have many different temples throughout. Jerusalem was, as N.T. Wright notes, "not so much a city with a temple in it"; she was "more like a temple with a small city round it."[4] Additionally, while most temples in the Mediterranean world would have multiple tokens and symbols of Roman allegiance, that was not the case in Jerusalem because the temple had no statues of any sort inside it.[5]

While much of Mark's portrayal of Jerusalem had been negative, it remained the city of David and the nation's chosen capital that God had chosen to be a light to the nations. Additionally, as the site of the temple, Jerusalem was the visible center of the worship of Israel's God.[6] The elaborate project that Herod had built was meant not to glorify God but to appease the Jews; this resulted

---

[1] R. T. France, *The Gospel of Mark: A Commentary on the Greek Text*, New International Greek Testament Commentary (Grand Rapids: Eerdmans, 2002), 436–437; Gavin Drew, "'Show Me the Money!' Part 1: Speculations Concerning Jesus and the Temple," *Stimulus* 17 (2009): 39.

[2] *Holman Illustrated Bible Dictionary* (2003), s.v. "Temple of Jerusalem."

[3] Robert Stein, *Mark*, Baker Exegetical Commentary on the New Testament (Grand Rapids: Baker, 2008), 515; M. Eugene Boring, *Mark: A Commentary* (Louisville: Westminster John Knox Press, 2006), 320.

[4] N. T. Wright, *The New Testament and the People of God*, vol. 1, *Christian Origins and the Question of God* (London: Society for Promoting Christian Knowledge, 1992), 225.

[5] Ronald Kernaghan, *Mark*, The IVP New Testament Commentary Series (Downers Grove: InterVarsity, 2007), 216–217.

[6] France, *The Gospel of Mark*, 426–427.

in a tense relationship between Jews and their Roman occupants. Regardless, even though the temple in Jesus's day might not have been precisely what it was supposed to be, both the Jews and Jesus saw it as God's dwelling place even though it was in Roman control.[7] It is against this backdrop that Jesus's interaction inside of the temple in Mark 11–12 serves as a springboard for a contemporary discussion of patriotism.

The Court of the Gentiles:
Setting of Nationalism or Worship?

The one place in Jerusalem where the people of Jerusalem seemed to be in some sort of control was the temple; however, there were also many different powerful groups with interests occupying it.[8] Romans, Pharisees, Sadducees, Zealots, sojourners, and Jerusalem citizens all were involved in the life of the temple and interacted with one another, attempting to make their version of the temple come to fruition. Jesus entered the temple in Mark 11 in the days leading up to Passover and discovered a sight that angered Him so much that he engaged in one of the only examples of violence recorded in the Gospels. Jesus encountered buyers and sellers of temple sacrifices and immediately expelled them both, overturned the money-changers' tables and those who sold doves for sacrifices, then prevented all transportation of temple vessels (Mk 11:15–16). In essence, Jesus stopped, then destroyed all of the commercial infrastructure necessary to engage in the sacrificial system.[9]

However, was Jesus only concerned with the commercialization of the sacrificial system, or was there more at

---

[7] Mt 21:21.

[8] Karen Wenell, "Contested Temple Space and Visionary Kingdom Space in Mark 11–12," *Biblical Interpretation* 15 (2007): 328.

[9] E. P. Sanders makes the argument that Jesus's actions could not have stopped "all" the buying and selling of sacrifices that was going on in the temple because that would have taken an army. E. P. Sanders, *Jesus and Judaism* (Philadelphia: Fortress Press, 1985), 70. James Edwards concurs with this assessment. James Edwards, *The Gospel According to Mark*, The Pillar New Testament Commentary (Grand Rapids: Eerdmans, 2002), 342. However, it does not matter that Jesus stopped "all" of the buying and selling in the temple but that He addressed the entire system that was taking place.

play? Herod's temple consisted of four divisions. The first and largest division was the court of the Gentiles, while the other three divisions of the temple were the court of the women, the court of Israel (which was only for circumcised Jewish males), and the holy of holies, which was within the sanctuary. The sanctuary was separated from the court of the Gentiles by a wall, with the following warning in Greek, Latin, and Aramaic: "No foreigner may enter within the railing and enclosure that surround the temple. Anyone apprehended shall have himself to blame for his consequent death."[10] While it seems that Herod's temple attempted to segregate all groups to "fulfill a stricter understanding of purity regulations," what can be said is that by attempting to keep the temple pure, it had caused it to be greatly divided.[11] The commercial sale of sacrificial animals that was taking place was, in effect, making it hard for the Gentiles to pray and worship God in the temple in the only way they were able.

Animals, especially pigeons, had been sold on the Mount of Olives for sacrifices for a long time, but around AD 30, the temple authorized such sales in the temple precinct itself, eventually taking up shop in the court of the Gentiles. This was perhaps done so the temple could get a portion of the profits and have some control over the procedures.[12] The court of the Gentiles was literally the closest the Gentiles were able to get to the temple, but the commercial selling of sacrificial animals in this area kept the temple from being used in the way that it was designed. The commercialization of the court of the Gentiles prevented the area, the only area available to the Gentiles, from actually being correctly used; this shows the Jews

---

[10] Edwards, *The Gospel According to Mark*, 340–341. This knowledge and understanding of Herod's temple depend on three ancient sources, Josephus (*Ant.* 15.391–425), the Mishnah, and the *Temple Scroll* (11QT) in the Dead Sea Scrolls. For a more comprehensive reconstruction of Herod's temple, see Joseph Patrich, "Reconstructing the Magnificent Temple Herod Built," *Bible Review* 4 (1988): 16–29; Kathleen and Leen Ritmeyer, "Reconstructing Herod's Temple Mount in Jerusalem," *Biblical Archaeology Review* 15 (1989): 23–42.

[11] Craig Keener, "One New Temple in Christ (Ephesians 2:11–22; Acts 21:27–29; Mark 11:17; John 4:20–24)," *Asian Journal of Pentecostal Studies* 12 (2009): 76.

[12] Ben Witherington III, *The Gospel of Mark: A Socio-Rhetorical Commentary* (Grand Rapids: Eerdmans, 2001), 315.

believed the court of the Gentiles held little, if any, sacred significance because they did not care if the Gentiles were able to use it for worship.[13]

Herod's temple separated the Gentiles by its very design, so when Jesus overturned the tables of the money changers, he challenged the activity in the one section of the temple where Gentiles were welcome. Jesus was upset at the total disregard for the court's sanctity that was designated for the Gentiles who had not yet become full members of the Jewish faith. All of the court's commercial activity was effectively denying the Gentiles, and the nations of the world, access to the temple.[14] The Jews continued to care about themselves at the expense of the nations around them, which was a direct rejection of the Old Testament perspective of the temple.

Isaiah 56:7:
A Call for the Nations to Worship as One

Jesus's rebuke of the commercialization of the sacrificial system was not so much directed toward the buying and selling of necessary sacrifices as it was a challenge to the Jew's nationalistic tendencies.[15] The Jews should have cared about whether the nations could freely worship in the temple, but that was not the case. After stopping the activity in the temple, Jesus began to teach the crowd by stating, "Is it not written, 'My house shall be called a house of prayer for all the nations'?" (Mk 11:17). Jesus clearly cared about what was happening in the temple, for He quoted Isaiah 56:7 in His rebuke of what was going on in the court of the Gentiles. Jesus's rebuke focused on how the temple was *not* the house of prayer for the nations that Isaiah expressed. Jesus's statement should not be seen merely about a desired state of affairs that He did not find in

---

[13] William Lane, *The Gospel According to Mark*, The New International Commentary on the New Testament (Grand Rapids: Eerdmans, 1974), 405.

[14] Kernaghan, *Mark*, 218.

[15] It is hard to see how the sacrifices in the temple could continue without the changing of money. Additionally, as Sanders notes, "[I]t appears that Jesus' demonstration was against what all would have seen as necessary to the sacrificial system." Sanders, *Jesus and Judaism*, 66.

the temple but more of a critique of how the Jews were causing their temple activity to keep the Gentiles from worshipping.[16] In Isaiah 56:7, God promises to cause the foreign people of the nations to come into his "holy mountain," a guarantee that picks up previous concepts found in Isaiah of the nations coming to the temple in Zion and later references to the nations coming to Zion (57:13; 60:3–11; 66:18–21).[17] When the nations come to worship God, they will spend time in God's "house of prayer."

Jesus saw that the Jews cared more about their own special relationship to God than they cared about the nations that God wanted to have the same relationship. The Jews cared more about whether they could have access to the proper sacrifices that they had forced the Gentiles out of their own sacred space in order to do so. In placing the commercial buying and selling of approved sacrifices in the court of the Gentiles, the Jews were keeping the Gentiles from being able to worship in the only way they could. In effect, the Jews were more concerned about their own worship than whether the nations could join them. Jesus sought the fulfillment of God's international mission for the nations, as seen in Isaiah 56:7, but also sought the temple's impending judgment in its failure to be that "house of prayer" for the nations. Foreigners were supposed to have an assured place in the temple because they enable it to be what God intended for it to be: a place open to all people of all nations, not just Israel.[18]

In Isaiah 56:7, God promises to cause foreigners to come into His "holy mountain" and that they will spend time in his "house of prayer." Therefore, according to Isaiah 56:7, Jews should have rejoiced and welcomed all foreigners who come to Zion, but Jesus saw that they had made it incredibly difficult for Gentiles to

---

[16] J. R. Kirk, "Time for Figs, Temple Destruction, and Houses of Prayer in Mark 11:12–25," *The Catholic Biblical Quarterly* 74 (2012): 516–517.

[17] For promises in Isaiah of the nations coming to the temple, see 2:2b–3; 9:10–12; 14:1–2; 25:6; 45:20–25; 49:6, 22. For promises in Isaiah of the nations coming to Zion, see 57:13; 60:3–11; 66:18–21.

[18] John Goldingay, *Isaiah*, Understanding the Bible Commentary Series (Grand Rapids: Baker, 2012), 317. John Goldingay goes on to say, "Foreigners have an assured place in the enthusiastic worship of that house. They indeed enable it to be what Yahweh intends, not a house where Israelites along are welcome, but one open to all peoples."

worship. By referring to Isaiah 56:7, Jesus made it clear the Jews were more concerned in protecting their national boundaries by not attempting to attract people of other nations to the God of Israel.[19] In other words, the Jews had made it easy for themselves to worship but seemingly did not care enough about the nations' ability to do the same to make it easier for them to do so. For the Jews, as long as they were able to worship, it mattered little to them if the Gentiles were able to enjoy the "house of prayer."

Isaiah 56:7 has an eschatological focus where God's temple will be called a house for all nations to come and pray.[20] By welcoming all of the nations to the temple, God was ensuring there were no second-class citizens among the worshippers of God, and Jesus's rebuke and quoting of Isaiah 56:7 shows that the eschatological nature of the temple should have already come. By not being a house of prayer for the nations, the temple had lost sight of the eschatological mission that it was meant to aspire.[21] However, the Jews cared more about their own identity and ability to worship than biblical faithfulness. As a result, the nations were not truly able to worship. Jesus's outright critique of the situation shows that He saw the temple as being a place that existed for all of the nations and not just Israel.

Jeremiah 7:11:
What the Temple has Become

While Jesus's quote of Isaiah 56:7 describes what the temple *should* be, Jesus's quote of Jeremiah 7:11 shows what it *was*. The temple was supposed to be a house of prayer for the nations; instead, it had become a "den of robbers." In Mark 11:17, λῃστής means "robber" or "bandit" and is fitting because it vividly recalled Jeremiah's sermon about the misplaced confidence of those whose behavior

---

[19] Timothy Geddert, *Mark*, Believers Church Bible Commentary (Scottsdale: Herald Press, 2001), 273.

[20] Gary Smith, *Isaiah 40–66*, The New American Commentary (Nashville: Broadman & Holman Publishers, 2009), 535–536.

[21] Geddert, *Mark*, 273.

contradicted their profession of honor for the temple (Jeremiah 7).[22] Instead of being faithful, Israel had made the temple like a "den of robbers" where villains could retreat after taking advantage of people. Jesus's use of this phrase did not necessarily accuse the Jews of His day of the same crimes as Jeremiah's hearers, but it shows their lack of honor for the temple by connecting it with a recognized abuse of it. Additionally, Jesus's hearers would have understood that Jeremiah's sermon went on to predict the eventual destruction of the temple (7:12–15), which came soon after. In this way, Jesus makes the same prediction (13:2).[23]

The present circumstances in the temple had turned the sacred space into a habitat for bandits because they had taken advantage of others and had kept the temple from fulfilling its biblical purpose.[24] The Gentiles had a right to pray in the temple just as much as the Jews. Mark's mostly Gentile audience would have understood Jesus's quotation's significance.[25] The Jews had allowed the temple to become a place where the Gentiles were cast aside and a den where Gentiles were robbed of their right to worship.

Mark 11:

Jesus as Political Prophet

Mark 11 describes a temple that is a place where the people of Israel envision themselves safe. The temple should have been a place where the nations were represented and gathered to worship alongside the people of Israel; instead, the nations had been cast aside in order for the people of Israel to be the center of all aspects of worship. Jesus's use of both Isaiah 56:7 and Jeremiah 7:11 color His entire confrontation with the temple in eschatological tones because it shows that Jesus was more concerned with the nations being able to worship inside the temple than he was concerned with

---

[22] Donald Juel, *Messiah and Temple: The Trial of Jesus in the Gospel of Mark* (Missoula: Scholars Press, 1977), 132–134.

[23] France, *The Gospel of Mark*, 446.

[24] Darrell Bock, *Mark*, New Cambridge Bible Commentary (New York: Cambridge, 2015), 293.

[25] Witherington, *The Gospel of Mark*, 316.

the Jewish preoccupation with being God's chosen nation.[26] Isaiah 56:7 and Jeremiah 7:11 present the temple as a house of prayer that is concerned with the nations being able to gather for collective worship instead of a den of robbers taking advantage of the people. In this way, Jesus's use of both texts provides a window to understand the narrative of Mark 11 as an example of how not to let patriotic tendencies get in the way of faithful worship.[27] Jesus's public rebuke of the temple serves as a reminder that God intended for the temple to be a place of worship for all people of all nations. Jesus rejected popular Jewish messianic hopes that looked for the Messiah to rid Jerusalem and the temple of the Gentiles and instead criticized the Jewish leaders for getting in the way of the Gentiles' access to the temple, which was one of the temple's most important purposes.[28] Jesus's indignation for what the temple had become presented Him as a political prophet who was greatly concerned about Israel's love of country keeping them from their eschatological mission of reaching the nations.[29]

Mark 12:
Church and Caesar, Adversaries or Allies?

A second event that helps frame a contemporary discussion of patriotism is Jesus's statement about rendering to Caesar what is his and to God what is His (Mk 12:17). This section has frequently been treated as the locus classicus of Jesus's political theology and is one of the most widely known and quoted of all of Jesus's teachings; it stands as one of the most quoted biblical texts in the Gospels about

---

[26] Timothy Gray, *The Temple in the Gospel of Mark: A Study in Its Narrative Role* (Tübingen: Mohr Siebeck, 2008), 45.

[27] Kirk, "Time for Figs, Temple Destruction, and Houses of Prayer in Mark 11:12–25," 510.

[28] Allen Black, *Mark*, The College Press NIV Commentary (Joplin: College Press, 2001), 201–202; Stein, *Mark*, 517.

[29] Richard Horsley, *Jesus and Empire: The Kingdom of God and the New World Order* (Minneapolis: Fortress, 2003), 93; Richard Bauckham, *The Bible in Politics: How to Read the Bible Politically* (Louisville: Westminster, 2011), 77.

the Christian's attitude toward the state.[30] Interestingly enough, the main issue in this periscope also centers around taxes. Mark 11 centers around exchanging money—most notably the temple tax mentioned in Exodus 30:13–16—while Mark 12 centers around the poll tax required by Rome. The poll tax required by Rome was a contentious issue in the lives of most Jews because it served as a tribute, or a direct tax payable to Rome. Being forced to pay this tax brought home to them their subjection to a foreign power. It reminded the Jews of their subjection not just to a foreign power but to a pagan one, especially since it had to be paid in Roman coins, which bore Caesar's image, who claimed to be divine. So, for most Jews, to pay this tax was to acknowledge Caesar's lordship.[31]

Pharisees and Herodians:
Strange Bedfellows

Mark had already mentioned the Pharisees and Herodians working together in Mark 3:6 when they are mentioned as collectively trying to find a way to kill Jesus, and here they again joined forces to test Jesus.[32] The Pharisees whom the chief priests, elders, and scribes sent to trap Jesus were devoted nationalists who hoped that God would send the messiah to defeat the foreign powers and expel them—and the Gentiles—from their land. They saw Roman

---

[30] Richard Bauckham, *The Bible in Politics*, 73; Arnold Monera, "The Christian's Relationship to the State According to the New Testament: Conformity or Non-Conformity?" *Asia Journal of Theology* 19 (2005): 113.

[31] Bauckham, *The Bible in Politics*, 79–80.

[32] Additionally, Jesus may have connected the two groups in Mark 8:15 when Jesus claimed, "Watch out; beware of the leaven of the Pharisees and the leaven of Herod." Mark 8:15 speaks of the "leaven of Herod," while the parallel passage in Matthew 16:6 speaks of the "leaven of the Sadducees." Were the Sadducees and the Herodians the same? Matthew tended to label the religious leaders as Jesus's opponents, whereas Mark emphasized that Jesus's opponents were *both* religious *and* political. Therefore, it is possible the Herodians were a political party composed primarily of Sadducees. *Baker Encyclopedia of the Bible* (1988), s.v. "Herodians."

occupation as proof of God's judgment, but they strongly objected to Israel's ruler's trust in Rome for national security.[33]

While less is known of the Herodians than the Pharisees, it is obvious they were connected with the Herodian dynasty in some regard and must have supported Rome, their rule, and their occupation of Israel.[34] The Herodians, who also accompanied them, lived at the other end of the political spectrum and were, in many ways, collaborators with the Roman Empire. They supported the Roman occupation and their ultimate control over the temple, even though it was a symbol of Jewish nationalism.[35] In the world of first-century Judea, it is difficult to imagine a stranger political alliance than the team of Pharisees and Herodians who were sent to Jesus, as they were, as William Hendriksen stated, a "strange coalition between the sanctimonious and the sacrilegious."[36]

Money and Taxes

The poll tax was introduced in the Roman Empire around AD 6 and was paid with a denarius bearing Caesar's image, which was fairly typical of imperial coins of the period.[37] The tax was imposed on every male Jew from ten to sixty-five years of age as a token of their submission to Caesar. This was a constant source of division and irritation to the Jews and served as a constant reminder of their Roman captivity.[38] The tax was a painful reminder that the Jewish

---

[33] Drew, "'Show Me the Money!'" 39.

[34] R. Alan Cole, R. *Mark*, Tyndale New Testament Commentaries (Downer Grove: InterVarsity, 2008), 267. While it is important to note that there is a broad understanding of who the Herodians were, it is safe to say that they were, at the very least, connected to the Herodian dynasty and supportive of it. For more, see J. P. Meier, who gives at least fourteen different theories about who the Herodians were. J. P. Meier, "The Historical Jesus and the Historical Herodians," *JBL* 119 (2000): 740–746.

[35] Drew, "'Show Me the Money!'" 38.

[36] Kernaghan, *Mark*, 229; William Hendriksen, *Mark*, New Testament Commentary (Grand Rapids: Baker, 2002), 480.

[37] Sara Harding, "'Astonished at His Teaching': The Structure and Authority of Jesus' Sayings in the Gospel of Mark" (PhD dissertation: Marquette University, 1999), 155; Martin Rist, "Caesar or God (Mark 12:13–17)? A Study in 'Formgeschichte'," *The Journal of Religion* 16 (1936): 317–318.

[38] Drew, "'Show Me the Money!'" 38; Stein, *Mark*, 544.

land that had been promised to them by God was no longer truly theirs but belonged to Rome and as such, it was, as William Lane notes, an "odious token of subjugation."[39] In essence, the tax served as a way to flame the tensions of nationalism and patriotism because it reminded the Jews that their country was not what they wanted. As long as they paid the tax, they were accepting that fate; this led to deep resentment by the Jews.

Rendering to Caesar

The question that the Herodians and Pharisees posed to Jesus was a clear trap. By asking Jesus, "Is it lawful to pay taxes to Caesar, or not? Should we pay them, or should we not," they were attempting to trap Jesus into making a claim. Either He must declare Himself to be a political rebel who will not pay the tax to Rome, or He will be a religious traitor by supporting Rome. Despite the Herodians and Pharisees' attempt to trap Jesus in the question of whether it was right to pay the poll tax or not, Jesus refused to be manipulated into either position. Jesus knew both their hypocrisy and wicked intent. Using His own authority, Jesus requested a denarius and asked, "Whose likeness and inscription is this?" There was some heavy irony in the fact that the testers possessed the coin for the tax, whereas Jesus did not. This implies they both shared more complicity in the tax system than their question suggested and suggests they were not as religious or patriotic as they wanted people to believe. According to Jesus, since the image and inscription were Caesar's, the coin belonged to Caesar.[40]

By claiming that the coin belonged to Caesar, Jesus was acknowledging the legitimacy of the Roman government and also distancing Himself from all forms of political anarchy, which was best exemplified in His day by the Zealots.[41] Jesus was not evading the question but saying that the tax was to be paid because the Roman government was the one who had the authority to mandate the tax in the first place. Jesus answered their hostile question by

---

[39] Lane, *The Gospel According to Mark*, 423.
[40] Edwards, *The Gospel According to Mark*, 363.
[41] Edwards, *The Gospel According to Mark*, 363.

going beyond their politically minded religious perspectives. Jesus understood that Caesar had as much right to mandate taxation as a native Jewish ruler, but this put Him out of step with contemporary Jewish nationalism.[42]

Church and State

It seems hard to square Jesus's attitude toward the temple tax and taxes to Caesar. On the one hand, Jesus rejected theocratic taxation as inappropriate to God's rule because it got in the way of the Gentiles being able to worship, but on the other hand, he seemed to accept the legitimacy of Roman taxation despite its oppressive character. To pay the tax would make Jesus look like an unfaithful and unpatriotic Jew, while not paying the tax would make Him look like a political rebel. However, Jesus did not take the bait and instead offered a brilliant response that properly dealt with both a Christian's duty to the state and God.

Jesus was not making an absolute demarcation between Caesar's sphere and God's authority as if God was not over Caesar. Instead, Jesus's point was that God has absolute rights but that does not mean that Caesar did not also have rights.[43] This statement by Jesus does not provide a full account of the Christian's obligation to the state, but it affirms that obedience to a secular power does not necessarily conflict with a Christian's obligation to God.[44] Loyalty to state authorities does not always mean that a person is disloyal to God. As Eckhard Schnabel rightly notes, "[L]oyalty to God and loyalty to legitimate claims of Caesar are not in opposition to each other."[45] This is the heart of what Jesus was claiming in this

---

[42] Bauckham, *The Bible in Politics*, 81.

[43] Bauckham, *The Bible in Politics*, 79–81.

[44] James Brooks, *Mark*, The New American Commentary (Nashville: Broadman & Holman, 1991), 193.

[45] Eckhard Schnabel, *Mark*, Tyndale New Testament Commentaries (Downers Grove: InterVarsity, 2017), 294.

periscope. Jesus placed Caesar and God together and prevented the reader from thinking of either realm in isolation.[46]

The Nature of the Church and State
in Light of Mark 11 and 12

Mark 11 and 12 present a Jesus who is concerned with both the church and the state. In Mark 11, Jesus condemned how the Jews have cast aside the nations by allowing commercial activity to overwhelm the court of the Gentiles, thus making it incredibly difficult for the Gentiles to be able to worship God. Instead of being a light to the nations and allowing the temple to be a "house of prayer," it had instead become a "den of robbers." In this way, Jesus is intimately concerned with how the church exists in connection to people of the nations. Mark 12 presents a Jesus who is concerned with how people see the role and function of the state. When He was faced with making a comment on whether taxes should be paid to Rome, He made it clear that the state has a certain level of authority and should be respected. In this way, Jesus shows that state authority is one that is legitimate, and as a result, believers must not seek to ignore it.

The Christian's understanding of the relationship between church and state is one that continues to be important even as it is complex. How is a Christian supposed to see his role within the church as it seeks to live out in the context of a nation? This is an issue that many have sought to understand. Jesus's actions in Mark 11 and 12 offer an opportunity to look at the relationship between church and state because He brought to light issues that are pertinent for both. First, Jesus made it clear that He was concerned with the nations and not just Israel when He stopped the money changing in the court of the Gentiles that was preventing the Gentiles from being able to worship. In so doing, Jesus was confronting how Jews in Jerusalem were more concerned with whether their own people were able to worship rather than the nations. Taken further, the Jews in Jerusalem were more concerned with their own national identity being able to worship than the nations around them. Second, Jesus's

---

[46] Boring, *Mark*, 336.

response to the Pharisees and the Herodians shows that the state has a specific authority in the culture and cannot be ignored. Mark 11 and 12 bring the conceptions of church and state to the forefront and give an appropriate starting point for a brief discussion on how a Christian must understand both church and state.

A Dual Understanding of Church and State

There have been various attempts to understand the nature of the church and the state, but most of the most significant center around the dual relationship between the two. Augustine's two-cities doctrine, Pope Gelagius I's two-swords doctrine, Luther's two-kingdoms doctrine, and even Kuyper's one-kingdom-with-separate-spheres doctrine all bring to mind that the church and the state are separate realms with specific roles in the world. While much can be said about the nature of these prominent conceptions of church and state, what follows is a brief discussion on Christian views on church and the state that will help in framing a discussion of patriotism.

Augustine's Two Cities

The locus classicus for Augustine's imagery of the two cities is *The City of God*: "We see then that the two cities were created by two kinds of love: the earthly city was created by self-love reaching the point of contempt for God, the Heavenly City by the love of God carried as far as contempt of self. In fact, the earthly city glories in itself, the Heavenly City glories in the Lord."[47] In other words, there are two cities in the world ruled by two different loves, and Christians, or citizens of the heavenly city of God, live in both and struggle in balancing their allegiances and loyalties to both, preferably reserving their highest allegiance and loyalty for God. For Augustine, Christians are citizens of the heavenly city while everyone else are citizens of the worldly city that is doomed for destruction, and the Christian is a simply a sojourner or pilgrim in this world on their way to his eternal home. In Augustine's view of

---

[47] Augustine, *City of God*, trans. H. Bettenson (London: Penguin, 2003), 593.

the two cities, Christians as pilgrims might intermingle somewhat and share some things in common with people who are citizens of the world, but they are never to truly focus on the world around them, for they are simply passing through on their way to the heavenly city.[48]

Pope Gelasius I's Two Swords

Another dual concept of church and state is Pope Gelasius I's two-swords theory. This theory presents two separate powers with a division between church and state that have two different means of authority. The state has a sword, which is execution, which is meant to enforce proper political rule, while the church wields the sword of excommunication, which is meant to keep the church pure. Gelasius recognized the church powers "have the greater responsibility" while the state powers are "subordinate."[49] These two swords (or powers) both come from God and have authority that also comes from God. Both rule over the same people but have different jurisdictions. For Gelasius, the state rules over worldly affairs while the church (through the priest) is concerned with spiritual activities. Additionally, Gelasius's framework posits that

---

[48] Augustine, "Book XIX", in *City of God*, trans. Henry Bettenson (London: Penguin, 2003), ch. 17: "But a household of human beings whose life is not based on faith is in pursuit of an earthly peace based on the things belonging to this temporal life, and on its advantages, whereas a household of human beings whose life is based on faith looks forward to the blessings which are promised as eternal in the future, making use of earthly and temporal things like a pilgrim in a foreign land, who does not let himself be taken in by them or distracted from his course toward God." Augustine, *City of God*, 877.

[49] Gelasius I, "Letters to Emperor Anastasius," in *From Irenaeus to Grotius: A Sourcebook in Christian Political Thought*, ed. Oliver O'Donovan and Joan Lockwood O'Donovan (Grand Rapids: Eerdmans, 1999), 179.

both church and emperor should submit to each other in their proper spheres of authority.[50]

Abraham Kuyper's One Kingdom with
Separate Spheres

Abraham Kuyper offered much in the discussion of the relationship between the church and state. According to Kuyper, all authority earthly ultimately comes from the sovereignty of God. This is especially true in regards to the authority of the state. According to Kuyper, without sin entering into the world, there would be no need for any sort of governmental order because all political life would have naturally evolved from the family. There would be one world government and there would no need for justice, police, or military in a world without sin. Kuyper went on to say the "shady-side" of earthly states should not exist, but because of sin, it now does.[51]

God is sovereign over all spheres of life but each sphere has authority within its own realm while receiving its respective authority from God. Within the sphere of the state, Kuyper argued that authority over men cannot arise from other men but must derive from the authority of God.[52] As God allows the state or rulers to exist within their sphere of authority, God grants them authority in order to show "common grace" to citizens and to "shield the good against the evil."[53] In this way, rulers are God's servants. Kuyper argued that magistrates of the state, as God's servants, must

---

[50] David VanDrunen, *Natural Law and the Two Kingdoms: A Study in the Development of Reformed Social Thought* (Grand Rapids: Eerdmans, 2010), 40. Gelasius's theory was expanded by Pope Boniface VIII in 1302 through his papal bull, *Unam Sanctam.* This reshaped the two swords doctrine to state both swords come from God but are now mediated through the Catholic Church. Robert Crouse, "Two Kingdoms and Two Cities: Mapping Theological Traditions of Church, Culture, and Civil Order," (PhD diss., Wheaton College, 2016), 30.

[51] Abraham Kuyper, *Lectures on Calvinism: Six Lectures from the Stone Foundation Lectures Delivered at Princeton* (N.p.: readaclassic.com, 2009), 59.

[52] Kuyper, *Lectures on Calvinism*, 60.

[53] Kuyper, *Lectures on Calvinism*, 60–61.

recognize they are God's servants and that they are "duty bound" to seek His will through His Word.[54]

The sphere of the state stands under the majesty and authority of God even as both church and state must, in their own spheres, obey God and serve Him. As such, each sphere, according to Kuyper, must let God's Word rule. In order to do this, Kuyper stated that all nations should be governed in a Christian way in accordance with the principles of statecraft that flow from Christ.[55] This does not mean that the church and state spheres exist in the same space; but rather, they "exist side by side, and they mutually limit each other."[56] The church has sovereignty over the affairs of the church only and no authority on those outside of the church, and the state has no authority within the sphere of the church. In this way, both the church and the state must allow people the right of freedom of conscience.[57]

David VanDrunen's Two Kingdoms

David VanDrunen is a contemporary scholar who adds much to the discussion of the relationship between church and state. VanDrunen builds on some of the concepts already discussed by adding to the Lutheran and Reformed conceptions of church and state. VanDrunen believes the entire human race makes up a "common" or civil kingdom established by God's covenant with Noah.[58]

---

[54] Kuyper, *Lectures on Calvinism*, 76–77.

[55] Kuyper, *Lectures on Calvinism*, 77. Kuyper put it well: "The lamp of the Christian religion only burns within that institute's walls, its light shines out through its windows to areas far beyond, illumining all the sectors and associations that appear across the wide range of human life and activity. Justice, law, the home and family, business, vocation, public opinion and literature, art and science, and so much more are all illuminated by that light, and that illumination will be stronger and more penetrating as the lamp of the gospel is allowed to shine more brightly and clearly in the church institute." Abraham Kuyper, *Abraham Kuyper: A Centennial Reader*, ed. James D. Bratt (Grand Rapids: Eerdmans, 1998), 194.

[56] Kuyper, *Lectures on Calvinism*, 79. The state's distinctive role is to keep all other spheres within their God-given boundaries of authority.

[57] Kuyper, *Lectures on Calvinism*, 80.

[58] David VanDrunen, *Living in God's Two Kingdoms: A Biblical Vision for Christianity and Culture* (Wheaton: Crossway, 2010), 15.

VanDrunen states the "civil kingdom pertains to temporal, earthly, provisional matters not matters of ultimate and spiritual importance."[59] Additionally, humankind also lives in a "redemptive" spiritual kingdom that is made up of God's chosen people through the Abrahamic covenant. The spiritual kingdom, according to VanDrunen, "is also ruled by God, but he rules it not only as creator and sustainer but also as its redeemer in Christ. This kingdom pertains to things that are of ultimate and spiritual importance, the things of Christ's heavenly, eschatological kingdom."[60] God rules both of these kingdoms, but does so in different ways: God rules the spiritual kingdom as its redeemer in Christ, and He rules the civil kingdom not as its redeemer but as its creator and sustainer.[61]

The two-kingdoms doctrine affirms that God has created all things but that sin has corrupted all aspects of human life. Despite this, Christians are called to be active in human culture. According to this doctrine, God is not trying to redeem the world but preserve it through the Noahic covenant. However, at the same time, God is redeeming a people for Himself through the Abrahamic covenant, which was brought to fulfillment through the work of Christ. For VanDrunen, the kingdom of heaven is ultimately an eschatological realm that will be fully revealed in the age to come, but the church is the community in present that embodies that kingdom.[62]

The fact that the kingdom of God is a coming kingdom means that Christians are always homeless in the present world to some degree. Using biblical terms, VanDrunen argues Christians are always sojourners and exiles in the present world and in their own respective political communities. This perspective calls for Christians to be cautious and thus to avoid the temptations of both

---

[59] David VanDrunen, *Biblical Case for Natural Law*, Studies in Christian Social Ethics and Economics (Grand Rapids: Acton Institute, 2006), 24.

[60] VanDrunen, *Biblical Case for Natural Law*, 24.

[61] David VanDrunen, "Abraham Kuyper and the Reformed Natural Law and Two Kingdoms Traditions," *Calvin Theological Journal* 42 (2007): 283–284.

[62] David VanDrunen, "Bearing Sword in the State, Turning Cheek in the Church: A Reformed Two-Kingdoms Interpretation of Matthew 5:38–42," *Themelios* 34 (2009): 323; also David VanDrunen, *Politics after Christendom: Political Theology in a Fractured World* (Grand Rapids: Zondervan, 2020), 18.

cultural pessimism and optimism.[63] The two-kingdoms doctrine stresses that Christians should not deny the importance of politics since it has great bearing on justice, peace, and prosperity of the world. However, it also stresses that Christians should not exalt politics as a means to usher in God's redemptive kingdom. The two-kingdoms doctrine effectively guards against both of these dangerous extremes in understanding the church and the state.[64]

Exiles and Sojourners

While there are many viewpoints in regards to the relationship between the church and the state, it is an issue of great importance for the Christian seeking to be faithful to God while also seeking to be faithful within the state.[65] Stanley Hauerwas is helpful here, stating that the "[c]hurch is not out of the world. There is no other place for the church to be than here. . . . The church need not worry about whether to be in the world. The church's only concern is *how* to be in the world, in what form, for what purpose."[66] The Bible is "clear": Christians exist within two kingdoms and have not been created in order to separate from the world.[67]

This point is shown again in Jeremiah 29 in God's challenge to Israel to be good citizens while in Babylon. In essence, understanding church and state involves understanding both being rooted and being sent. On one hand, the church is sent into the culture, but on the other hand, it also exists with a mission in a

---

[63] VanDrunen, *Politics after Christendom*, 18.

[64] VanDrunen, *Living in God's Two Kingdoms*, 194–195.

[65] See Stanley Hauerwas and William Willimon, *Resident Aliens: Life in the Christian Colony* (Nashville: Abingdon, 1993). Stanley Hauerwas argues the people of God, the church, exist as a social alternative to living in the world as an individual concerned with simply making life better. The church exists as a redeemed people who faithfully follow Jesus and are seeking to see the culture redeemed. Hauerwas and Willimon, *Resident Aliens*, 44–45.

[66] Hauerwas and Willimon, *Resident Aliens*, 43.

[67] Lesslie Newbigin was helpful on the importance of living a faith within the context of being "in the world" by stating, "A privatized eschatology causes Christians to pull away from culture which diminishes the perceived personal responsibility for public affairs." Lesslie Newbigin, *The Gospel in a Pluralist Society* (Grand Rapids: Eerdmans, 1986), 113.

specific culture. As Hauerwas says, Christians cannot be "deceived into thinking that they can be Christians and remain strangers" with those around her.[68] The world needs the church but only if it is properly fulfilling the mission of Jesus. As Israel was challenged to seek the welfare of the city in Jeremiah 29, so too should the church seek the welfare of the state.

In a sense, Christians are complete strangers in the world despite how they view the state.[69] Christians are "sojourners and exiles" in that they are strangers in this world. The language of strangers and exiles is meant theologically, indicating that the readers are "like" foreigners because of their allegiance to Jesus Christ. Peter intended us to read them together to say that believers are aliens and strangers in this world. We should not read the words literally as if they depict the actual political status of the readers. The language of strangers and exiles is appropriated theologically, signifying that the readers are "like" foreigners because of their allegiance to Jesus Christ.[70] Paul Achtemeier rightly observed, "It was precisely the precarious legal status of foreigners that provided the closest analogy to the kind of treatment Christians could expect from the hostile culture in which they lived."[71] The citizen of the city of God will always find himself thrown into a situation of being a resident alien living in some outpost of the earthly city.

Mark 11–12's Effect on Patriotism

When Jesus dealt with the temple's commercialization, He did so because it had made it difficult for the Jews to reach the nations. Jesus saw that the temple system was getting in the way of its missiological mission by forcing the Gentiles to the outskirts in order to make it easier for the Jews to worship in the way they saw

---

[68] Hauerwas and Willimon, *Resident Aliens*, 108.

[69] Christians are "exiles" in 1 Peter 1:1; the church is in "exile" in 1 Peter 1:17; Christians are called "sojourners and exiles" in 1 Peter 2:11. Christians are "strangers and exiles" in Ephesians 2:19 and Hebrews 11:13.

[70] Thomas Schreiner, *1, 2 Peter, Jude*, The New American Commentary (Nashville: Broadman & Holman, 2003), 119–120.

[71] Paul Achtemeier, *1 Peter: A Commentary on First Peter* (Minneapolis: Fortress, 1996), 174.

fit. Gentiles could come close but not close enough to be included in worship like the natural-born Jews. Further, with the crowded commercialization found in the court of the Gentiles, the limited ability they had to worship was made substantially harder. Additionally, by forcing the commercial activity of the temple to the court of the Gentiles, the Jews were also showing their own personal worship was more important than including the people of the nations because they were cast aside. Jesus was clearly affirming that Gentiles should be included in the prayer and worship in the temple, but the activity in the temple was preventing this from happening. The Jews did everything in order to secure their own ability to worship in Jerusalem at the temple. The fact that the Jews were able to worship at the expense of the Gentiles (in their own court no less) shows that Jews cared for their own people at the expense of their call to include the nations. In this way, the temple was a mild example of Jewish nationalism being a hindrance to faithfully reaching the nations.

Patriotic Jews would not readily accept paying a tax to their oppressors, especially considering it had Caesar's picture on it, which was seen as blasphemy. When Jesus claimed that Caesar had a legitimate claim to taxes, He also showed that the state had a legitimate sphere of influence despite the Jews' abhorrence for their oppressive authority. However, there is much irony in the fact that the Pharisees and Herodians, in the midst of attempting to trap Jesus, had the very coin in question. This shows that they already acknowledged, in some sense, the authority of Caesar. What Jesus did by accepting Caesar's authority was to acknowledge that the state had an authority that was distinct to it while also clearly stating that God is to be honored and obeyed. God and state are not always in direct opposition to one another, a point made clear by Darrell Bock:

What the Jewish leaders had set up as a choice between rival options, Jesus turned into a set of relationships where no absolute choice is required, merely discerning what belongs to whom. Jesus is no revolutionary, nor is he a servant of Rome. He urges that the government be honored, and God obeyed. So Jesus avoids the trap, leaving his listeners amazed. The text is not so much of speaking of two realms so that one should separate church and state, as it is affirming that government and God are each a part of the creation with their own set of relationships, with God having priority.[72]

God has the ultimate authority, but He also allows the state to have its own authority, which is significant because it notes that the Christian lives in the spheres of both. Caesar is not God and is not to be followed blindly. Both church and state have a role and should be appropriately honored. Jesus recognized that Caesar had a specific sphere of authority, as did God. The coins that belonged to Caesar helped him to run the economy, so people should pay him what was owed. However, they should also understand that God should also get what was due to Him.[73]

Mark 11–12 shows that Jesus rejects an intimate connection between church and state because He recognizes both the relative autonomy of the state in His response to give to Caesar what is rightly his, but He also rejects a form of theocratic worship that rejects the importance of other nations. In this way, Mark 11–12 helps frame two serious issues that American Christians must consider in how they connect a patriotic understanding of church and state: the flag's role in the church and patriotic liturgy in worship.

Visual Hermeneutics:
The American Flag

In the United States, American flags are significant symbols of patriotism; this is also true in most American congregations. In the United States, 60 percent of churches across all denominations and faiths have flags featured in their church building. Protestant churches in the United States have a high percentage of flags in their buildings, with a 76.5 percent chance of having one.[74] Symbols of

---

[72] Bock, *Mark*, 306.

[73] Bock, *Mark*, 306.

[74] Yoshito Ishio, et al., "American Flags in Religious Congregations in the United States," *Journal of Church and State* 61 (2018): 442. Interestingly, Jewish congregations fly the flag at 90 percent. The Protestant denomination with

civil religion are most visible during times of trial. The use of flags in America and American churches grew significantly after 9/11, where they became symbols of national identity and were flown to symbolize people's commitment and connections to their fellow citizens.[75]

The flag is the central symbol of a highly patriotic nation, and displaying it is readily seen as a statement affirming one's allegiance to the United States. In this way, the flag is essential to maintaining and reproducing American national identity and is one of the most "evocative American national symbols" because it plays a critical role in focusing on national attachment.[76] If American flag display is so prevalent among American churches, and if it is one of the central symbols of American patriotism and identity, it is appropriate to ask how the flag should be viewed in the American church.[77] Should the American flag—and the patriotic loyalty that accompanies it—be embraced in totality, or should care be taken to ensure that the church is not embracing a view of the state that it should not?

There are at least four views regarding how the American flag should be viewed within the context of the American church. First, some engage the church because of their love for the state,

---

the highest percentage of flag usage is the Southern Baptist Convention, with 81.7 percent of churches with at least one flag in their building. Black Protestants have the lowest percentage of having a flag in their building, with 37.1 percent reporting a flag.

[75] Linda Skitka, "Patriotism or Nationalism? Understanding Post-September 11, 2001, Flag-Display Behavior," *Journal of Applied Social Psychology* 35 (2005): 2009. Seventy-four to eighty-two percent of Americans responded to the events of 9/11 by displaying flags on homes, cars, or their person.

[76] Markus Kemmelmeier and David Winter, "Sowing Patriotism, but Reading Nationalism? Consequences of Exposure to the American Flag," *Political Psychology* 29, no. 6 (2008): 859–861.

[77] Ferdinand Piper stated that certain monuments and symbols have a spiritual character. His "monumental theology" connected gothic architecture with theology. While the flag is not technically a monument, its symbolism carries a certain weight that closely resembles the point that Piper was trying to communicate. His analogy is helpful in that it helps people come to terms with the enormous "spiritual" weight that symbols like the flag possess. See Ferdinand Piper, *Einleitung in die Monumentale Theologie: Eine Geschichte der chrislichen kunstarchälogie und Epigraphik* (Mittenwald: Mäander, 1978), 1–8.

which leads the flag to have such a heavy presence that it is sacrosanct. So, removing it is seen as an affront to the state *and* the church. Second, some are thankful for the state but understand that the state is not ultimate. In this way, people see the flag as representing the country for which they are very thankful. The flag as a symbol for America is essential but not sacrosanct. Third, some see tensions with the state, so they prioritize the church while respecting the state's authority as seen in Scripture. In this way, the flag represents the biblical authority of the state. To them, the flag reminds them of the honor that is due to the nation because of the created order, but it has no real power in the church. Fourth, some stress the church's purity while losing sight of the state's authority. In this way, some have no patriotic attachment to the country or the country's symbols and, as a result, do not see having flags in the church as being appropriate. It is essential to see how these views of the American flag affect how Christians view patriotic loyalty within the church.

The Flag as a Necessary Symbol

For people who engage the church because of their love for the state, the flag is an indispensable symbol for the church's life and health. Carolyn Marvin and David Ingle —following Émile Durkheim— posit that the American flag is the totem symbol of American civil religion and is the central object of group cohesion.[78] As the totem symbol of America, civil religion has an extreme religious power: Americans have rarely sacrificed, bled, or died for their faith, but they have quite often done so for their country.[79] The themes of honor and sacrifice are important to most Americans and figure very prominently in the military, deepening the sense of patriotism and national attachment.[80] However, deepening the sense of patriotism

---

[78] S. P. Huntington stated, "It seems probable that in almost no other country is the flag so pervasively present and so central to national identity." S. P. Huntington, *Who Are We? The Challenges to America's National Identity* (New York: Simon & Schuster, 2004), 126.

[79] Carolyn Marvin and David Ingle, *Blood Sacrifice and the Nation: Totem Rituals and the American Flag* (Cambridge: Cambridge, 1999), 1–2, 9.

[80] Kemmelmeier and Winter, "Sowing Patriotism?" 860.

around the flag allows for an almost sacralization of the flag, which is problematic because it can lead to patriotism becoming a central part of worship.[81]

Seeing the flag as a necessary symbol within the church can lead it to be seen and treated as a sacred object, leading to idolatry because it is synonymous with a person's faith. As Marvin and Ingle note, the flag "is not *like* religion; it *is* religion. Nor is it casually religious."[82] While the nation is not ultimate, many make the flag an indispensable patriotic symbol present in worship, making it appear almost sacred. This is dangerous because to make a national symbol sacred contributes to the state becoming a primary potential source of idolatry. James Wood notes this danger:

> The proclivity of Americans to make sacred their national symbols and the nation-state they represent and invoking God's name in support of American nationalism and patriotism threatens the very essence of America's nationhood and the

---

[81] There have been many attempts to ratify a flag desecration amendment to the United States Constitution. While these have ultimately failed, the use of the term "desecration" implies that there is a sacred character to the flag. For an assessment of the theological implications of some of these attempts, see Robert Jewett and Constance Collora, "On Turning the Flag into a Sacred Object," *Journal of Church and State* 37 (1995): 741–752; James Wood, "Making a Nation's Flag a Sacred Symbol," *Journal of Church and State* 31 (1989): 375–380. Robert Jewett notes, "Any attempt to make the nation's flag sacred—to endow this secular symbol with the holiness required for "desecration"—not only undermines our political freedom but belittles our worship of the Creator. . . . Should we respect the flag? Always. Should we worship the flag? Never. We salute the flag, but we reserve worship for God." Jewett and Collora, "On Turning the Flag into a Sacred Object," 742. For a more legal view of the issues surrounding flag desecration, see Sheldon Nahmod, "The Sacred Flag and the First Amendment," *Indiana Law Journal* 66 (1991): 511–548; Mohammed Wattad, "The Meaning of Wrongdoing—A Crime of Disrespecting the Flag: Grounds for Preserving National Unity," *San Diego International Law Journal* 5 (2008): 5–62.

[82] Marvin and Ingle, *Blood Sacrifice and the Nation*, 25.

integrity of authentic religious faith. In doing so, the state becomes an idol, and religion is profaned.[83]

The flag in churches may have a similar function to signifying to devotees that Christianity is intimately connected to national identity and patriotism through the national flag's sacredness. Exposure to this seemingly sacred flag can reinforce a loyalty toward a national identity at others' expense.[84] Few things threaten the separation of church and state than a flag seen as sacred, and any attempt to make the flag sacred undermines both political freedom and belittles the worship of a holy God.[85] If the flag is a necessary symbol within the church, there is a connection between one's absolute loyalty being directed toward the nation and its symbols, and the issue remains if the loyalty toward the country is at odds with the proper loyalty that should be directed toward God. There is much danger in sacralizing secular ideals and symbols because they made something represented by the symbol into something that is in itself sacred. This necessitates a level of worship towards the symbol, which is, by definition, idolatry, and must be avoided at all costs.

The Flag as a Needed Symbol

Many Christians see America as something to be truly thankful for, and while the nation is not ultimate, this leads to the American flag as being a needed symbol within the church because it is a reminder of God's providence. For many, America is a country that, through God's providence, has become a shining light in the world, and as a result, the flag should be seen as a symbol that links the past with the present.[86] In this way, the flag represents something that a

---

[83] Wood, "Making a Nation's Flag a Sacred Symbol," 380.

[84] As Markus Kemmelmeier and David Winter note, "[P]atriotic Americans who display the flag may indeed be sowing patriotism, but reaping nationalism." Kemmelmeier and Winter, "Sowing Patriotism, but Reading Nationalism?" 871.

[85] Jewett and Collora, "On Turning the Flag into a Sacred Object," 742.

[86] In this way, the flag can be seen to be "living history." Kelebogile Resane, "Statues, Symbols, and Signages: Monuments towards Socio-Political Divisions, Dominance and Patriotism?" *HTS* 74 (2018): 7. David Batstone and

Christian should be thankful for, and having a flag within the church is simply a way to show "respect to whom respect is owed" and "honor to whom honor is owed" (Rm 13:7). Additionally, the flag can represent a collective memory, which leads to strong attachment and patriotism. The flag and what it represents can lead to an almost intimate connection between church and state because it sees God's hand in the nation to be most clearly seen in the church. Many churches, for instance, could be interpreted not only as places of worship but also, and perhaps even primarily, as quasi-religious extensions of the state's power if an idealized version of the nation is too connected to the workings of the church.[87] Patriotism that leads a Christian to be thankful is a patriotism that can be encouraged; however, care must be urged so that the American flag's presence in congregations does not lead to signifying to devotees that religious faith is intertwined with national identity and patriotism.[88]

The Flag as a Neutral Symbol

Many see the American flag as a national symbol only and not a religious one. In this way, the flag is neutral in the church's life because there should be no religious attachment to it. It is important that the church does not confuse Christianity with the state and that Christianity is not wrapped up in the nation's flag.[89] For people who hold to this view, the flag is not a religious symbol but leads to a proper sense of patriotic attachment. The church and state are separate here, even if the Christian sees God's providence in the nation's working. In this way, patriotism is primarily focused on

Eduardo Mendieta also pick up on this idea in regards to the flag. They see the "flag not as an object but as a history—the history of the acts of representation undertaken by a community of citizens." Batstone and Mendieta, *The Good Citizen* (New York: Routledge, 1999), 2.

[87] John Cilliers, "God in Granite? Aesthetic-Theological Perspectives on the Monumentalisation of Religion," *Scriptura* 114 (2015): 3.

[88] Yoshito Ishio, et al., "American Flags in Religious Congregations in the United States," 434.

[89] Joshua Berrus, "The Church's Relationship with Patriotism and Politics: An Evaluation of Francis A. Schaeffer and John Howard Yoder" (master's thesis, Southeastern Baptist Theological Seminary, 2008), 30.

promoting the welfare of one's nation but is neutral concerning the evaluation of others and within the walls of the church.[90]

Christians who see the flag as a neutral symbol understand that it represents their nation, but this does not lead them to be such ardent patriots that they place loyalty to the state as equal the loyalty to God. In essence, they look to their patriotic attachments in the same way as Israel was supposed to in Jeremiah 29. Just as Israel was supposed to seek Babylon's welfare while they were in captivity, Christians in America should seek the welfare of the nation. Seeing the flag as a neutral symbol allows Christians to seek the nation's welfare while they stay faithful to Christ while not equating the two as equals. To be sure, the flag does have symbolic meaning, but viewing it in this manner allows it to have an important place in the life of the Christian citizen but not a sacred place in danger of becoming idolatrous. In this way, the flag can be seen not just as an object of patriotism but as an object of humble patriotism because it is rooted in being a faithful citizen.

The Flag as a Negative Symbol

While many see the flag positively, some see the flag as a symbol to be avoided. While 60 percent of churches across all Protestant denominations in the United States have an American flag in their church building, many do not. Less than half of all Roman Catholic congregations have a flag in their church, while only 37.1 percent of Black Protestant churches have a flag in their worship space. Additionally, many churches of a more minority faith tradition, such as Eastern Orthodox, Jehovah's Witness, Mormons, Buddhists, Hindus, and Muslims, do not display an American flag. In these religious traditions, only 15.5 percent of congregations display a flag.[91]

While there is no specific reason for American congregations *not* to display the American flag, many choose not to. This means that many hold different perspectives on whether the flag is an appropriate symbol within a church's walls. For some, the

---

[90] Kemmelmeier and Winter, "Sowing Patriotism?" 863.

[91] Yoshito Ishio, et al., "American Flags in Religious Congregations in the United States," 442.

national flag's presence in religious settings blurs the line between church and state, and creates a connection of exposure to the flag that spans many major social institutions, including religion, sports, education, and politics. Americans encounter the flag in almost every social sphere: congregations, schools, sporting events, businesses, and government buildings.[92] It is possible that seeing the flag in so many places can lead people of faith to divorce themselves from this to be faithful to their unique nature as people of faith. Experimental research reveals that exposure to the flag has implications for people's attitudes and actions.[93] Some, by rejecting the flag as a symbol, may be attempting to divorce themselves—and the church—from negative associations.

People who see the flag as a negative symbol keep the flag out of their churches. While the reasoning for why may be varied, they are keeping their conception of church and state entirely separate. While this may be an attempt to keep away from idolatry, it may also be an overreaction because it may lead to negative views on a Christian's role in citizenship. Both Jesus and Paul noted that the state has a specified role in the world due to its God-given authority. If one does not recognize that authority, there may be a potential danger of rejecting that authority altogether. True, Americans can get quite obsessed with their flag, but is a total rejection of the state in the church necessary? While care must be taken so that the presence of the American flag in congregations

---

[92] Yoshito Ishio, et al., "American Flags in Religious Congregations in the United States," 447.

[93] David Buts, et al., "Liberty and Justice for All? Implications of Exposure to the U.S. Flag for Intergroup Relations," *Personality and Social Psychology Bulletin* 33 (2007): 396–408; Kemmelmeier and Winter, "Sowing Patriotism, but Reading Nationalism?"; Travis Carter, et al., "A Single Exposure to the American Flag Shifts Support toward Republicanism up to 8 Months Later," *Psychological Science* 22 (2011): 1011–1018.

does not lead to an intertwining of patriotism and faith, care must also be taken to not reject the role of the state for the church.

A Nuanced Approach to the
Flag in Church

In the United States, patriotic symbols and rituals bear a striking resemblance to traditional rites and symbols. If the symbol of national faith is the American flag, it can also be the central object of its worship. This is not to say that flags, in and of themselves, are always idolized, but great care must be taken to distinguish between the flag and the country it represents and the proper object of worship, which is God. God knows the power of symbols, which is why he forbid Israel from making symbols or representations of Himself in the second commandment. God was warning against the potential pull of idols in commanding that no image be made of Himself; if God's image is not made and used in worship, why would people place so much importance on the nation's symbol? The flag remains a potential for idolatry because of its very present nature in Americans' lives and the church. Modern people usually misunderstand idolatry because it is not merely the practice of worshipping through statues, pictures, or symbols as actual focal points for veneration; instead, it is an entire religious system and lifestyle counter to what God desired worship to be. The attractions of idolatry were compelling and tended to continually draw the Israelites away from true worship and obedience to God.[94]

Great pastoral care and wisdom must be used in dealing with the American flag within a church and within her buildings. Since the flag is such a powerfully visual symbol, it communicates a message. In essence, the American flag can serve as a visual hermeneutic that declares the nation's importance and its loyalty to her. If loyalty to America is associated with the worship of God, how will people not commit idolatry? For some, the cross looks best when it is side by side with an American flag, and Christian faithfulness looks safest when seen through a lens of civil religion

---

[94] Douglas Stuart, *Exodus*, The New American Commentary (Nashville: Broadman & Holman, 2006), 450.

that sees America as God's chosen nation. This is both wrong, sinful, and arrogant. God is the God of the nations and uses all nations to bring about His will on earth. To see God through an American lens conflates the worship of the country with God and results in idolatry. It is more important to be Christ-like than to attempt to be a patriotic American; therefore, conflating Christianity with American exceptionalism through the flag's symbolism necessitates an ethic of national superiority that demands ultimate loyalty.

Does one's absolute loyalty belong to the nation or its symbols? While the obvious answer is "no," the average observer may not see its symbols' danger. The United States flag code states, "When displayed from a staff in a church or public auditorium, the flag of the United States of America should hold the position of superior prominence, in advance of the audience, and in the position of honor at the clergyman's or speaker's right as he faces the audience."[95] Where churches display the Christian flag, what is being communicated when the national flag holds "superior prominence"? Does the United States flag code, in itself, almost declare a visual hermeneutic that the nation-state is to be the recipient of higher honor and greater respect than the church itself?

The symbolic significance of this display of the flag is highly relevant. Most churches follow the American flag code when displaying the American flag. This code declares that when the flag is displayed, it is put on the speaker's right hand, giving it the position of "superior prominence" and the highest honor.[96] Other flags, such as the Christian flag in Protestant worship settings, are supposed to be displayed on the speaker's left, which indicates a lesser prominence. While the average onlooker is probably ignorant of what is being communicated, and Jesus did not command that we create a Christian flag, what is being stated by the flag's positioning? If the American flag is supposed to have a more prominent place than even the Christian flag, does that not communicate a message that should be avoided? Should America, through the flag, be the recipient of higher honor and, quite possibly, greater respect than of

---

[95] 36 U.S.C. chap. 10 §175 (1994).

[96] "Superior prominence" is the specific language used in the code. Ibid.

Jesus and the church itself? Of course not. Therefore, removing national symbols from the church might be a relatively small gesture, but it might be essential. It is in the gathering of the church that the church identifies herself as the body of Christ. Therefore, especially during the gathered assembly, to make a national symbol sacred is as much a violation of the first and second commandments as the worship of the golden calf at Sinai.[97] The claim is *not* that one cannot be patriotic or pledge allegiance to the United States flag without breaking the second commandment but that to do so in the confines of a worship setting that is supposed to worship "Jesus as Lord" is extremely close to idolatry.[98] Great care must be taken in a church's endorsement of the flag inside the confines of the church building, where allegiance must be to God alone.

Patriotic Hymns:
The Dangers of Patriotic Liturgy

Across the nation, during almost any national holiday, such as Memorial Day, Independence Day, or Veteran's Day, one will find Sunday morning church services filled with the playing of hymns centered around national ideology such as "My Country 'Tis of Thee," "America the Beautiful," and "Battle Hymn of the Republic." Patriotic hymns sung in church can be seen as a type of civil religion. Following Robert Bellah, many speak of the prevalence in America of this type of civil religion, which is used to unify Americans around a shared sense of culture and purpose, but perhaps singing patriotic songs in worship services ought to be seen as a type of national liturgy.[99] These songs, and the patriotic services that often accompany them, serve as a national and patriotic liturgy

---

[97] Shane Akerman, "Classical Trinitarian Theology and the Idolatry of Nationalism: The Doctrine of the Trinity as a Critique of Political Theology" (PhD diss., Claremont Graduate University, 2020), 274–275.

[98] Nancy Duff, "Locating God in all the Wrong Places: The Second Commandment and American Politics," *Interpretation* 60 (2006): 197.

[99] Robert Bellah, "Civil Religion in America," *Dædalus* 96 (1967): 1–21.

because they use rituals and songs to reinforce a particular type of American group identity and view of the world.[100]

Building on concepts of death, sacrifice, and honor, many patriotic songs are sung in church and present the United States as an almost mythical creature that is both chosen by God and innocent in the world's affairs. Building on the American Revolution, many see America as a nation created by God with a God-given mission in the world. Thus, for example, singing the popular refrain in "America the Beautiful" that says, "America! America! God shed his grace on thee," posits that America is a chosen nation:

> Oh beautiful for patriot dream
> That sees beyond the years
> Thine alabaster cities gleam,
> Undimmed by human tears!
> America! America!
> God shed his grace on thee,
> And crown they good with brotherhood
> From sea to shining sea.

It presents an America that is pure and undimmed by the world's events. Seeing America as chosen—or special—is a crucial element of civil religion and patriotic liturgy.

The way one worships shapes the way one believes. Christians must be continuously formed and shaped in their faith, belief, and holiness. This is especially true in the church's missional endeavors, where Christians attempt to share Christ with others and reach the nations. Any mission activity that rejects or minimizes the sacramental presence and worship of Jesus Christ is greatly impoverished and weakened. In Christian liturgy, the congregation publicly confesses their faith in Christ, a public witness of whom

---

[100] John Wilsey, *American Exceptionalism and Civil Religion: Reassessing the History of an Idea* (Downers Grove: InterVarsity, 2015), 27; William Cavanaugh, *Migrations of the Holy: God, State, and the Political Meaning of the Church* (Grand Rapids: Eerdmans, 2011), 115–116.

they worship and what is important to them.[101] However, in some patriotic-centered church services, people will proudly stand and pledge allegiance to the American flag and sing patriotic hymns with a strangely religious fervor. Patriotic-centered hymns in church services combined with the American flag's heavy presence can send the wrong message that a church's liturgy—and focus of worship—is the nation.

The Nations in Worship:
Toward a Proper Liturgy

Christian nationalism and patriotism run the risk of wrapping American exceptionalism in the Christian language of political rhetoric, which is especially dangerous in the context of worship. If civil religion is heavily present in many American churches through the highly symbolic flag and patriotic-centered worship services, how must one look at the proper understanding of a church's liturgy? Paul stated that all praise should be directed toward the Lord. For example, every use of "Lord" refers to Jesus, so Paul clearly showed that proper worship should be directed toward Christ alone.[102] Patriotic liturgy looks back on the sacrifice of service members and blood spilled for the nation, while Christian liturgy looks both back on the blood shed by Christ for His people but also forward at His eventual return. What does the Bible say about patriotic-centered worship services that are so prevalent in churches across America?

Colossians 3:16/Ephesians 5:19

Colossians 3:16 (and similarly, Ephesians 5:19) gives a framework on what is supposed to be present in the gathered church assembly. Paul said, "[T]he word of Christ" must be present in "teaching and admonishing one another in all wisdom." Additionally, Paul told the church at Colossae that they should be "singing psalms and hymns

---

[101] Timothy Quill, "Liturgical Worship," in *Perspectives on Christian Worship: 5 Views*, ed. Ligon Duncan, et al. (Nashville: Broadman & Holman, 2009), 75.

[102] Clinton Arnold, *Ephesians*, Zondervan Exegetical Commentary on the New Testament (Grand Rapids: Zondervan, 2010), 354.

and spiritual songs, with thankfulness in your hearts to God." Paul's point was that songs are meaningful and complement teaching in worship.

In Christian liturgy, songs can clarify biblical theology's great themes and prepare people's hearts for proclamation and worship. The grammar shows that singing in the church is viewed as one of the major church forms of teaching and admonition.[103] The three terms "psalms," "hymns," and "songs" are the most common words used in the LXX for religious songs and generally occur interchangeably in the titles of the psalms. Firm distinctions cannot be made between the three terms, but they refer to the full range of singing, which the Holy Spirit leads.[104] Whatever the songs Paul spoke of were, he cautioned that they must be spiritual and not secular. Together, "psalms and hymns and spiritual songs" speak to the entire extent of musical expression in the worship of the early church and show that the message in the music is incredibly important. Music in the church is only appropriate when used in pointing beyond itself to the worship of Christ.[105]

Revelation's Contribution to Christian Liturgy

Revelation 7:9 gives a beautiful picture of what worship will look like in heaven. John noted that there is a multitude made up of people from every nation, tribe, people, and language, which stressed that this group is ethnically distinct from the Jews who are sealed in the first part of the chapter. Additionally, they are incredibly diverse from one another: ethnically, tribally, and linguistically. The multitude comes from different nations, which shows how the gospel of Jesus Christ has filled the entire earth.[106]

---

[103] Ben Witherington III, *The Letters to Philemon, the Colossians, and the Ephesians: A Socio-Rhetorical Commentary on the Captivity Epistles* (Grand Rapids: Eerdmans, 2007), 181.

[104] Peter O'Brien, *The Letter to the Ephesians*, The Pillar New Testament Commentary (Grand Rapids: Eerdmans, 1999), 395–396.

[105] Richard Melick, *Philippians, Colossians, Philemon*, The New American Commentary (Nashville: Broadman & Holman, 1991), 305.

[106] Paige Patterson, *Revelation*, The New American Commentary (Nashville: Broadman & Homan, 2012), 200.

This is the picture that Jesus had in mind when he criticized the temple because it was not a house of prayer for the nations. When God is worshipped, people join a multitude of saints from all peoples and eras of history. Understanding this should make Christians less likely to have idolatrous allegiance to any nation.[107]

True worship of Christ transcends all time, culture, language, and nation. Jesus is the supreme center of Christian worship; thus, all worship must be directed toward Him. Additionally, Christian worship has allegiance shaping power. Worshipping Jesus shapes loyalty to the kingdom of God just as emperor worship consolidated allegiance to Rome.[108] Therefore, care must be taken to worship Jesus, who is the "King of the nations" (Rv 15:3), which further explains that God is the sovereign ruler over all nations.[109] To offer songs in Christian worship that celebrate America rather than the King of the nations is potentially troubling because it can lead to celebrating a narrow view of God that void of his relationship to the nations. Worshippers run a risk of failing to see how the nation's songs and rituals compete with the worship of Christ. Therefore, Christians must use discernment when singing patriotic songs that foster solidarity among Americans and heighten patriotic attachment, but might not fully express who they are in Christ. Patriotic liturgy runs a risk of not focusing proper attention upon the God of the Bible, who demands loyalty, honor, and praise.[110]

Jeremiah 29:
The Church as Humble Exiles

The prophet Jeremiah can be seen through the lens of theopolitics. There was much tension between Jeremiah and the nation of Israel

---

[107] J. Nelson Kraybill, *Apocalypse and Allegiance: Worship, Politics, and Devotion in the Book of Revelation* (Grand Rapids: Brazos, 2010), 187.

[108] Kraybill, *Apocalypse and Allegiance*, 187.

[109] G. K. Beale, *The Book of Revelation: A Commentary on the Greek Text*, New International Greek Testament Commentary (Grand Rapids: Eerdmans, 1999), 795.

[110] Craig Watts, "Singing the Songs of Babylon in the Worship of the Church," *Encounter* 74 (2013–2014): 10, 15.

and her prophets. This tension was partly political because the people saw Jeremiah as both a traitor and a Babylonian sympathizer (37:11–16). However, the tension was also theological because Jeremiah was convinced the nation was under God's judgment and would be punished, whereas his prophetic opponents argued (6:14; 28:10–11) that since God had given them the land as part of the covenant, there was nothing to fear, for the exile would be quick.[111] Jeremiah 29 was written sometime after 586 BC during the Babylonian exile, where the people of Israel suffered great hardships, including the loss of their culture. More importantly, for the Jews, they lost both their ability to worship at the temple and their way of life.[112] The Babylonian exile threatened everything for the Jews. When the Jews were defeated and captured, they immediately lost their sense of identity and power and had to come to terms with how they were no longer a dominant political nation. Initially, the Jews were in a state of shock at this, but they came to recognize this as a result of God's punishment for their sinfulness and unfaithfulness.

Jeremiah 29 stands as God's plan for the nation of Israel, who now found themselves without much political hope. What were they to do now that they had lost all of their political and national power? God commanded that the Jews not cower in shame; instead, God commanded Israel to engage the city actively.[113] By "seeking the welfare of the city," they were to engage with the dominant culture around them. This would require the understanding that God had "sent" them into the exile that they were experiencing. Nowhere in the context of Jeremiah 29 were the Jews told that their stay would be brief; instead, it seemed that they were to settle down to

---

[111] F. B. Huey, *Jeremiah, Lamentations*, vol. 16, *The New American Commentary* (Nashville: Broadman & Holman, 1993), 31–32.

[112] Psalm 137:1 shows the Jews' apparent brokenness: "By the waters of Babylon, there we sat down and wept, when we remembered Zion."

[113] Jeremiah 29:4–7, "Thus says the LORD of hosts, the God of Israel, to all the exiles whom I have sent into exile from Jerusalem to Babylon: Build houses and live in them; plant gardens and eat their produce. Take wives and have sons and daughters; take wives for your sons, and give your daughters in marriage, that they may bear sons and daughters; multiply there, and do not decrease. But seek the welfare of the city where I have sent you into exile, and pray to the LORD on its behalf, for in its welfare you will find your welfare."

understand that their stay would be lengthy. In other words, the people needed to settle in for the long haul and live a normal life in a foreign country. Additionally, Jeremiah 29 understands that Israel's and Babylon's welfare were tied to each other: if Babylon prospered, then the people of Israel would as well.

The church in America seems to have lost its way and influence in the culture. The church is no longer the dominant culture but is seemingly subservient to the world around it and no longer seems to be the "city on a hill" that Jesus envisioned. What is the American church to do? Do we live in a defeated manner while we await the return of Jesus, or do we live in isolation, staying away from the sinful culture that exists around us? Jeremiah 29 and the concept of exile is a rich metaphor for the church today because the church and the culture that it resides in are no longer in a mutual alliance. Just as the nation of Israel questioned what their role and purpose was in Babylon, the church today must also seek to find its purpose. The parallels are there for a discussion of what the church today can learn from the nation of Israel's exile.

Walter Brueggemann argues that being in exile brings to mind a sense of "rootlessness" for people who live as a group that seems to have been orphaned.[114] Being in exile means one is wandering while he is away from his real home. In this state of wandering, the Jews lost their purpose, which was rooted in God's worship at the temple. Thus, the people of Israel had not only lost their home; they had lost their roots. In this way, the church is a group that has been uprooted and transplanted to a foreign place where, on the outside, there seems to be little purpose due to the perceived rootlessness. This rootlessness is one that makes us yearn for another place—a place that we understand. It can easily seem as if the church is still wandering around with no purpose in life, much like the exilic Jews.

While the exilic period was a specific time in history for the Jews, it is a metaphor for the time that the church finds itself. According to Brueggemann, the challenge is to understand that the metaphor of exile allows the church to understand its true place in

---

[114] Walter Brueggemann, *Cadences of Home: Preaching among Exiles* (Louisville: Westminster, 1997), 5.

the world. It allows the church to have access to scriptural resources in new ways.

> The suffering of exile is for the Old Testament, the matrix in which the hope of God is most powerfully and characteristically at work. The exile is the place where God's faithful promises work a profound newness. . . . Prophetic faith is hard-nosed realism that is resistant to romantic, ideological escapism. No pretense based in religious fantasy can extricate God's people from their actual place in history. Those who permit religion to abrogate historical-political reality is a lie.[115]

Just as the Old Testament exile did not lead the Jews to abandon their faith nor retreat into isolation, the church today must be willing to stand her ground in such a way as to see the mission of God continued within the culture of today. The church must reject notions of national superiority by understanding that it is an exilic citizen sent by God into the world to live faithful lives and not patriotic ones.

Despite God's judgment on Israel, He still had a plan for them, and the very plan included those who had taken them into captivity. This is a reminder that the "LORD of hosts" (Jer 29:4) is not bound to Jerusalem or Judah or any other nation. God is the God of the entire world and can use any nation to bring about his sovereign plan. This is important for Americans to understand. Often, America is presented as some sort of new Israel, but in reality, she is more like Babylon, a foreign country where Christian citizens, like ancient Israel, are in exile living attempting to seek the welfare of the city.[116] However, just as God used the real Babylon to bless Israel, God can use America to bless the church in America. After

---

[115] Brueggemann, *Cadences of Home*, 256–258.

[116] Augustine also used this Babylon imagery as a way to see a Christian's life in the midst of church and state. Christians seek the welfare of the city by possessing "peace in this life, since so long as the two cities are intermingled we also make use of the peace of Babylon—although the People of God is by faith set free from Babylon, so that in the meantime they are only pilgrims in the midst of her." Augustine, "Book XIX," ch. 26, 892.

all, patriotic Americans should find it easy to seek the welfare of America and to connect their welfare with it.

Jeremiah 29 gives three critical lessons on living as political exiles in a distracted and divided nation. First, it suggests that Christians should live a life of peace (shalom) in their country. Verse 7, translated "welfare" in the ESV, is the Hebrew word שָׁלוֹם, which means "peace." Christians in America (and all other nations) must seek to be humble citizens by living a life of biblical faithfulness. Humility is more important to a Christian than who is the president or who controls the United States Senate or any other host of political issues. This is not to say that politics are not important, but it is not ultimate, and political leanings of Christians should not result in arrogant citizens. Second, Jeremiah 29 suggests that Christians in America should live a life of prayer for their country. Understanding that a Christian is a citizen requires that prayer must be offered on the nation's behalf. Indeed, if Christians find their own welfare in the nation they reside in, they must be prayerful toward it, which requires a humility that supersedes national attachments. Third, Jeremiah 29 suggests that Christians must live a life of hope. Just as Israel had to come to terms with the fact that they were no longer in their natural home, Christians in America must understand that we have a supranational identity that is not confined to the nation. This requires us to see that no matter how good or bad America is, our hope is in a greater kingdom.

As American Christians come to terms with being exiles in a country that is not truly their home, there is an excellent opportunity for faithfulness. Exile in Babylon was a great opportunity for the Jews to return to the true nature of being God's chosen nation because it offered them an opportunity for faithfulness. In the same way, when American Christians see that they are exiles in America, they have an opportunity to return to what the church is supposed to be: a missional church living as humble citizens.

Conclusions

Christians run the risk of falling prey to the appeal of various ideologies, despite their commitment to the exclusivity of the gospel. So, it is not surprising that many have fallen prey to a form of Christian nationalism. This is especially true in America, where the nation is seen as divinely chosen by God to be a shining light in the world. However, God's grace is not reserved for one specific nation, and there is no scriptural basis for suggesting that God has specifically chosen the United States for a salvific role in the world. To wrongly connect God directly to the United States while ignoring His sovereign claim to the rest of the world engenders conflict between competing centers of loyalty. If God is only concerned with the United States, then being loyal to the nation is proper, right, and godly, but if God is truly sovereign and uses all nations to bring about his plan, can a Christian see his country as the only one that truly matters? It is arrogant and foolish to think that America is the only God-favored country in the world, when it is clear that He has a love and plan for all nations.

Christians must be careful not to pay their nation honor due only to God, but that does not mean that one cannot be patriotic. When rightly defined, patriotism offers a Christian an opportunity to live as humble citizens who are living as exiles until they reach their final home. Christians who connect patriotism with worship cannot exist as humble citizens because they are in danger of exchanging their citizenship in heaven with their citizenship in America. So, great care must be exercised so that a Christian truly knows where his true allegiances lie.

Overly patriotic Americans run a significant risk in intimately connecting God and country. While not consciously worshipping America as God or worshipping a different God, extremely patriotic Americans confuse the worship of one with the need to worship both simultaneously. As Nancy Duff states: while not committing outright apostasy, "in seeking to be faithful to God, they discern God's purposes being worked out through the purpose and mission, policies, actions, and destiny of the United States." In so doing, they are breaking the second commandment by locating God too closely with America and accepting "cross and flag to stand for virtually the same thing diminishes the integrity of the Gospel; and allows it to be taken over by the entity that stands behind the symbol of the flag rather than the One who has been revealed through the cross."[117] A Church that is as much American as it is Christian has lost its distinctive identity and cannot be a church that takes the commands of Scripture seriously.

On the other hand, there are some who think Christians should not be patriotic, so there should not be any loyalty toward the country. This fails the test of good citizenship according to the Bible because Scripture is clear that the state has a God-given authority and to not respect that authority is to not respect the God who established it. While various levels of patriotism can be advocated, a Christian must have a biblical conception of citizenship, which leads to an understanding that the nation is worthy of a certain level of respect and loyalty. This necessitates a certain level of patriotism.

There is some irony in the fact that many Christians can look out across the cultural landscape and see the dangers of many contemporary movements without seeing the potential dangers of patriotism. The dangers of socialism and Marxism are pronounced by Christian conservatives and pastors alike. When Black Lives Matter protests tear up the American flag, or professional athletes kneel at the national anthem, it ruffles many patriotic Christian's feathers.[118] In this way, patriotic attachment to America is almost seen as a test for being an American. So, if Christians want to be good citizens, the logic implies that they must be patriotic.

While many of these contemporary issues are seen as evil (and many rightly are) by patriotic Christians in America, many are also among the first to jump on the "God and country" bandwagon. While patriotism is, at present, tenable for Christians in America, idolatry must always be rejected.[119] Therefore, patriotism must be

---

[117] Duff, "Locating God in all the Wrong Places," 184–185.

[118] While not directly commenting on the role of patriotism in the church, Leonard Doob makes a great statement regarding how important the flag is as a symbol in regards to contemporary demonstrations against the national flag: "The concept of the nation, through verbalizations and slightly extended symbols, in short, acquires a superorganic sacredness of its own. To cast even a verbal slur upon it or its name or other symbol is blasphemy, hence taboo, and quickly and decisively punishable." Leonard Doob, *Patriotism and Nationalism: Their Psychological Foundations* (New Haven: Yale Press, 1964), 33.

[119] It is likely that there will be a day where people who would consider themselves to be patriotic Christian conservatives will no longer pledge allegiance to the flag or stand for the national anthem. Depending on the political changes

seen as a way to be humble citizens and not used as a slow drift toward idolatry. In this way, an American who wants to be faithful to Jesus must do all he can to stay faithful to Christ while living in exile in America. To be appropriately patriotic in America is to realize that exile is an ever-present reality, much like Augustine saw in his day. As he beautifully stated, "[S]ince so long as the two cities are intermingled we also make use of the peace of Babylon— although the People of God is by faith set free from Babylon, so that in the meantime they are only pilgrims in the midst of her."[120]

---

over the next decade or so (this chapter is being finalized in the days after the contentious 2020 presidential election that is still not entirely settled), America could make a significant move toward socialism. Additionally, Democratic policies that define abortion as proper healthcare may eventually include legal infanticide. If America continues to trend toward some of these issues, it is entirely conceivable that Christians may no longer be able in good conscience to be patriotic. If this happens, in an ironic twist, patriots who currently condemn people who are not patriotic for not honoring the flag (and so on) because it does not represent something to them to be proud of will eventually be doing the same thing for the same reasons.

[120] Augustine, *City of God*, 892.

7

Conclusions

American patriotism is a concept that is difficult to understand because the terminology surrounding it is unclear. Some connect patriotism too closely to nationalism, which leads to negative connotations, while others see it as a virtue leading to one's attempt to seek out the good for one's country.[1] The diverse understandings and concepts of patriotism make it a concept that is a worthy topic for academic study, and the misunderstandings of the topic make it clear that there is a need in research. Not only does patriotism need academic study, but it also needs an in-depth theological study. Christians in America find themselves in a very eclectic, diverse, and profoundly political nation. If they are going to attempt to navigate the American cultural landscape, they need to understand how patriotism interacts and affects their faith.

The early Puritan settlers of America had a deep sense that God had ordained the founding and colonization of the New World as an extension of God's sovereign will in the world and was thus a "city on a hill" for the world to see.[2] This belief gave America and her early citizens a sense of mission and purpose that came directly from God and helped form a sense of patriotic duty in America's fabric. This sense of patriotism has stood the test of time, even if it has become something with various definitions within America's citizenry.

Due to the United States' contemporary political culture, there is much polarization on what it means to be a patriotic American. The 9/11 terrorist attacks and the subsequent war on

---

[1] See Alasdair MacIntyre, "Is Patriotism a Virtue?" in *Patriotism*, ed. Igor Primoratz (New York: Humanity, 2002), 43–58.

[2] John Winthrop, "A Modell of Christian Charity," in *Political Thought in America: An Anthology*, ed. Michael Levy (Prospect Heights: Waveland, 1992), 12.

terror, which has lasted almost twenty years; the election of Donald Trump as the forty-fifth president of the United States; and professional athletes kneeling during the national anthem have added to this polarization. Even during the writing of this project, many other issues have arisen that show there is a serious need for biblical scholarship on what it means to be a patriotic Christian in America.[3] These contemporary issues have made the need for a biblical assessment of patriotism more urgent.

Summary of Thesis

"Patriotism" needs a proper definition that can be biblically assessed for Christians to navigate the political landscape in America. In so doing, this project's thesis defines patriotism as "loyalty to one's particular country that involves a personal identification with their country, culture, and people." Building on this definition of patriotism requires a discussion of loyalty as a central aspect to understanding patriotism by looking at familial relationships, friendships, and land, ultimately leading to looking at the apostle Paul as a biblical example of a proper sense of patriotism.

---

[3] The year 2020 has given many opportunities to see how important a biblical sense of patriotism is. 2020 has seen a minor civil rights movement due to perceived police brutality directed toward African Americans through tragic and high-profile deaths of many African Americans (George Floyd, for example). This led to the Black Lives Matter movement becoming a very prominent political voice, stressing social justice. Eventually, some of these protests turned violent through rioting. Building on the Black Lives Matter movement, even more professional athletes and college and high school athletes continued to kneel during the national anthem, furthering a division between people who claimed that doing so was un-American and unpatriotic. While this was going on, COVID-19 shut most of the country (and world) down, which led to even more civil unrest. Mask mandates and mandatory closures of businesses and churches across the nation sparked more discussions of patriotism and tested many people's understanding of what it means to be a good citizen in following local, state, and national authorities. Further, while all of these issues were going on, there was a very contentious presidential election cycle between Donald Trump and Joe Biden. While this chapter is being written almost a month after the election, there still is much confusion and division surrounding it because Trump has not yet conceded, citing voter irregularities.

Summary of Chapter 2

Chapter 2 examined the historical underpinnings of American patriotism that helped guide the country to embrace patriotism's cultural importance. The Puritans' settling of America played an important role in developing a sense of patriotism because they saw America's settling as a heroic and noble errand into the wilderness where Christians were being sent to do God's work in the world. In this way, American Puritans saw themselves as being chosen by God and saw America as God's own city on a hill. The second historical underpinning was the Revolutionary War era, which helped turn the errand into the wilderness into a political venture. The revolutionaries and clergy saw America through a millennial lens, combining millennial theology and republican virtues that became central themes in the relationship between church and state and the revolution itself. This millennial understanding infused patriotism with much religious significance and gave contemporary actions a major place in Americans' lives.

The third historical underpinning in the development of patriotism in America was the Civil War. The Civil War brought about a strong sense of divine providence in the lives of both Northerners and Southerners. Both sides of the Civil War saw themselves as fighting for the Lord and were convinced of their moral rightness. As a result, both anticipated a God-given victory.[4] The Civil War added a nationalistic framework to patriotism since both sides of the war started to see themselves through shared identities found in their respective nations (Confederacy and the Union). Additionally, during this time, national symbols (such as flags) became transcendent symbols of patriotism.

World War II and the Vietnam War also added to the underpinnings of American patriotism. During WWII, America became a world power and was established as a major political player in the world's affairs. Further, America's role in the war left a sense of patriotic pride in most Americans who saw in the country a united front fighting a righteous war against evil. As a result,

---

[4] Kimlyn Bender, "The American Experience of a Darkening and Receding Providence: The Civil War and the Unmaking of an American Religious Synthesis," *Cultural Encounters* 9 (2013): 115.

American militarism became a part of American life, and people began to see troops as citizen soldiers who were, by extension, a symbol of national unity and pride. While WWII was seen as a good war and left a positive effect on patriotism, Vietnam led to a more critical understanding of patriotism. During the Vietnam War, Americans were, for the first time, able to be involved in the front lines of war due to television and the news media. The news gave a much less optimistic view of the war, which influenced Americans' minds. Due to a lack of total enthusiastic support of the war combined with a sense of moral ambiguity about the justification for the war, Americans began to be more open to criticism of the government, leading to a more critical sense of patriotism.

Summary of Chapter 3

Chapter 3 developed a definition of patriotism that was centered around loyalty. "Patriotism" was defined as "loyalty toward one's own home country—and one's home country alone—and personal identification with one's home country, culture, and people." This definition of patriotism is specific enough to be separated from the notions of nationalism and cosmopolitanism and can be biblically assessed. Additionally, this chapter examined how biblical concepts of loyalty are framed through a biblical understanding of filial relationships, friendships, and land.

Loyalty to parents is commanded in the Old Testament and helps in framing patriotic loyalty in two major ways. First, just as a person does not choose to be born within his family, he does not choose the country in which he is born. The command to show honor to one's parents has no qualification, and the command to honor parents is inherent in who they are. In much the same way, patriotism is linked to a person's country via his connection to it through his birth, and there is no qualification that a country must meet in order to be one's object of patriotism. Second, just as a person is commanded to show loyalty to his parents and not someone else's, people are patriotic to their own country and not to another.

Friendship loyalties help frame an understanding of patriotism because they show that they can make a judgment call on to whom they show loyalty. Friendships are based on an individual's decision that calls for a certain level of loyalty to the recipient based upon the nature of the friendship. In the same way, people chose to be loyal to their country. This choice of loyalty is a decision that must be made by an individual to remain patriotic toward his country.

Loyalty to the land is the third way to frame an understanding of patriotic loyalty. First, loyalty to the land is shaped by an understanding that God has given and established all countries' boundaries (Dt 32:8; Acts 17:26). Because God has established all national boundaries and chosen to use the nations for His purpose, it is acceptable to show patriotism toward them. Second, one's homeland is a type of Promised Land—or Eden—in that it is a place for him to belong. One's homeland is now seen as a place with an intimate connection to God, leading to a sense of loyalty.

Summary of Chapter 4

Part of the thesis of this project was that a definition must be given in order to be able to biblical assess the nature of patriotism. To that end, while Chapter 3 defined "patriotism" for the project's scope, Chapter 4 looked at popular and prominent views of patriotism. Additionally, this chapter noted how patriotism, when properly defined, is a far better alternative than nationalism and cosmopolitanism, which are the bookends of a proper understanding of patriotism. Additionally, "nationalism" was shown to be "an attempt to elevate one's nation above all others," which is unbiblical since God established all nations. "Cosmopolitanism" was shown to be "an attempt to ignore the nations in order to become a world citizen." This, too, is unbiblical because it rejects the notion that God has established all nations. Thus, both nationalism and cosmopolitanism were shown to be untenable to the Christian, while a biblical understanding of patriotism can exist.

Summary of Chapter 5

Chapter 5 examined how the apostle Paul stands as a test case for a biblically informed patriotism. Paul was a genuinely multicultural person: he was a Jew and a Roman citizen, but also had dual citizenship with the important and influential ancient city of Tarsus. Paul, and what made Paul who he was, was shown to be a proper basis for a Christian's understanding and practice of patriotism today. This chapter explored Paul's multicultural identity that allowed him to become very aware of politics and culture. Each part of Paul's Greco-Roman character, merged with his Jewish ancestry, made him diverse and helped frame a biblical understanding of patriotism.

Tarsus was an important city of the day and was known as the seat of one of the world's most famous universities. The intellectual nature of Tarsus helped shape Paul's upbringing and set the stage for his understanding of citizenship because he understood how to walk in diverse worlds and cultures simultaneously. Paul's Jewish nature and heritage helped shape his understanding of the gospel, which was heavily influenced by his understanding of the Old Testament. In Philippians 3:5–6, Paul claimed to have advanced in his ancestors' religion and culture far beyond many of his age. Further, he claimed that he was not of "mixed stock" like so many Jews in his day who were living in Palestine.[5] In this way, Paul stressed his pure Jewish heritage, and as a result, Paul had a relationship with Palestine in a way that the average Hellenist did not.

Paul was shaped by being from Tarsus and being a faithful Jew with a pure heritage. In addition to that, Paul was shaped by his Roman citizenship. Paul's citizenship played a significant role in understanding the life of Paul. Paul's claiming to be a Roman citizen gives clear evidence that a Christian does not necessarily need to reject the entire notion of citizenship or empire but can claim to be a part of it while using it for protection that comes from God.[6] Paul's

---

[5] William Hendriksen, *Philippians*, New Testament Commentary (Grand Rapids: Baker, 1962), 156, 159.

[6] Christopher Bryan, *Render to Caesar: Jesus, the Early Church, and the Roman Superpower* (Oxford: Oxford University Press, 2005), 103.

multicultural background made him comfortable with his Roman citizenship. Politically, Paul was Roman; religiously, he was Christian, although heavily influenced by his former life in Judaism.[7] Furthermore, while Paul lived in a deeply political culture, he never allowed it to influence the person that he was in a negative way. He embraced his citizenship and was not against the Roman Empire.

This chapter made the case that Romans 13 is the key to understanding Paul's sense of patriotism. In Romans 13, Paul claimed that every person is to be subject to the governing authorities because God Himself has established them. He claimed that one should not resist the authorities because they are God's servants and ministers for the citizens' good. Romans 13 shows that Paul was neither a political radical nor uninterested in the affairs of the Roman Empire. Instead, it shows that Paul had an understanding of patriotism. First, Romans 13 shows that Paul saw the state as a legitimate authority for believers. Second, Romans 13 shows that Paul was not anti-empire; nor was he intentionally trying to disrupt or subvert the Roman order. Third, Romans 13 also shows that he was not necessarily pro-empire. While Paul was respective toward the empire, he did not wholeheartedly endorse them in all things. Fourth, Romans 13 shows that Paul was not apolitical; nor was he consumed with politics. Fifth, Romans 13 shows that Paul understood that being faithful to Christ would require a Christian to be able to navigate the political tension in the world. In these ways, Romans 13 shows that Paul was a concerned citizen who wanted Christians to understand their role in a structured political society.

By balancing both his Roman citizenship and Jewish heritage, along with his time in Tarsus and Rome, Paul was able to write to his audience, encouraging them to live in tension with the state while being faithful to Christ. Paul's sense of patriotism was rooted in his understanding of the gospel. First, Paul understood that God was the one who established all earthly powers, thereby giving all of them validity, making Christians "subjects" to them. Second, Paul made it clear that all states were allowed to have specified

---

[7] Gordon Zerbe, "Citizenship and Politics According to Philippians," *Direction* 38 (2009): 194.

national boundaries allowing all nations to coexist. Third, Paul understood that the power of all states is limited and finite, and one day, Jesus will return to establish His eternal kingdom. Paul would have been a productive and patriotic citizen because he had a proper understanding of the state's role, but more importantly, he had a proper understanding of the lordship of Christ. Therefore, just like Paul, all Christians must seek to model a proper sense of patriotism toward their nation, showing a proper sense of loyalty to the land, people, and culture.

Summary of Chapter 6

Chapter 6 gave pastoral implications of a proper understanding of patriotism. In a diverse and divisive America, Christians need to understand how patriotism should cause them to live in their political context. This chapter looked at Mark 11 and 12 to discuss Jesus's understanding of both church and state. In Mark 11, Jesus was deeply concerned by how Jews had allowed money changers to overrun the court of the Gentiles, which kept them from being able to worship. Further, this chapter argued that the Jews neglected the court of the Gentiles and made it the center of commerce because they were unconcerned about the Gentiles' ability to worship. The Jews were more concerned about their ability to worship as a people group that they neglected their call to make the temple a place of prayer for the nations. Mark 11 shows Jesus as a political prophet who wanted the church to be a place where all nations were represented, and His indignation for what the temple had become presented Him as a political prophet who was greatly concerned about Israel's love of country, keeping them from their eschatological mission of reaching the nations.[8]

In Mark 12, Jesus addressed His view of how the church should view the state. While the Pharisees and Herodians attempted to trap Jesus in a question about taxes, Jesus used it as a way to show that He viewed the Roman government as a legitimate authority. By

---

[8] Richard Horsley, *Jesus and Empire: The Kingdom of God and the New World Order* (Minneapolis: Fortress, 2003), 93; Richard Bauckham, *The Bible in Politics: How to Read the Bible Politically* (Louisville: Westminster, 2011), 77.

stating that people were to "render to Caesar" what was his, Jesus acknowledged the legitimacy of the Roman government while also distancing Himself from forms of political anarchy, which put him out of step with most understandings of Jewish nationalism of the day.

Additionally, this chapter looked at various understandings of church and state and their importance to understanding citizenship. Augustine's two-cities doctrine called Christians to see themselves as pilgrims in the contemporary political world, while Pope Gelasius I's two-swords doctrine called for Christians to recognize the power of both church and state. Abraham Kuyper's one-kingdom-with-many-spheres doctrine called for Christians to see God as sovereign over both church and state. David VanDrunen's conception of the two-kingdoms doctrine was looked at as a way to see that while God rules both church and state, He does so in different ways. God rules the spiritual kingdom as its redeemer in Christ, and He rules the civil kingdom not as its redeemer but as its creator and sustainer.[9] The two-kingdoms doctrine stresses that Christians should not deny the importance of politics since it has a great bearing on justice, peace, and prosperity of the world. However, it also stresses that Christians should not exalt politics as a means to usher in God's redemptive kingdom. The two-kingdoms doctrine effectively guards against both of these dangerous extremes in understanding the church and the state.[10]

Additionally, this chapter attempted to understand the role of church and state by discussing two significant issues: the American flag's role in the church and the nature of patriotic liturgy in worship. The American flag is the central symbol of a patriotic nation, so the church must understand the flag's nature and what it represents when it is displayed in the church. To that end, a rubric was given to navigate the flag as a patriotic symbol.

Regarding the flag, there are four views regarding how the American flag should be viewed within the church. First, some see the flag as a necessary symbol, which leads the flag to have such a

---

[9] David VanDrunen, "Abraham Kuyper and the Reformed Natural Law and Two Kingdoms Traditions," *Calvin Theological Journal* 42 (2007): 283–284.

[10] David VanDrunen, *Living in God's Two Kingdoms: A Biblical Vision for Christianity and Culture* (Wheaton: Crossway, 2010), 194–195.

heavy presence that it is sacrosanct. Second, some see the flag as a needed symbol because they are thankful for the state, while understanding that it is not ultimate. Third, some recognize tensions with the state, so they prioritize the church while respecting the state's authority as seen in Scripture, seeing the flag as a neutral symbol. Fourth, some stress the church's purity while losing sight of the state's authority, making the flag a negative symbol. It is essential to see how these views of the American flag affect how Christians view patriotic loyalty within the church while developing a nuanced approach to the flag's presence within the church.

This chapter argued against patriotic liturgy within the church because the church should gather to worship Christ. Jesus is the supreme center of Christian worship; thus, all worship must be directed toward him. Therefore, care must be taken to worship Jesus, who is the "King of the nations" (Rv 15:3) and to offer songs in Christian worship that celebrate America rather than the King of the nations is potentially disturbing because it can lead to celebrating a narrow view of God that voids His relationship to other nations. Singing patriotic songs may foster solidarity among Americans and heighten patriotic attachment, but it does very little to express who the people of God are because it does not focus proper attention upon the God of the Bible, who demands loyalty, honor, and praise.[11]

Concluding Thoughts

This project was an attempt to understand the nature of patriotism within the local church's context through the lens of Scripture. While many Christian Americans see patriotism as a virtue, there must also be a critical assessment of what that means. While America is a great country and a country with many virtues, it is not as virtuous or as great as the kingdom of God. Christians in America must critically evaluate what being a good citizen is while also pledging their ultimate loyalty to God alone. This is right, proper, and good. Christians can be patriotic citizens as long as they define

---

[11] Craig Watts, "Singing the Songs of Babylon in the Worship of the Church," *Encounter* 74 (2013–2014): 10, 15.

what that means through a critical assessment of Scripture. Hopefully, this project will lead to some of these critical assessments at the local church level. When this happens, may Christian citizens faithfully navigate the political culture while also remaining true to the truth of Scripture. This is the only way to be the type of patriotic citizens who endure the exile while sojourning through a wonderful country that is not truly our home.

Common Grace and the
American Experiment

While this project claims that nationalism is not tenable for the Christian because God has created all nations with love and care according to His plan, there is something unique to the American experiment. Even a cursory look at American history shows that God has indeed used this country and blessed it in a way that few countries have had the honor to experience. Therefore, patriotism can recognize the common grace that Americans have experienced. This is not to say that all countries have not experienced God's common grace in their own way, but that America has been especially blessed in this way.

Patriotism offers the Christian a way in which to understand three specific blessings in connection to common grace. First, patriotism allows an opportunity to understand the God-created order to America has. Just as Paul had a clear understanding of both the state and citizenship, he understood that God had established the nations. A biblical understanding of patriotism allows a Christian to recognize that God has truly established the state authority of America and, as such, there is ample opportunity to have a patriotic loyalty towards her.

Second, patriotism offers American citizens an opportunity to recognize how they have a role to play in this God-created order through their citizenship. Americans have an opportunity to recognize that all men are indeed created equal, and because of this distinction, they have an opportunity to participate in the political process. This also gives Americans an ample opportunity to recognize the common grace that has been specially bestowed upon this nation.

Third, Americans have an opportunity to see the inherent value in our nation. A biblical understanding of patriotism allows Christians to see the loyalty towards America but also allows for a personal understanding of the nation's value as a whole. This is not to say that America has not had its share of faults. Indeed, issues such as slavery and the Civil War are a blight on the nation's character and must be understood as such. However, America is also a country that, despite its faults, has allowed citizens the opportunity to correct itself. The opportunity to correct America through the political process is an aspect of God's common grace that cannot go unnoticed or unpraised. Through His goodness and grace, God has allowed Americans the opportunity to speak freely and worship freely, and, as a result, American Christians have an opportunity to live as freemen. This is a good blessing of a good God towards America. By recognizing God's common grace, American Christians can see value in their patriotic loyalty to the state while also recognizing that they have an opportunity to play a part in the American experiment. This is right and good. May American Christians find comfort in the nature of God's common grace by seeking to be active, patriotic members of this great American experiment.

Bibliography

Abernethy, David. "The Heir of Saul: Jonathan's Life and Death in Theological Perspective." In *Characters and Characterization in the Book of Samuel*, edited by Keith Bodner and Benjamin Johnson, 139–156. London: T & T Clark, 2020.

Achtemeier, Paul. *1 Peter: A Commentary on First Peter*. Minneapolis: Fortress, 1996.

Akerman, Shane. "Classical Trinitarian Theology and the Idolatry of Nationalism: The Doctrine of the Trinity as a Critique of Political Theology." PhD diss., Claremont Graduate University, 2020.

Albanese, Catherine. *America: Religions and Religion*. Belmont: Wadsworth, 1981.

______. *America: Religions and Religion*. Belmont: Wadsworth, 1992.

______. *Sons of the Fathers: The Civil Religion of the American Revolution*. Philadelphia: Temple University Press, 1976.

Albertz, Ranier. "Hintergrund und Bedeutung des Elterngebots im Dekalog." *ZAW* 90 (1978): 348–374.

Alexander, Jon. "Christian Attitudes toward War in Colonial America." *Church and Society* 64 (1974): 16–24.

Alter, Peter. *Nationalism*. London: Arnold, 1985.

Anderson, Benedict. *Imagined Communities: Reflections on the Origin and Spread of Nationalism*. London: Verso, 2016.

Anderson, Bernhard. *Out of the Depths: The Psalms Speak for Us Today*. Philadelphia: Westminster, 2000.

Anderson, Jennifer. "Prime Time Politics: Television News and the Visual Framing of War." PhD diss., Vanderbilt University, 2011.

Antle, W. James. "Trump's Nationalist Moment: Voters Are Speaking up for Country, Border, and Sovereignty." *The American Conservative* 19, no. 1 (2019): 14–17.

Appiah, Kwame. "Cosmopolitan Patriots." *Critical Inquiry* 23 (1997): 617–639.

Arnold, Clinton. *Ephesians*. Zondervan Exegetical Commentary on the New Testament. Grand Rapids: Zondervan, 2010.

Ateek, Naim. "Zionism and the Land: A Palestinian Christian Perspective." In *The Land of Promise: Biblical, Theological and Contemporary Perspectives*, edited by Philip Johnston and Peter Walker, 201–214. Downers Grove: InterVarsity, 2000.

Audi, Robert. "Nationalism, Patriotism, and Cosmopolitanism in an Age of Globalization." *Journal of Ethics* 13 (2009): 365–381.

Augustine. *City of God*. Translated by Henry Bettenson. London: Penguin, 2003.

Bailey, Sarah. "White Evangelicals Voted Overwhelmingly for Donald Trump, Exit Polls Show." *Washington Post*, November 9, 2016, https://www.washingtonpost.com/news/acts-of-faith/wp/2016/11/09/exit-polls-show-white-evangelicals-voted-overwhelmingly-for-donald-trump/?noredirect=on&utm_term=.9b754341acf1.

Baldwin, Joyce. *1 and 2 Samuel: An Introduction and Commentary*. The Tyndale Old Testament Commentaries. Leicester: Inter-Varsity, 1998.

Baron, Marcia. "Patriotism and 'Liberal' Morality." In *Patriotism*, edited by Igor Primoratz, 59–86. Amherst: Humanity, 2002.

Batstone, David and Eduardo Mendieta, eds. *The Good Citizen*. New York: Routledge, 1999.

Bauckham, Richard. *The Bible in Politics: How to Read the Bible Politically*. Louisville: Westminster, 2011.

Beale, G. K. *The Book of Revelation: A Commentary on the Greek Text*. New International Greek Testament Commentary. Grand Rapids: Eerdmans, 1999.

———. "Eden, the Temple, and the Church's Mission in the New Creation." *JETS* 48 (2005): 5–31.

______. *A New Testament Biblical Theology: The Unfolding of the Old Testament in the New.* Grand Rapids: Baker, 2011.

Beecher, Henry. *Freedom and War.* Boston: Ticknor & Fields, 1863.

Beitz, Charles. "Cosmopolitanism and Global Justice." *The Journal of Ethics* (2005): 11–27.

Bellah, Robert. "Civil Religion in America." *Dædalus* 96 (1967): 1–21.

______. *The Broken Covenant: American Civil Religion in the Time of Trial.* Chicago: Chicago University, 1970.

Bercovitch, Sacvan. "How the Puritans Won the American Revolution." *The Massachusetts Review* 17 (1976): 597–630.

______. "The Typology of America's Mission." *American Quarterly* 30 (1978): 135–155.

Berens, John. "'Good News from a Far Country': A Note on Divine Providence and the Stamp Act Crisis." *Church History* 45 (1976): 308–315.

Bergen, Robert. *1, 2 Samuel.* The New American Commentary. Nashville: Broadman & Holman Publishers, 1996.

Berrus, Joshua. "The Church's Relationship with Patriotism and Politics: An Evaluation of Francis A. Schaeffer and John Howard Yoder." Master's thesis, Southeastern Baptist Theological Seminary, 2008.

Bird, Michael. *An Anomalous Jew: Paul among Jews, Greeks, and Romans.* Grand Rapids: Eerdmans, 2016.

______. *The Saving Righteousness of God: Studies on Paul, Justification and the New Perspective.* Eugene: Wipf and Stock, 2007.

Black, Allen. *Mark.* The College Press NIV Commentary. Joplin: College Press, 2001.

Black, Clifton. "American Scriptures." *Theology Today* 67 (2010): 127–168.

Bloch, Ruth. "The Social and Political Base of Millennial Literature in Late Eighteenth-Century America." *American Quarterly* 40 (1988): 378–396.

______. *Visionary Republic: Millennial Themes in American Thought, 1756–1800*. Cambridge: Cambridge University Press, 1985.

Blum, Lawrence. "Best Traditions Patriotism: A Commentary on Miller, Wingo and Ben-Porath." *Theory and Research in Education* 5 (2007): 61–68.

Bock, Darrell. *Mark*. New Cambridge Bible Commentary. New York: Cambridge, 2015.

Bonanno, George and John Jost. "Conservative Shift among High-Exposure Survivors of the September 11th Attacks." *Basic and Applied Social Psychology* 28 (2006): 311–323.

Bonikowski, Bart and Paul DiMaggio. "Varieties of American Popular Nationalism." *American Sociological Review* 81 (2016): 949–980.

Bonner, Robert. "Flag Culture and the Consolidation of Confederate Nationalism." *The Journal of Southern History* 68 (2002): 293–332.

Bonomi, Patricia. *Under the Cope of Heaven: Religion, Society, and Politics in Colonial America*. New York: Oxford University Press, 1986.

Borggren, Erik. "Romans 13:1–7 and Philippians 3:17–21: Paul's Call to True Citizenship and to Gaman." *The Covenant Quarterly* 73 (2015): 26–40.

Boring, M. Eugene. *Mark*: A Commentary. Louisville: Westminster John Knox Press, 2006.

Borradori, Giovanna. *Philosophy in a Time of Terror: Dialogues with Jügen Habermas and Jacques Derrida*. Chicago: University of Chicago, 2004.

Boyce, Travis. "Radical Teacher: A Socialist, Feminist, and Anti-Racist." *Journal of the Theory and Practice of Teaching* 109 (2017): 21–28.

Brand, Chad, ed. *Holman Illustrated Bible Dictionary*. Nashville: Broadman and Holman, 2003, S.v. "temple of Jerusalem."

Bratt, James. *Abraham Kuyper: A Centennial Reader*. Grand Rapids: Eerdmans, 1998.

Bratta, Phillip. "Flag Display Post-9/11: A Discourse on American Nationalism." *The Journal of American Culture* 32 (2009): 232–243.

Bredin, Mark. *Jesus, Revolutionary of Peace: A Nonviolent Christology in the Book of Revelation.* Milton Keynes: Paternoster, 2003.

Brewer, Susan. *Why America Fights: Patriotism and War Propaganda from the Philippines to Iraq.* Oxford: Oxford University Press, 2009.

Bridges, Carl, Jr. "Friend, Friendship." In *Evangelical Dictionary of Biblical Theology*, 272. Grand Rapids: Baker, 1996.

Brighouse, Harry. "Justifying Patriotism." *Social Theory and Practice* 32 (2006): 547–558.

Brooks, James. *Mark.* The New American Commentary. Nashville: Broadman & Holman, 1991.

Browning, Judkin. "'I Am Not So Patriotic as I Was Once': The Effects of Military Occupation on the Occupying Union Soldiers during the Civil War." *Civil War History* 55 (2009): 217–243.

Bruce, F. F. *Commentary on the Book of the Acts.* The New International Commentary of the New Testament. Grand Rapids: Eerdmans, 1980.

Brueggemann, Walter. *Cadences of Home: Preaching among Exiles.* Louisville: Westminster, 1997.

———. "The Covenanted Family: A Zone for Humanness." *Journal of Current Social Issues* 14 (1977): 18–23.

———. *First and Second Samuel.* Interpretation: A Bible Commentary for Teaching and Preaching. Louisville: John Knox, 1990.

———. *Genesis 1-11:26*, The New American Commentary. Nashville: Broadman & Holman, 1996.

———. *The Land: Place as Gift, Promise, and Challenge in Biblical Faith.* 2nd ed. Minneapolis: Fortress, 2002.

Bryan, Christopher. *Render to Caesar: Jesus, the Early Church, and the Roman Superpower.* Oxford: Oxford University Press, 2005.

Burge, Gary. *Jesus and the Land: The New Testament Challenge to "Holy Land" Theology.* Grand Rapids: Baker, 2010.

Burk, Denny. "Is Paul's Gospel Counterimperial? Evaluating the Prospects of the 'Fresh Perspective' for Evangelical Theology." *JETS* 51 (2008): 309–337.

Buts, David, E., Ashby Plant, and Celeste Doerr. "Liberty and Justice for All? Implications of Exposure to the U.S. Flag for Intergroup Relations." *Personality and Social Psychology Bulletin* 33 (2007): 396–408.

Cafferky, Michael. "Honor the King. Yes. But Emulate the King?" The Journal of Applied Christian Leadership 4 (2012): 32-51.

Callan, Eamonn. "The Better Angels of Our Nature: Patriotism and Dirty Hands." *The Journal of Political Philosophy* 18 (2010): 249–270.

______. *Creating Citizens: Political Education and Liberal Democracy*. Oxford: Oxford University Press, 1997.

Carlson, John and Jonathan Ebel. *From Jeremiad to Jihad: Religion, Violence, and America.* Berkeley: University of California Press, 2012.

Carter, Travis, Melissa Ferguson, and Ran Hassin. "A Single Exposure to the American Flag Shifts Support toward Republicanism up to 8 Months Later." *Psychological Science* 22 (2011): 1011–1018.

Carter, Warren. "Adult Children and Elderly Parents: The Worlds of the New Testament." *Journal of Religious Gerontology* 12 (2001): 45–59.

Cartledge, Tony. *1 and 2 Samuel*. Smyth and Helwys Bible Commentary. Macon: Smyth & Helwys, 2001.

Casey, Edward. "Between Geography and Philosophy: What Does It Mean to Be in the Place-World?" *Annals of the Association of American Geographers* 91 (2001): 683–693.

Casey, Michelle. "Working as Civic and Patriotic Duty for Consumption: A Critical Discourse Analysis of American Presidential Inaugural Speeches since World War II." PhD diss., University of Nevada, Las Vegas, 2016.

Cavanaugh, William. *Migrations of the Holy: God, State, and the Political Meaning of the Church.* Grand Rapids: Eerdmans, 2011.

Chapman, Colin. *Whose Promised Land?* Tring: Lion, 1983.

Cherry, Conrad. *God's New Israel: Religious Interpretations of American Destiny*. Chapel Hill: University of North Carolina Press, 1998.

Chesebrough, David. "The Civil War and the Use of Sermons as Historical Documents." *OAH Magazine of History* (1993): 26–29.

Child, Samuel. *The Colonial Parson of New England: A Picture.* New York: The Baker and Taylor Co, 1896.

Christensen, Daniel. "Roman Citizenship as a Climatic Narrative Element: Paul's Roman Citizenship in Acts 16 and 22 Compared with Cicero's *Against Verres." Conversations with the Biblical World* 38 (2018): 55–75.

Cilliers, Johan. "God in Granite? Aesthetic-Theological Perspectives on the Monumentalisation of Religion." *Scriptura* 114 (2015): 1–13.

Cole, R. Alan. *Mark.* Tyndale New Testament Commentaries. Downer Grove: InterVarsity, 2008.

Connor, Joseph. "Off Key: America's National Anthem was a Lightning Rod for Controversy Long before Colin Kaepernick Stayed in His Seat." *American History* (2017): 43–51.

Craigie, Peter. *The Problem of War in the Old Testament.* Grand Rapids: Eerdmans, 1978.

Crittendon, David. "Differentiating Patriotism and Nationalism: Influence of Valence of Primes." *The New School Psychology Bulletin* 15 (2018): 1–10.

Crouse, Robert. "Two Kingdoms and Two Cities: Mapping Theological Traditions of Church, Culture, and Civil Order." PhD diss., Wheaton College, 2016.

Culbertson, Philip. *The Future of Male Spirituality.* Minneapolis: Fortress Press, 1992.

Davies, W. D. *The Gospel and the Land: Early Christianity and Jewish Territorial Doctrine.* Berkeley: University of California Press, 1974.

Davis, Kenneth. *FDR, the War President, 1940–1943: A History.* New York: Random House, 2000.

de Figueiredo, Rui, Jr. and Zachary Elkins. "Are Patriots Bigots? An Inquiry into the Vices of In-Group Pride." *American Journal of Political Science* 47 (2003): 171–188.

Deissmann, Adolf. *Paul: A Study in Social and Religious History.* Translated by William Wilson. New York: Harper, 1957.

Deitz, Mary. "Patriotism: A Brief History of the Term." In *Patriotism*, edited by Igor Primoratz, 201–215. Amherst: Humanity, 2002.

Delanty, Gerald. "Nationalism and Cosmopolitanism: The Paradox of Modernity." In *The SAGE Handbook of Nations and Nationalism,* edited by Gerald Delanty and Krishan Kumar, 357–368. London: SAGE, 2006.

Denker, Angela. *Red State Christians: Understanding the Voters Who Elected Donald Trump.* Minneapolis: Fortress, 2019.

Deweese-Boyd, Ian and Margaret Deweese-Boyd. "'Flying the Flag of Rough Branch': Rethinking Post-September 11 Patriotism through the Writings of Wendell Berry." *Appalachian Journal* 32 (2005): 214–232.

Diehl, Judy. "Empire and Epistles: Anti-Roman Rhetoric in the New Testament Epistles." *Currents in Biblical Research* 10 (2012): 217–263.

Divine, Robert. *Roosevelt and World War II.* Baltimore: Johns Hopkins Press, 1969.

Dixon, Nicholas. "The Friendship Model of Filial Obligations." *Journal of Applied Philosophy* 12 (1995): 77–87.

Doob, Leonard. *Patriotism and Nationalism: Their Psychological Foundations.* New Haven: Yale Press, 1964.

Dorn, A., David Mandel, and Ryan Cross. "How Just Were America's Wars? A Survey of Experts Using a Just War Index." *International Studies Perspectives* 16 (2015): 270–285.

Drew, Gavin. "'Show Me the Money!' Part 1: Speculations Concerning Jesus and the Temple." *Stimulus* 17 (2009): 37–48.

Driver, Julia. "Cosmopolitan Virtue." *Social Theory and Practice* 33, no. 4 (2007): 595–608.

Duff, Nancy. "Locating God in All the Wrong Places: The Second Commandment and American Politics." *Interpretation* 60 (2006): 182–193.

Duncan, Ligon, Dan Kimball, Michael Larence, Mark Dever, Timothy Quill, and Dan Wilt. *Perspectives on Christian Worship: 5 Views.* Nashville: Broadman & Holman, 2009.

Edwards, James. *The Gospel According to Mark*. The Pillar New Testament Commentary. Grand Rapids: Eerdmans, 2002.

Elliott, Neil. "The Apostle Paul's Self-Presentation as Anti-Imperial Performance." In *Paul and the Roman Imperial Order*, edited by Richard Horsley, 67–88. Harrisburg: Trinity Press, 2004.

Elwell, Walter and Barry Beitzel, eds. *Baker Encyclopedia of the Bible*. Grand Rapids: Baker, 1988, S.v. "Herodians."

______. *Baker Encyclopedia of the Bible*. Grand Rapids: Baker, 1988, S.v. "land."

______. *Baker Encyclopedia of the Bible*. Grand Rapids: Baker, 1988, S.v. "Tarsus."

Endy, Melvin, Jr. "Just War, Holy War, and Millennialism in Revolutionary America." *The William and Mary Quarterly* 42 (1985): 3–25.

Engberg-Pedersen, Troels. "Paul's Stoicizing Politics in Romans 12–13: The Role of 13:1–10 in the Argument." *JSNT* 29 (2006): 163–72.

Esler, Philip. *Community and Gospel in Luke-Acts: The Social and Political Motivations of Lucan Theology*. Cambridge: Cambridge University Press, 1987.

Fahs, Alice. *The Imagined Civil War: Popular Literature of the North and South, 1861–1865*. Chapel Hill: University of North Carolina, 2001.

Falcous, Mark and Michael Silk. "Manufacturing Consent: Mediated Sporting Spectacle and the Cultural Politics of the 'War on Terror'." *International Journal of Media and Cultural Politics* 1 (2005): 59–65.

Fee, Gordon. *Philippians*. The IVP New Testament Commentary Series. Westmont: InterVarsity, 1999.

Fernández, Oscar and Roberto Cachán-Cruz. "An Assessment of the Dynamic of Religious Ritualism in Sporting Environments." *Journal of Religious Health* 53 (2014): 1653–1661.

Fitzmyer, Joseph. *Romans: A New Translation with Introduction and Commentary*. Anchor Yale Bible. New Haven: Yale University Press, 2008.

Fleche, Andre. *The Revolution of 1861: The American Civil War in the Age of Nationalistic Conflict.* Chapel Hill: University of North Carolina, 2012.

Foucault, Michael. *Collected Interviews, 1961–1984.* Edited by Sylvere Lotringer. New York: Semiotext(e), 1996.

Fozdar, Farida and Mitchell Low. "'They Have to Abide by Our Laws . . . and Stuff': Ethnonationalism Masquerading as Civic Nationalism." *Nations and Nationalism* 21 (2015): 524–543.

France, R. T. *The Gospel of Mark: A Commentary on the Greek Text.* New International Greek Testament Commentary. Grand Rapids: Eerdmans, 2002.

Frankel, Jerry. *The Land of Canaan and the Destiny of Israel: Theologies of Territory in the Hebrew Bible.* Winona Lake: Eisenbrauns, 2011.

Gamble, Richard. *In Search of the City on a Hill: The Making and Unmaking of an American Myth.* New York: Continuum, 2012.

Geddert, Timothy. *Mark.* Believers Church Bible Commentary. Scottsdale: Herald Press, 2001.

George, Timothy. *Galatians.* The New American Commentary. Nashville: Broadman & Holman, 1994.

Gilbert, Margaret. "Pro Patria: An Essay on Patriotism." *Journal of Ethics* 13 (2009): 319–346.

Godwin, Promise. "Tarsus and Jerusalem: The Interplay of Knowledge and Spirituality Reading Acts 17:22–28 as a Theological Response to the Quest for Gospel." *Journal for Biblical Theology* 3 (2020): 42–69.

Goepner, Erik. "Measuring the Effectiveness of America's War on Terror." *Parameters* 46 (2016): 107–120.

Goldingay, John. *Isaiah.* Understanding the Bible Commentary Series. Grand Rapids: Baker, 2012.

______. *Old Testament Theology: Israel's Life.* Downers Grove: InterVarsity, 2009.

Gorski, Philip. *American Covenant: A History of Civil Religion from the Puritans to the Present.* Princeton: Princeton University Press, 2017.

______. "Why Evangelicals Voted for Trump: A Critical Cultural Sociology." *American Journal of Cultural Sociology* 5 (2017): 338–354.Grasso, Christopher. "Images and Shadows of Jonathan Edwards." *American Literary History* 8 (1996): 683–698.

Grant, Jamie. *The King as Exemplar: The Function of Deuteronomy's Kingship Law in the Shaping of the Book of Psalms*. Atlanta: SBL, 2004.

Gray, Timothy. *The Temple in the Gospel of Mark: A Study in its Narrative Role*. Tübingen: Mohr Siebeck, 2008.

Green, Gene. *The Letters to the Thessalonians*. The Pillar New Testament Commentary. Grand Rapids: Eerdmans, 2002.

Greenfeld, Liah. *Advanced Introduction to Nationalism*. Cheltenham: Edward Elgar, 2016.

______. *Nationalism: A Short History*. Washington, D.C.: Brookings, 2019.

Gregory, Sean. "Colin Kaepernick." *TIME Magazine*, 2017.

Grimsrud, Ted. *The Good War That Wasn't—and Why It Matters: World War II's Moral Legacy*. Eugene: Cascade, 2014.

Grosby, Steven. *Biblical Ideas of Nationality: Ancient and Modern*. Winona Lake: Eisenbrauns, 2002.

______. "Religion and Nationality in Antiquity." *European Journal of Sociology* 32 (1991): 229–65.

Grüneberg, Keith. *Abraham, Blessing and the Nations: A Philological and Exegetical Study of Genesis 12:3 in its Narrative Context*. Berlin: Walter de Gruyter, 2003.

Goldingay, John. *Old Testament Ethics: A Guided Tour*. Downers Grove: InterVarsity, 2019.

______. *Old Testament Theology: Israel's Life*.Downers Grove: InterVarsity, 2009.

Goswell, Gregory. "'David Their King': Kingship in the Prophecy of Hosea." *Journal for the Study of the Old Testament* 42 (2017): 213–31.

Habel, Norman. *The Land Is Mine: Six Biblical Land Ideologies*. Minneapolis: Fortress, 1995.

Habermas, Jürgen, ed. "Citizenship and National Identity." In *Between Facts and Norms: Contributions to a Discourse*

Theory of Law and Democracy, 491–516. Cambridge: MIT Press, 1996.

Haberski, Raymond, Jr. *God and War: American Civil Religion since 1945*. New Brunswick: Rutgers, 2012.

Hall, Eric. "Policy Point—Counterpoint: Do African American Athletes Have an Obligation to Fight Against Racial Injustice?" *International Social Science Review* 93 (2017): 1–9.

Hansen, G. Walter. *The Letter to the Philippians*. The Pillar New Testament Commentary. Grand Rapids: Eerdmans, 2009.

Harding, Sara. "'Astonished at His Teaching': The Structure and Authority of Jesus' Sayings in the Gospel of Mark." PhD diss., Marquette University, 1999.

Harrill, J. Albert. *Paul the Apostle: His Life and Legacy in Their Roman Context*. Cambridge: Cambridge University Press, 2012.

Harrison, James. *Paul and the Imperial Authorities at Thessalonica and Rome: A Study in the Conflict of Ideology*. Wissenschaftliche Untersuchungen zum Neuen Testament. Tübingen: Mohr Siebeck, 2011.

______. "Paul and the Imperial Gospel at Thessaloniki." *JSNT* 25 (2002): 71–96.Hatch, Nathan. "The Origins of Civil Millennialism in America: New England Clergymen, War with France, and the Revolution." *The William and Mary Quarterly* 31 (1974): 407–430.

______. *The Sacred Cause of Liberty: Republican Thought and the Millennium in Revolutionary New England*. New Haven: Yale University Press, 1977.

Hauerwas, Stanley and William Willimon. *Resident Aliens: Life in the Christian Colony*. Nashville: Abingdon, 1993.

Hays, Daniel. *From Every People and Nation: A Biblical Theology of Race,* New Studies in Biblical Theology 14. Downers Grove: InterVarsity, 2003.

Heimert, Alan. *Religion and the American Mind: From the Great Awakening to the Revolution*. Cambridge: Harvard University Press, 1966.

Heimert, Alan and Andrew Delbanco, eds. *The Puritans in America: A Narrative Anthology*. Cambridge: Harvard University

Press, 1985.Hellerman, Joseph. *Philippians.* Exegetical Guide to the New Testament. Nashville: Broadman, 2015.

______. *Reconstructing Honor in Roman Philippi: Carmen Christ as Cursus Pudorum.* Society for New Testament Studies Monograph Series 132. Cambridge: Cambridge University Press, 2005.

Hendriksen, William. *Mark.* New Testament Commentary. Grand Rapids: Baker, 2002.

______. *Philippians.* New Testament Commentary. Grand Rapids: Baker, 1962.

Holifield, E. Brooks. "The Penurious Preacher? Nineteenth-Century Clerical Wealth: North and South." *Journal of the American Academy of Religion* 58 (1990): 17–36.

Holst, Daniel. "From Patriotism's Christian Narrative to Ironic War Poetry." Master's thesis, Western Illinois University, 2018.

Horrell, David. "The Peaceable, Tolerant Community and the Legitimate Role of the State: Ethics and Ethical Dilemmas in Romans 12:1–15:13." *Review and Expositor* 100 (2003): 81–99.

Horsley, Richard. *Jesus and Empire: The Kingdom of God and the New World Order.* Minneapolis: Fortress, 2003.

Horsley, Richard, ed. *Paul and Empire: Religion and Power in Roman Imperial Society.* Harrisburg: Trinity Press, 1987.Houser, Sarah. "Loving Pimlico: Patriotism in the Age of Cosmopolis." PhD diss., Notre Dame, 2009.

Howard, David. "The Case for Kingship in the Old Testament Narrative Books and the Psalms." *Trinity Journal* 9 (1988): 19–35.

Huey, F. B. *Jeremiah, Lamentations.* The New American Commentary. Nashville: Broadman & Holman, 1993.

Hughey, Michael. "The Political Covenant: Protestant Foundations of the American State." *State, Culture, and Society* 1 (1984): 113–156.

Huntington, S. P. *Who Are We? The Challenges to America's National Identity.* New York: Simon & Schuster, 2004.

Hutchinson, John and Anthony Smith, eds. *Nationalism.* Oxford Readers. Oxford: Oxford University Press, 1994.

Ikuenobe, Polycarp. "Citizen and Patriotism." *Public Affairs Quarterly* 24 (2010), 297–318.

Inge, John. "A Christian Theology of Place." PhD diss., University of Durham, 2001.

Isaak, Jon. "The Christian Community and Political Responsibility: Romans 13:1–7." *Direction* 32 (2003): 32–46.

Ishio, Yoshito, Kevin Dougherty, and Izumi Niki. "American Flags in Religious Congregations in the United States." *Journal of Church and State* 61 (2018): 431–450.

Jewett, Robert. *Romans: A Commentary.* Hermeneia. Minneapolis: Fortress, 2007.

Jewett, Robert and Constance Collora. "On Turning the Flag into a Sacred Object." *Journal of Church and State* 37 (1995): 741–752.Jones, Charles. *Global Justice: Defending Cosmopolitanism.* Oxford: Oxford University Press, 1999.

Juel, Donald. *Messiah and Temple: The Trial of Jesus in the Gospel of Mark.* Missoula: Scholars Press, 1977.

Juster, Susan. *Doomsayers: Anglo-American Prophecy in the Age of Revolution.* Philadelphia: University of Pennsylvania Press, 2003.

Kateb, George. "Is Patriotism a Mistake?" *Social Research* 67 (2000): 901–924.

Kaufman, Chloe. "Speaking about Politics, A Fireable Offense? The Legality of Employee Speech Restrictions in the Entertainment Industry." *Journal of Intellectual Property and Entertainment Law* 8 (2019): 376–408.

Kaveny, Cathleen. "The Remnants of Theocracy: The Puritans, the Jeremiad and the Contemporary Culture Wars." *Law, Culture and the Humanities* 9 (2013): 59–70.

Kealy, Sean. "Friendship in the Bible." *Scripture in Church* 31 (2001): 507–512.

Keener, Craig. "One New Temple in Christ (Ephesians 2:11–22; Acts 21:27–29; Mark 11:17; John 4:20–24)." *Asian Journal of Pentecostal Studies* 12 (2009): 75–92.

———. *Romans.* New Covenant Commentary Series. Eugene: Cascade Books, 2009.

Keller, Simon. "Are Patriotism and Universalism Compatible." *Social Theory and Practice* 33 (2007): 609–624.

______. "The Case against Patriotism." In *The Ethics of Patriotism: A Debate*, edited by John Kleinig, Simon Keller, and Igor Primoratz, 48–72. Malden: Wiley, 2015.

______. "Four Duties of Filial Duty." *The Philosophical Quarterly* 56 (2006): 254–274.

______. "Patriotism as Bad Faith." *Ethics* 115 (2005): 563–592.Kemmelmeier, Markus and David Winter. "Sowing Patriotism, but Reading Nationalism? Consequences of Exposure to the American Flag." *Political Psychology* 29, no. 6 (2008): 859–879.

Kernaghan, Ronald. *Mark.* The IVP New Testament Commentary Series. Downers Grove: InterVarsity, 2007.

Keszler, Werner. "Die Literarische, Historische und Theologische Problematik des Dekalogs." *VT* 7 (1957): 1–16.

Kidd, Thomas. *The Protestant Interest: New England after Puritanism.* New Haven: Yale University Press, 2004.

Kimball, Warren. "The Incredible Shrinking War: The Second World War, Not (Just) the Origins of the Cold War." *Diplomatic History* 25 (2001): 347–365.

Kirk, J. R. "Time for Figs, Temple Destruction, and Houses of Prayer in Mark 11:12–25." *The Catholic Biblical Quarterly* 74 (2012): 509–527.

Kleinig, John. "The Virtue in Patriotism." In *The Ethics of Patriotism: A Debate*, edited by John Kleinig, Simon Keller, and Igor Primoratz, 19–47. Malden: Wiley, 2015.

Kleinig, John, Simon Keller, and Igor Primoratz. *The Ethics of Patriotism: A Debate*. Malden: Wiley, 2015.

Knoblauch, Austin. "NFL Expected to Enact National Anthem Policy for 18." NFL, http://www.nfl.com/news/story/0ap3000000933952/article/nfl-expected-to-enact-national-anthem-policy-for-18.

______. "NFL Player Protests Sweep League after President Trump's Hostile Remarks." *USA Today*, September 24, 2017, usatoday.com/story/sports/nfl/2017/09/24/donald-trump-nfl-player-protests-national-anthem-week-3-response/697609001/.

Kohn, Hans. *Nationalism: Its Meaning and History*. Malabar: Krieger, 1982.

Köstenberger, Andreas and Peter O'Brien. *Salvation to the Ends of the Earth: A Biblical Theology of Mission.* New Studies in Biblical Theology. Downers Grove: InterVarsity, 2001.

Kraybill, J. Nelson. *Apocalypse and Allegiance: Worship, Politics, and Devotion in the Book of Revelation.* Grand Rapids: Brazos, 2010.

Kruse, Colin. *Paul's Letter to the Romans.* The Pillar New Testament Commentary. Grand Rapids: Eerdmans, 2012.

Kuyper, Abraham. *Lectures on Calvinism: Six Lectures from the Stone Foundation Lectures Delivered at Princeton.* Readaclassic.com, 2009.

Laborde, Cécile. "From Constitutional to Civic Patriotism." *British Journal of Political Science* 32 (2002): 591–612.

Laertius, Diogenes. *Lives of the Eminent Philosophers.* Edited by James Miller. Translated by Pamela Mensch. Oxford: Oxford University Press, 2018.

LaGrand, James. *The Earliest Christian Mission to 'All Nations' in the Light of Matthew's Gospel.* Tampa: Scholars Press, 1995.

LaMothe, Ryan. "The Problem of Patriotism: A Psychoanalytic and Theological Analysis." *Pastoral Psychology* 58 (2009): 151–166.

Lane, William. *The Gospel According to Mark.* The New International Commentary on the New Testament. Grand Rapids: Eerdmans, 1974.

Lawson, Melinda. "'A Profound National Devotion': The Civil War Union Leagues and the Construction of a New National Patriotism." *Civil War History* 48 (2002): 338–362.

Leibig, Ann and Katherine Green. "The Development of Family Loyalty and Relational Ethics in Children." *Contemporary Family Therapy* 21 (1999): 89–112.

Levine, Baruch. *Leviticus.* The JPS Torah Commentary. Philadelphia: Jewish Publication Society, 1989.

Lewis, Penny. *Hardhats, Hippies, and Hawks: The Vietnam Antiwar Movement as Myth and Memory.* Ithaca: ILR Press, 2013.

Li, Qiong and Marilynn Brewer. "What Does It Mean to Be an American? Patriotism, Nationalism, and American Identity after 9/11." *Political Psychology* 25 (2004): 727–739.

Lienesch, Michael. "Contesting Civil Religion: Religious Responses to American Patriotic Nationalism, 1919–1929." *Religion and American Culture: A Journal of Interpretation* 28 (2018): 92–134.

______. "The Role of Political Millennialism in Early American Nationalism." *The Western Political Quarterly* 36 (1983): 445–465.

Lieven, Anatol. *America Right or Wrong: An Anatomy of American Nationalism*. Oxford: Oxford University Press, 2012.

Loh, I-Jin and Eugene Nida. *A Handbook on Paul's Letter to the Philippians*. UBS Handbook Series. New York: United Bible Societies, 1995.

Lukacs, John. *The Legacy of the Second World War*. New Haven: Yale University Press, 2010.

MacIntyre, Alasdair. "Is Patriotism a Virtue?" In *Patriotism*, edited by Igor Primoratz, 43–58. Amherst: Humanity, 2002.

Mackenzie, Ed. "The Quest for the Political Paul: Assessing the Apostle's Approach to Empire." *EJT* 20 (2011): 40–50.

Maclear, J. F. "New England and the Fifth Monarchy: The Quest for the Millennium in Early American Puritanism." *The William and Mary Quarterly* 32 (1975): 223–260.

Madsen, Deborah. *American Exceptionalism*. Jackson: University Press, 1998.

Mandel, Seth. "The Failed War on the 'War on Terror': Everybody Hates It and It's Not Going Anywhere." *Commentary* November (2013): 17–25.

Marsden, George. *Religion and American Culture*. New York: Broadway, 2001.

______. *Religion and the American Culture*. New York: Harcourt, 1990.

Marshall, I. Howard. *Acts*. Tyndale New Testament Commentaries. Downers Grove: InterVarsity, 2008.

Marshall, Scott. "The Vietnam War on Prime Time Television: Focus Group Aided Rhetorical Criticism of American Myths in Tour of Duty and China Beach." PhD diss., Ohio State University, 1993.

Martin, Leisa. "Blind Patriotism or Active Citizenship? How Do Students Interpret the Pledge of Allegiance?" *Action in Teacher Education* 34 (2012): 55–64.

Martin, Oren. *Bound for the Promised Land: The Land Promise in God's Redemptive Plan*. New Studies in Biblical Theology. Downers Grove: Apollos, 2015.

Martinez, Jessica and Gregory Smith. "How the Faithful Voted: A Preliminary 2016 Analysis." Pew Research, https://www.pewresearch.org/fact-tank/2016/11/09/how-the-faithful-voted-a-preliminary-2016-analysis/.

Marvin, Carolyn and David Ingle. *Blood Sacrifice and the Nation: Totem Rituals and the American Flag*. Cambridge: Cambridge, 1999.

Masco, Joseph. "Auditing the War on Terror: The Watson Institute's Costs of War Project." *American Anthropologist* 115 (2013): 312–313.

Mathews, Kenneth. *Genesis 1–11:26*. The New American Commentary. Nashville: Broadman & Holman Publishers, 1996.

McClay, Wilfred. "America—Idea or Nation?" *The Public Interest* (2001): 44–58.

McCleary, Daniel, Meagan Nalls, and Robert Williams. "Types of Patriotism as Primary Predictors of Continuing Support for the Iraq War." *Journal of Political and Military Sociology* 37 (2009): 77–94.

McConville, J. G. *Deuteronomy*. Apollos Old Testament Commentary. Downers Grove: InterVarsity, 2002.

McDonald, Jermaine. "A Fourth Time of Trial: Towards an Implicit and Inclusive American Civil Religion." *Implicit Religion* 16 (2013): 47–64.

McKenna, George. *The Puritan Origins of American Patriotism*. New Haven: Yale, 2007.

McMahon, Robert. "Contested Memory: The Vietnam War and American Society, 1975–2001." *Diplomatic History* 26 (2002): 159–184.

McPherson, James. *For Cause and Comrades: Why Men Fought in the Civil War*. New York: Oxford University Press, 1997.

Meier, J. P. "The Historical Jesus and the Historical Herodians." *JBL* 119 (2000): 740–746

Melick, Richard. *Philippians, Colossians, Philemon*. The New American Commentary. Nashville: Broadman & Holman, 1991.

Merrill, Eugene. *Deuteronomy*. The New American Commentary. Nashville: Broadman & Holman Publishers, 1994.

Miller, David. *On Nationality*. Oxford: Clarendon, 1995.

Miller, Patrick. "The Gift of God: The Deuteronomic Theology of the Land." *Interpretation* 23 (1969): 451–465.

Miller, Perry. *Errand in the Wilderness*. New York: Harper, 1954.

______. "Preparation for Salvation." In *Essays in American Colonial History*, edited by Paul Goodman, 152–83. New York: Holt, 1967.

Miller, Randall, Harry Stout, and Charles Wilson. *Religion and the Civil War*. New York: Oxford University Press, 1998.

Monera, Arnold. "The Christian's Relationship to the State According to the New Testament: Conformity or Non-Conformity?" *Asia Journal of Theology* 19 (2005): 106–142.

Monnet, Agnieszka. "War and National Renewal: Civil Religion and Blood Sacrifice in American Culture." *European Journal of American Studies* 7 (2012): 1–17.

Moo, Douglas. *The Epistle to the Romans*. New International Commentary of the New Testament. Grand Rapids: Eerdmans, 1996.

Moore, Margaret. "Is Patriotism an Associative Duty?" *Journal of Ethics* 13 (2009): 383–399.

Morgan, Edmund. "The Puritan Ethic and the American Revolution." *The William and Mary Quarterly* 24 (1967): 3–43.

Morgan, Matthew, ed. *The Impact of 9/11 on the Media, Arts, and Entertainment: The Day That Changed Everything?* New York: Palgrave, 2009.

Morris, Leon. *The Epistle to the Romans.* The Pillar New Testament Commentary. Grand Rapids; Eerdmans, 1988.

Morrissey, Mary. "Elect Nations and Prophetic Preaching: Types and Examples in the Paul's Cross Jeremiad." In *The English Sermon Revised: Religion, Literature and History, 1600–1750*, edited by Lori Ferrell and Peter McCullough. Manchester: Manchester University Press, 2000.

Moser, Richard. *The New Winter Soldiers: GI and Veteran Dissent during the Vietnam Era.* New Brunswick: Rutgers, 1996.

Mounce, Robert. *Romans.* The New American Commentary. Nashville: Broadman & Holman, 1995.

Müller, Jac. *The Epistles of Paul to the Philippians and to Philemon.* The New International Commentary on the New Testament. Grand Rapids: Eerdmans, 1978.

Mummendey, Amélie, Andreas Klink, and Rupert Brown. "Nationalism and Patriotism: National Identification and Out-Group Rejection." *British Journal of Social Psychology* 40 (2001): 159–172.

Munther, Isaac. "From Land to Lands, from Eden to the Renewed Earth: A Christ-Centred Biblical Theology of the Promised Land." PhD diss., Middlesex University, 2014.

Murphy-O'Conner, Jerome. *Paul: A Critical Life.* Oxford: Clarendon, 1996.

Myers, Allen. "Friend." *The Eerdmans Bible Dictionary.* Grand Rapids: Eerdmans, 1987, 392–393.

Nahmod, Sheldon. "The Sacred Flag and the First Amendment." *Indiana Law Journal* 66 (1991): 511–548.

Nathanson, Stephen. "Is Cosmopolitan Anti-Patriotism a Virtue?" In *Patriotism: Philosophical and Political Perspectives*, edited by Aleksander Pavkovic and Igor Primoratz, 75–91. London: Routledge, 2007.

______. "On Deciding Whether a Nation Deserves Our Loyalty." *Public Affairs Quarterly* 4 (1990): 287–298.

______. "Patriotism, War, and the Limits of Permissible Partiality." *Journal of Ethics* 13 (2009): 401–422.

Naws, Brigitte. *Mass-Mediated Terrorism: The Central Role of the Media in Terrorism and Counterterrorism.* New York: Rowman and Littlefield, 2002.

Nelson, Michael. *Trump's First Year*. Charlottesville: University of Virginia, 2018.

Newbigin, Lesslie. *The Gospel in a Pluralist Society.* Grand Rapids: Eerdmans, 1986.

Nincic, Miroslav and Jennifer Ramos. "The Sources of Patriotism: Survey and Experimental Evidence." *Foreign Policy Analysis* 8 (2012): 373–388.

Noll, Mark. *America's God: From Jonathan Edwards to Abraham Lincoln.* New York: Oxford University Press, 2002.

______. *God and Race in American Politics: A Short History.* Princeton: Princeton University Press, 2008.

______. *One Nation under God? Christian Faith and Political Action in America.* San Francisco: Harper & Row, 1988.

Nussbaum, Martha. *For Love of Country?* Edited by Joshua Cohen. Boston: Beacon, 1996.

______. *Upheavals of Thought: The Intelligence of Emotion.* Cambridge: Cambridge University Press, 2009.

O'Connor, Raymond. *Diplomacy for Victory: FDR and Unconditional Surrender.* New York: W. W. Norton, 1971.

O'Donovan, Oliver. *The Desire of the Nations: Rediscovering the Roots of Political Theology.* Cambridge: Cambridge, 1996.

______. "The Loss of a Sense of Place." *The Irish Theological Quarterly* 55 (1989): 39–58.

O'Donovan, Oliver and Joan Lockwood O'Donovan. *From Irenaeus to Grotius: A Sourcebook in Christian Political Thought.* Grand Rapids: Eerdmans, 1999.

O'Brien, Peter. *The Epistle to the Philippians: A Commentary on the Greek Text.* New International Greek Testament Commentary. Grand Rapids: Eerdmans, 1991.

Oakes, Peter. "Re-Mapping the Universe: Paul and the Emperor in 1 Thessalonians and Philippians." *JSNT* 27 (2005): 301–322.

Olyan, Saul. *Friendship in the Hebrew Bible*. New Haven: Yale, 2017.

Omanson, Roger and John Ellington. *A Handbook on the First Book of Samuel*. UBS Handbook Series. New York: United Bible Societies, 2001.

Parsons, David. *Dangerous Grounds: Antiwar Coffeehouses and Military Dissent in the Vietnam Era*. Chapel Hill: University of North Carolina Press, 2017.

Parker, Christopher. "Symbolic versus Blind Patriotism: Distinction without Difference?" *Political Research Quarterly* 63 (2009): 97–114.

Patterson, Paige. *Revelation*. The New American Commentary. Nashville: Broadman & Homan, 2012.

Pauwels, Jacques. *The Myth of the Good War: America in the Second World War*. Toronto: Jame Lorimer, 2015.

Peterson, Anders. "Imperial Politics in Paul: Scholarly Phantom or Actual Textual Phenomenon?" In *People under Power: Early Jewish and Christian Responses to the Roman Empire*, edited by Outi Lehtipuu and Michael Labahn, 101–127. Amsterdam: Amsterdam University Press, 2015.

Peterson, David. *The Acts of the Apostles*. The Pillar New Testament Commentary. Grand Rapids; Eerdmans, 2009.

Piper, Ferdinand. *Einleitung in die Monumentale Theologie: Eine Geschichte der chrislichen kunstarchälogie und Epigraphik*. Mittenwald: Mäander, 1978.

Plöger, Josef. *Literarkritische, Forgeschichtliche und Stilkritische Untersuchungen Zum Deuteronomium*. Bonn: Bonner, 1967.

Pogge, Thomas. *World Poverty and Human Rights*. Malden: Polity, 2002.

Pojman, Louis. *Terrorism, Human Rights, and the Case for World Government*. Lanham: Rowman and Littlefield, 2006.

Polhill, John. *Acts*. The New American Commentary. Nashville: Broadman & Holman Publishers, 1992.

Porter, Stanley. *Paul: Jew, Greek, and Roman*. Leiden: Brill, 2008.

Porter, Stanley. "Romans 13:1–7 as Pauline Political Rhetoric." *Filologia Neotestamentaria* 3 (1990): 115–139.

Portolano, Marlana. "The Rhetorical Function of Utopia: An Exploration of the Concept of Utopia in Rhetorical Theory." *Utopian Studies* 23 (2012): 113–141.

Price, S. R. F. *Rituals and Power: The Romans Imperial Cult in Asia Minor*. Cambridge: Cambridge University Press, 1984.

Primoratz, Igor, ed. "Introduction." *Journal of Ethics* 13 (2009): 293–99.

______. *Patriotism*. Amherst: Humanity, 2002.

______. "Patriotism: A Two-Tier Account." In *The Ethics of Patriotism: A Debate*, edited by John Kleinig, Simon Keller, and Igor Primoratz, 73–103. Malden: Wiley, 2015

______. "Patriotism and Morality: Mapping the Terrain." *Journal of Moral Philosophy* 5 (2008): 204–226.

Punt, Jeremy. "Paul's Imperium: The Push and Pull of Empire, and the Pauline Letters." *Religion and Theology* 23 (2016): 339–363.

Rable, George. *God's Almost Chosen Peoples: A Religious History of the American Civil War*. Chapel Hill: University of North Carolina, 2010.

Rapske, Brian. *The Book of Acts in Its First-Century Setting: The Book of Acts and Paul in Roman Custody*. Grand Rapids; Eerdmans, 1994.

Reed, Esther. "Refugee Rights and State Sovereignty: Theological Perspectives on the Ethics of Territorial Borders." *Journal of the Society of Christian Ethics* 30 (2010): 59–78.

Reid, Daniel, Robert Linder, Bruce Shelley, and Harry Stout. *Dictionary of Christianity in America*, S.v. "civil religion."

Resane, Kelebogile. "Statues, Symbols, and Signages: Monuments towards Socio-political Divisions, Dominance and Patriotism?" *HTS* 74 (2018): 1–8.

Richey, Sean. "Civic Engagement and Patriotism." *Social Science Quarterly* 92 (2011): 1044–1056.

Rist, Martin. "Caesar or God (Mark 12:13–17)? A Study in 'Formgeschichte'." *The Journal of Religion* 16 (1936): 317–331.

Robertson, O. Palmer. *The Israel of God: Yesterday, Today, and Tomorrow*. Philipsburg: P & R, 2000.

Rooker, Mark. *Leviticus,* The New American Commentary. Nashville: Broadman & Holman Publishers, 2000.

Rorty, Richard. *Achieving Our Country: Leftist Thought in Twentieth Century America*. Cambridge: Cambridge University Press, 1998.

Roshwald, Aviel. *The Endurance of Nationalism: Ancient Roots and Modern Dilemmas*. Cambridge: Cambridge University Press, 2006.

Rothbart, Myron and James Johnson. "Social Class and the Vietnam War: Some Discrepant Motives for Supporting or Opposing U.S. Involvement in Southeast Asia." *Pacific Sociological Review* 17 (1974): 46–59.

Royce, Josiah. *The Philosophy of Loyalty*. Nashville: Vanderbilt, 1908.

Rutgers, Mark and Lijing Yang. "Virtue or Vice: The Nature of Loyalty. *Public Integrity* 21 (2019): 394–405.

Ryrie, Charles. *Biblical Theology of the New Testament*. Dubuque: ECS Ministries, 2005.

Sanders, E. P. *Jesus and Judaism*. Philadelphia: Fortress Press, 1985.

Sandoz, Ellis, ed. *Political Sermons of the American Founding Era, 1730–1805*, vol. 1. Indianapolis: Liberty Fund, 1998.

Sardoč, Mitja. "The Anatomy of Patriotism." *Anthropological Notebooks* 23 (2017): 43–55.

Sarna, Nahum. *Genesis*. The JPS Torah Commentary. Philadelphia: Jewish Publication Society, 1989.

Schatz, Robert, Ervin Staub, and Howard Lavine. "On the Varieties of National Attachment: Blind versus Constructive Patriotism." *Political Psychology* 20 (1999): 151–174.

Scheffler, Samuel. *Boundaries and Allegiances: Problems of Justice and Responsibility in Liberal Thought*. Oxford: Oxford University Press, 2001.

______. "Conceptions of Cosmopolitanism." *Utilitas* 11 (1999).

Schellenberg, Ryan. "Seed of Abraham (Friesen?): Universality and Ethnicity in Paul." *Direction* 44 (2015): 16–29.

Schnabel, Eckhard. *Mark*. Tyndale New Testament Commentaries. Downers Grove: InterVarsity, 2017.

Scholz, Bettina. *The Cosmopolitan Potential of Exclusive Associations: Criteria for Assessing the Advancement of Cosmopolitan Norms*. Lanham, Lexington, 2015.

Schreiner, Thomas. *1, 2 Peter, Jude*. The New American Commentary. Nashville: Broadman & Holman, 2003.

Scruton, Roger. *The Need for Nations*. London: Civitas, 2004.

Scobie, Charles. "Israel and the Nations: An Essay in Biblical Theology." *Tyndale Bulletin* 43 (1992): 283–305.

Sheehan-Dean, Aaron. *Why Confederates Fought: Family and Nation in Civil War Virginia.* Chapel Hill: University of North Carolina, 2007.

Silva, Elisabete. "Cosmopolitanism and Patriotism: Questions of Identity, Membership and Belonging." *Annals of the University of Craiova, Romania* (2008): 151–161.

Sin, William. "Adult Children's Obligations towards Their Parents: A Contractualist Explanation." *Journal of Value Inquiry* 53 (2019): 19–32.

Singer, Peter. "Famine, Affluence, and Morality." *Philosophy and Public Affairs* 1 (1972): 229–243.

Skitka, Linda. "Patriotism or Nationalism? Understanding Post-September 11, 2001, Flag-Display Behavior." *Journal of Applied Social Psychology* 35 (2005): 1995–2011.

Slaughter, Kirk. "Gaining Momentum: How Media Influences Public Opinion to Push Civil-Military Decision Makers into Formulating Foreign Policy." Paper presented to the Air University, February 2016.

Small, Melvin. *Antiwarriors: The Vietnam War and the Battle for America's Hearts and Minds (Vietnam: America in the War Years).* Lanham: SR Books, 2002.

Smeda, Karen. "Foul on the Play: Applying Mediation Strategies to Address Social Injustice Protests in the NFL." *Dispute Resolution Journal* 73 (2018): 51–60.

Smith, Anthony. *Ethno-Symbolism and Nationalism: A Cultural Approach.* London: Routledge, 2009.

Smith, Gary. *Isaiah 40–66.* The New American Commentary. Nashville: Broadman & Holman Publishers, 2009.

Snay, Mitchell. *Gospel of Disunion: Religion and Separatism in the Antebellum South.* Cambridge: Cambridge Press, 1993.

Spry, Carmen and Matthew Hornsey. "The Influence of Blind and Constructive Patriotism on Attitudes toward Multiculturalism and Immigration." *Australian Journal of Psychology* 59 (2007): 151–158.

Stansell, Gary. "David and His Friends: Social-Scientific Perspectives on the David-Jonathan Friendship." *Biblical Theology Bulletin* 41 (2011): 115–131.

Stein, Robert. *Mark.* Baker Exegetical Commentary on the New Testament. Grand Rapids: Baker, 2008.

Stenschke, Christoph. "Paul's Jewish Gospel and the Claims of Rome in Paul's Epistle to Romans." *Neotestamentica* 46 (2012): 338–378.

Stott, John. *The Spirit, the Church and the World: The Message of Acts.* Downers Grove: InterVarsity Press, 1990.

Stout, Harry. *The New England Soul: Preaching and Religious Culture in Colonial New England.* Oxford: Oxford University Press, 2012.

Stuart, Douglas. *Exodus.* The New American Commentary. Nashville: Broadman & Holman, 2006.

Tan, Andrew. *U.S. Strategy against Global Terrorism: How It Evolved, Why It Failed, and Where It Is Headed.* New York: Palgrave, 2009.

Tan, Kok-Chor. *Justice without Borders: Cosmopolitanism, Nationalism and Patriotism.* Cambridge: Cambridge, 2004.

______. "Patriotic Obligations." *The Monist* 86 (2003): 434–453.

Terkel, Studs. *"The Good War": An Oral History of World War II.* New York: The New Press, 1984.

Theiss-Morse, Elizabeth. *Who Counts as an American? The Boundaries of National Identity.* Cambridge: Cambridge, 2009.

Thomas, Etan. "What Kaepernick Started: A Former NBA Player Reflects." *The Progressive* (2016): 29–31.

Tierney, Dominic. "The Two Vietnam Wars: American Perceptions of the Use of Force." *Political Science Quarterly* 138 (2018): 641–667.

Tigay, Jeffrey. *Deuteronomy.* The JPS Torah Commentary. Philadelphia: Jewish Publication Society, 1996.

Trask, Kerry. *In the Pursuit of Shadows: A Study of Collective Hope and Despair in Provincial Massachusetts during the Era of the Seven Years War, 1748–1764.* Minneapolis: University of Minnesota Press, 1971.

van Hekken, Suus. "Parent and Child Perceptions of Boszormenyi-Nagy's Ethical Dimensions of the Parent-Child Relationship." *Contemporary Family Therapy* 12 (1990): 529–543.

VanDrunen, David. "Abraham Kuyper and the Reformed Natural Law and Two Kingdoms Traditions." *Calvin Theological Journal* 42 (2007): 283–284.

______. "Bearing Sword in the State, Turning Cheek in the Church: A Reformed Two-Kingdoms Interpretation of Matthew 5:38–42." *Themelios* 34 (2009): 322–334.

______. *Biblical Case for Natural Law, Studies in Christian Social Ethics and Economics*. Grand Rapids: Acton Institute, 2006.

______. *Living in God's Two Kingdoms: A Biblical Vision for Christianity and Culture*. Wheaton: Crossway, 2010.

______. *Natural Law and the Two Kingdoms: A Study in the Development of Reformed Social Thought*. Grand Rapids: Eerdmans, 2010.

______. *Politics after Christendom: Political Theology in a Fractured World*. Grand Rapids: Zondervan, 2020.

Verbruggen, Jan. "Filial Duties in the Ancient Near East." PhD diss., The Johns Hopkins University, 1997.

Vertovec, Steven and Robin Cohen, eds. *Conceiving Cosmopolitanism: Theory, Context, and Practice*. Oxford: Oxford, 2002.

von Rad, Gerhard. *Holy War in Ancient Israel*. Translated by Marva Dawn. Grand Rapids: Eerdmans, 1991.

Vos, Howard. *Nelson's New Illustrated Bible Manners and Customs: How the People of the Bible Really Lived*. Nashville: Nelson Publishers, 1999.

Waldstreicher, David. "Rites of Rebellion, Rites of Assent: Celebrations, Print Culture, and the Origins of American Nationalism." *The Journal of American History* 82 (1995): 37–61.

Waltke, Bruce and Charles Yu. *An Old Testament Theology: An Exegetical, Canonical, and Thematic Approach*. Grand Rapids: Zondervan, 2007.

Walzer, Michael. *Arguing about War*. New Haven: Yale University Press, 2004.

Watson, Samuel. "Religion and Combat Motivation in the Confederate Armies." *The Journal of Military History* 58 (1994): 29–55.

Wattad, Mohammed. "The Meaning of Wrongdoing—A Crime of Disrespecting the Flag: Grounds for Preserving National Unity." *San Diego International Law Journal* 5 (2008): 5–62.

Watts, Craig. "Singing the Songs of Babylon in the Worship of the Church." *Encounter* 74 (2013–2014): 1–17.

Webster, Gerald. "American Nationalism, the Flag, and the Invasion of Iraq." *The Geographical Review* 101 (2011): 1–18.

Welch, Brynn. "A Theory of Filial Obligations." *Social Theory and Practice* 38 (2012): 717–737.

Wenell, Karen. "Contested Temple Space and Visionary Kingdom Space in Mark 11–12." *Biblical Interpretation* 15 (2007): 323–337.

Wesley, Timothy. "The Politics of Faith: Religious Authority and Politics during the American Civil War." PhD diss., Pennsylvania State University, 2010.

Whitehead, Andrew and Samuel Perry. "Is a 'Christian America' a More Patriarchal America? Religion, Politics, and Traditionalist Gender Ideology. *Canadian Review of Sociology* 56 (2019): 151–177.

Whitehead, Andrew, Samuel Perry, and Joseph Baker. "Make America Christian Again: Christian Nationalism and Voting for Donald Trump in the 2016 Presidential Election." *Sociology of Religion: A Quarterly Review* 79 (2018): 147–171.

Williams, George. *Wilderness and Paradise in Christian Thought: The Biblical Experience of the Desert in the History of Christianity and the Paradise Theme in the Theological Idea of the University.* New York: Harper & Brothers, 1962.

Wilsey, John. "America as the City upon a Hill: An Historical, Philosophical and Theological Critique of the Historiographical Construal of America as a Christian Nation." PhD diss., Southeastern Baptist Theological Seminary, 2009.

———. *American Exceptionalism and Civil Religion: Reassessing the History of an Idea.* Downers Grove: InterVarsity, 2015.

———. *One Nation under God? An Evangelical Critique of Christian America.* Eugene: Pickwick, 2011.

Wilson, Kevin. "From Memory to History: American Cultural Memory of the Vietnam War." Master's thesis, Miami University, 2006.

Winthrop, John. "A Modell of Christian Charity." In *Political Thought in America: An Anthology*, edited by Michael Levy. Prospect Heights: Waveland, 1992.

Witherington, Ben, III. *The Acts of the Apostles: A Socio-Rhetorical Commentary*. Grand Rapids: Eerdmans, 1998.

______. *Conflict and Community in Corinth: A Socio-Rhetorical Commentary on 1 and 2 Corinthians*. Grand Rapids: Eerdmans, 1995.

______. *Paul's Letter to the Philippians: A Socio-Rhetorical Commentary*. Grand Rapids: Eerdmans Company, 2011.

______. *The Gospel of Mark: A Socio-Rhetorical Commentary*. Grand Rapids: Eerdmans, 2001.

Wolak, Jennifer and Ryan Dawkins. "The Roots of Patriotism across Political Contexts." *Political Psychology* 38 (2017): 391–408.

Wood, James. "Making a Nation's Flag a Sacred Symbol." *Journal of Church and State* 31 (1989): 375–380.

Wright, Christopher. *The Mission of God's People: A Biblical Theology of the Church's Mission*. Grand Rapids: Zondervan, 2010.

Wright, N. T. *The New Testament and the People of God. Christian Origins and the Question of God*, vol. 1. London: Society for Promoting Christian Knowledge, 1992.

Yeboah, Kofie. "A Timeline of Events since Colin Kaepernick's National Anthem Protest." The Undefeated, https://theundefeated.com/features/a-timeline-of-events-since-colin-kaepernicks-national-anthem-protest/.

Yoon, Cheol-Won. "Paul's Citizenship and Its Function in the Narratives of Acts." PhD diss., University of Sheffield, 1996.

Zelinsky, Wilbur. *From Nation into State*. Chapel Hill: University of North Carolina Press, 1988.

Zerbe, Gordon. "Citizenship and Politics According to Philippians." *Direction* 38 (2009): 193–208.